The Quest

A Journey of
SPIRITUAL
REDISCOVERY

Richard and Mary-Alice
Jafolla

unity®
HOUSE

Unity Village, Missouri

Eighth printing 2005

Published by the Unity Movement Advisory Council, a joint committee of the Association of Unity Churches and Unity School of Christianity.

To place an order, call the Customer Service Department at 1-800-669-0282 or visit us online at *www.unityonline.org.*

Cover photo © J. A. Kraulis/Masterfile
Cover photo of Dhaulagiri and Tukuche Peaks, Nepal
Authors' photo by Kim Crenshaw
Cover designed by Chad Pio
Text designed by Linda Gates

Library of Congress Catalog Card Number: 92-063345
ISBN 0-87159-276-2 (Guidebook)
ISBN 0-87159-277-0 (Set)

Canada BN 13252 9033 RT

Unity House feels a sacred trust to be a healing presence in the world. By printing with biodegradable soybean ink, we believe we are doing our part to be wise stewards of our Earth's resources.

*T*ABLE OF CONTENTS

$\mathcal{A}$CKNOWLEDGMENTS

Our warm gratitude goes to all of our colleagues for the loving support they provided during the development of *The Quest*.

Special thanks to all those who have served on the Unity Movement Advisory Council throughout the publication of this work—Bob Barth, Maya Brandenberger, Bill Dale, Marge Dale, Connie Fillmore, Stan Hampson, Chris Jackson, Wayne Manning, Glenn Mosley, Charles Neal, Nancy Neal, Jim Rosemergy, Alan Rowbotham, Scott Sherman, Edie Skalitzky, John Strickland, Larry Swartz, and their facilitator, Rita Cashman.

Our sincerest appreciation also goes to Nancy Hiscoe for so smoothly guiding this project and to our editor, Michael Maday, as well as to Kim Ames, Jack Barker, Pat Barker, Roy Healy, Joyce Kramer, Tim Shrout, Karen Todd, Barbara Young, Jerry Young, and the Unity ministerial classes of 1991 and 1992 for their helpful comments and feedback. Heartfelt thanks to Janna Beatty for her wisdom and vision and to all of our friends and family whose encouragement and faith inspired us along the path.

And finally, love and thanks to Roscoe Smith, who knows just how much he meant to the creation and completion of this work.

$\mathcal{P}$ROLOGUE

$\mathcal{H}$ELLO, $\mathcal{F}$RIEND!

It is not by chance that we meet. Your search to satisfy the longing in your heart has led you here.

What you hold in your hand is not a "book" in the usual sense—not a course of learning but a process. *The Quest* is a process of remembering the truths that have been hidden in the ancient forests of your mind. It is the next step in the evolution of your soul, which spirals ever upward in the rediscovery of its spiritual self. It is a journey which can transform your life far beyond any good that you can now envision.

COMING HOME

No more will you have to feel empty and lost, without hope, without direction. No more will your soul cry out in despair, "Is anybody there?" Never again will you scan the heavens with anxious eyes searching for a sign—some lifeline to grab which will rescue you once and for all. In many ways, *The Quest* is a coming home. You've been expected.

When Michelangelo was asked how he could carve his magnificent *David* out of a shapeless block of marble, he replied that *David* had always been in the stone. A sculptor merely had to remove what was not *David*.

The Quest will not "teach" you anything. Rather, it will help you to remove all that is not the *real* you. It will help the divine part of you to emerge, just as the statue, imprisoned in the marble for so long, was finally allowed to emerge.

IN CASE YOU'RE WONDERING

Before we go any further, we'd like to put your mind at ease by telling you that this is not a study of philosophy or science or religion. It is a quest for the eternal truth behind all philosophy, all science, all religion—behind everything. It deals with universal spiritual roots, common to all humankind. Our priority? Inner transformation rather than dogma and intellectual exercise. Our emphasis? Practice more than theory, purpose more than goals.

The Quest is for sincere seekers everywhere who are ready to discover the Power within them, and Its incomparable ability to heal, comfort, and prosper. The process is for those who are prepared to make a genuine commitment to the transformation this discovery brings and who will be faithful to the discipline required to complete the journey.

"SOMETHING MORE"

No matter what your circumstances, no matter what the past or present, there has always been the hope of connecting with "something more." Somehow, somewhere tucked away in the attic of your soul, a part of you has always considered the possibility of that connection and yearned for it. Sometimes the yearning was strong and urgent. Sometimes it was so remote and hidden that it was not even identifiable. But it was always there.

Perhaps, as you read these words, something within you stirs. "Could it be that these words were written for me? Have I reached the point in my life where I must get serious about my own spiritual evolution?"

Perhaps you have, friend. Perhaps it is now your turn.

If you feel yourself being drawn to the miracle-working process of *The Quest*, we invite you to join us as a kindred spirit on the Path. We travel light—no need to bring a lot of intellectual and emotional baggage with you. This will be a spiritual journey. There is but one simple necessity: your sincere desire to know God. Nothing more is required.

You stand at the gate. The spirit of life is alive and well, and living in you! It is longing to express Itself through you and as you in new and marvelous ways. You can let It ... Now.

Our blessings are with you.
Richard & Mary-Alice Jafolla

$\mathcal{T}$HE STORY OF THE QUEST

The title, *The Quest,* was chosen because it represents something so deep within us that it is etched into our very tissues. The story of the quest is an ancient theme, part of the heritage of all humanity. It strikes a familiar chord in every heart that ever beat.

In every era of history and in every culture, people have created and cherished the story of a hero or heroine whose life is transformed by traveling on a special journey. From primitive myth and beloved folktales to literary classics and modern science fiction, we humans continue to identify with this journey and its quest for the prize.

As children, we're entranced by fairy tales like "Jack and the Beanstalk" and "Sleeping Beauty." As adults, we thrill to the excitement of Homer's *Odyssey,* Herman Melville's *Moby Dick,* and Joseph Conrad's "Heart of Darkness."

Why is it that we are so drawn to stories of the quest? Because they are symbolic of our own journeys through life, with challenges to overcome and the ultimate prize to capture. These stories do not belong solely to their heroes or heroines. They are the stories of us all. They are *your* story. You are the champion of your own quest. And your quest, like those of fiction, follows a certain classical pattern.

THE CALL

The beginning of the quest always finds the hero or heroine on the brink of a major change, feeling that the world is closing in. There is a sense of despair or of being trapped. Life seems empty, or there is a realization of not using one's gifts in the highest way. Whatever the reason, present life is unrewarding, and so there is a yearning for "something more."

Then one day, quite unexpectedly, the hero or heroine receives a call. It can be an extraordinary event, a dramatic experience, an inner whispering. In Herman Melville's classic quest story *Moby Dick*, Ishmael's inner torment of depression is a summons to return to adventure at sea. In *The Wizard of Oz*, it is a tornado which serves as the call to whisk Dorothy into her journey to Oz. Maybe your call came in the form of a serious illness. Or maybe it was a nagging dissatisfaction with your life. Maybe it was suddenly finding yourself out of a job or a marriage. A call can be disguised in a thousand different forms.

Regardless of the form it takes, the summons stirs the heart of the one who hears it, moving him or her into action. It trumpets that "*Now* is the time. Wait no longer. This is the moment. Mount up!" Something within the hero or heroine, instinctively sensing the rightness of this call, leaps up with a resounding "Yes!" And the quest begins.

How about you? What call did you heed that made you realize you must begin your journey? Was it a dramatic event in your life or a particular need or an inner whisper? Where were you when you heard the call? Was anyone with you? Can you identify what you believe to be your personal summons?

THE JOURNEY

A major element of all quests is a journey. From old legends like King Arthur and the Knights of the Round Table or the pursuit of the Holy Grail, to more contemporary adventure stories like *Lord of the Rings, Star Wars,* and your own, the main story line of every quest is a journey filled with experiences and challenges to be used as stepping-stones.

In ancient tales, these challenges were external hazards like treacherous terrains or wild animals or demons and dragons. (Orpheus had to descend into hell. Jonah was swallowed by a gigantic fish. Hercules was sent to perform twelve superhuman feats. Daniel was thrown into a den of lions.)

Today we no longer think in terms of dragons and demons in our outer world. *The threatening beasts to be conquered are deep in the recesses of our own minds.* They are our own fears, our worries, our perceived limitations. Our biggest battles take place internally, within our souls.

It could be that you yourself are battling some fearsome challenge like financial lack or personal rejection. These demons rear their ugly heads, tempting you to revert to the old ways, to give up the quest. Like the dragons of old, they block the path and prevent you from reaching the treasure.

Sometimes the journey seems littered with one major calamity after another. But the hero or heroine prevails, overcomes all, and proceeds inexorably toward the prize. And so will you! Every dragon you now face, every obstacle in your path, every demon and ogre can be overcome. You can do it, and as you do so, you will learn more about yourself, about life, about your fellow human beings, and about God.

There is an innate knowing that one's spiritual, emotional, and even physical well-being depend upon heeding the call and making the commitment to endure whatever is necessary in order to attain the treasure and the transformation.

It has probably occurred to you that not everyone is willing to give himself or herself so completely to a quest. Indeed, most people are unaware that there *is* a quest with a prize to be won. They prefer to cling to old familiar ways, even when the old ways no longer fit. Daring to change is what distinguishes the hero or heroine from the rest of humanity.

THE PRIZE

The purpose of the journey, with all of its experiences and challenges, is the winning of the prize. All stories of the quest, since the beginning of time, revolve around a fabulous treasure. From the ancient Holy Grail and Golden Fleece adventures to our current tales in books and movies, any quest story you can think of has a valuable prize as its goal.

This might be a material prize such as a chest of gold or a magic sword. For you, the prize may be a physical healing or a more loving relationship with your estranged son or freedom from a long-standing alcohol dependency. Prizes come in all shapes and sizes. But the material prize is always accompanied by the *true* prize, which is spiritual gain—an expanded awareness, some new insight—which transforms your life. Whatever the prize, it always brings with it a new beginning.

As you recall stories of the quest, you remember

that the treasures are never attained without effort. While most of us do not have to endure the unimaginable difficulties of the legendary Greek hero Jason in his quest for the Golden Fleece, any hero or heroine must be willing to endure discomfort and make sacrifices, if necessary, in order to reach the goal. But this does not dissuade him or her. Totally committed, face set in one direction only, the hero or heroine continues to find the quest ... *irresistible.*

THE REBIRTH

But winning the prize, as wonderful as it is, is not enough. The physical healing, the loving relationship, the sobriety, these are not the end of the story. They are really the beginning. Victory signifies the death of the old life and the beginning of a new one. Once the treasure is obtained, the heroine or hero must return with it and put it to use in the world.

So, the finale of the quest is not only a triumphant return, but a resurrection, a rebirth. The person is transformed. And because *he* or *she* is, that person's whole world is changed as well. And nothing will ever be the same again.

TRAILBLAZER

The compelling stories of the quest inspire and encourage us because they strike a chord within our own hearts, hearts which also have been waiting for a call to action.

We are fascinated by the heroes and heroines of the legends, secretly yearning to emulate their victories and to set forth on our own quests, achieving our own transformations. We're especially heartened when a real-life individual triumphs over great hardships.

We feel good, since we know that what one person can do, others can also do. Because that person has blazed the trail, it makes our own journeys that much easier.

We each have our own visions of what our prize should be. You have yours. But the truth is that, in essence, our quests are all the same: to know God and to experience the transforming power of God in our lives. Although we might not realize it, this is what we all want. (Isn't this, after all, what *you* really want?)

If at first we feel overwhelmed by the prospect of our journeys, we need not. You see, we have the extraordinary advantage of having a "trailblazer" who has gone before us to show us the way.

Our trailblazer is Jesus Christ.

NOT RELIGIOUS

We told you at the outset that *The Quest* is not a religious venture, and we meant it. It isn't. *The Quest* is an inner, spiritual process. It has nothing to do with your specific religious practices or affiliations. How, where, or if you worship God is entirely your own business. No, this is something completely different. We will use Jesus to lead our way because He is the quintessential hero on the quest.

THE PATTERN FITS

Think for a moment of the pattern of the quest—the call, the journey, the prize, the transformation. Now think of the life of Jesus and recognize those same elements, that same pattern, in His life.

While we're not privileged to know the inner

10

workings of His mind, we can assume that at some point on His spiritual journey, Jesus had received a call. We know that at an early age He seemed to believe He was on a special path. Perhaps the call had come so early and so unrelentingly that it would be impossible to pinpoint its arrival at any particular time.

Or was it when John baptized Him in the River Jordan and the "Spirit ... like a dove" (Mk. 1:10) descended upon Him that Jesus fully recognized the call He had been hearing and began His quest? We can only guess.

THE ULTIMATE HERO

Can you see how the life of Jesus is the life of the ultimate hero? There was the journey, with its challenges leading to the despairing night in the garden of Gethsemane, the Crucifixion, the dark tomb. There was the prize of Resurrection and fully knowing His oneness with God. There was the return to the world with the treasure and the sharing of that treasure with others.

The transformation which Jesus underwent is as powerful today as it was at the time. Its effects are at work right now in our world. This is why *The Quest* is based on the provocative truths which Jesus so ingeniously uncovered. No one, in all of history, has had the impact on humankind that Jesus has. No quest, in all of history, has been as triumphant as His.

*D*IRECTIONS FOR YOUR JOURNEY

You are now about to embark on your own quest, your own journey of spiritual rediscovery.

Before you set forth, take the time to skim through the entire adventure to get an overall feel for it. As you do this, you may have some questions about *The Quest* and how to proceed. This is perfectly natural. We've tried to anticipate some of your questions and, hopefully, answer them for you here.

"I couldn't help noticing that each teaching in the Guidebook begins with a quote from Jesus. I thought The Quest was not religious."

The Quest is not religious. It is spiritual. This could use some further clarification.

Spirituality is our inner awareness of a Higher Presence, of a spirit within us, and our highly personal, very intimate connection to it.

Religion refers to organized systems of beliefs and rituals. Religions are movements created by people for the purpose of defining, understanding, and worshiping a Higher Presence.

Not everyone belongs to a religion. Many people are not in any way religious. But everyone is spiritual because, at our nucleus, we are spiritual beings. A quick glance at crime statistics shows that not all of us have come in contact with this higher aspect of ourselves, but that doesn't mean it's not there. The spirituality of humankind is a universal experience. It's our common denominator.

Please Note: The quotations of Jesus used in *The Quest* are not intended to generate or support any particular religious beliefs. In fact, *The Quest* regards Jesus not as a religious leader but as a master of life—a cosmic figure. To interpret His wisdom and teachings and example as "religious" is to completely miss their main thrust and will only blur and diminish them. *At their essence, they are spiritual.* They transcend all "religions." Eloquent, yet exquisitely simple, they are profound teachings, highly relevant to our everyday lives.

Individuals and organizations have made many different religions out of Jesus' words. Yet in actuality, a person of any (or no) religion, in any part of the world, can find meaning and help in Jesus' teachings. They speak to all people, everywhere, and they are as fresh and significant in the twenty-first century as when He walked the earth. In fact, more so. They stand today as an open invitation to anyone who has the awareness.

Only lately are we coming to understand how brilliant, how advanced, was Jesus' cosmic knowledge. Science is only now beginning to verify the truth of what He said. His concepts of the limitless power of the mind, the capacity of love and joy to heal inner (as well as outer) conditions—these and other breakthroughs are now measurable in research laboratories. We are just now starting to get a hint of what their full impact will be in the future.

This is why Jesus Christ will be *your* Guide and Trailblazer as you journey through the process of

The Quest. You can understand what an advantage it will be to you.

Don't let the fact that it's a solo journey into new territory frighten you. It will not be the uncharted wilderness you might have imagined. Your Trail-blazer has provided you with maps, charts, and signs. While the path may be foreign to you, it is not unmarked, for someone has gone before you to point the way. If one person did it, you can do it too.

"How long will this journey take?"

In *The Quest* there are fifty-two legs of the journey, divided into four 12-part sections. Each section is followed by a week of "vacation." Therefore, it seems natural to devote a year to *The Quest*, but we leave that decision entirely up to you. The length of time it takes to complete it is not as important as the discipline of a faithful, regular routine.

"Can I work with The Quest *alone, or should I be part of a group?"*

You can proceed along the path by yourself or with a group of friends, whichever suits you best. The advantage of working alone is that you can proceed entirely at your own pace; you don't have to go out to meetings on stormy nights, and you reap huge benefits from the self-discipline required. (There are no two ways about it, if you work alone, you will need lots of self-discipline.)

The advantage of a study group is that it's easier to stay motivated and to hold to a regular schedule. Also, there is a wonderful camaraderie developed with like-minded seekers, as each is able to help the others. The spirit of growth is infectious. We've found a good *Quest* group to be wonderfully effective, and we highly recommend it. Keep in mind, however, that even if you are in a study group which meets once a week or so, you'll still be following an individual daily routine. (On the chance that we haven't already stressed it enough, this seems like the perfect time to announce it once again: The key to your success with *The Quest* is a faithful, disciplined routine! In other words, make it a habit!)

Whichever way you choose to proceed, alone or with a group, *The Quest* is ultimately a solo journey. No one can learn or grow for you, so you won't want to move on to a new teaching until you feel you've mastered the previous one.

"What if I already understand the principle presented in a chapter?"

You most certainly will know some of these principles, probably many of them, maybe every one of them! After all, they are ancient truths which are known instinctively if we will listen to the deepest levels of our hearts. But, as a great scholar once remarked, "To know the truth is easy. To serve the truth? Ah, to serve the truth is another matter entirely."

We announced in the Prologue that the purpose of *The Quest* is not to teach you anything. It is to encourage you, walk with you through the transformation of your life by *applying* certain truths. If we truly believe the principles, then we have no choice but to live by them, put them to practical use, prove them daily. Otherwise, what possible good are they?

It is not only the *knowing* but the habitual practice which brings the results. No matter the level of our spiritual awareness, unless we have translated that awareness into our daily thoughts and actions, we are still spiritual neophytes. Therefore, *The Quest* is for all of us who want to serve the truth in a higher way.

"What if I see a topic I think will help me with a problem I have right now? Should I skip around, or should I follow the order of the book?"

A house is built from the foundation up, a ladder climbed one rung at a time. Each teaching builds on the previous one and has been designed to bring you the optimum experience. It's important that you don't go on to the next teaching or any future teachings without completing your current one.

Here's the reason: You don't have specific problems. No one does. We all have general life problems that manifest in specific ways. In *The Quest*, you will be working to change your life for the better. When your life changes for the better, all of the circumstances of your life (including any present "problems") change for the better.

For example, if you are on Teaching 5 and see your current need addressed in Teaching 32, don't jump ahead. If you keep working on the teachings one at a time, learning and changing as you proceed, chances are that your need will have disappeared by Teaching 32 without your even having specifically addressed it.

A flower's drooping petals may seem to be the problem, but it's really only a symptom. The problem is dry soil. You don't work on the drooping petals; you water the soil. You work from the foundation up.

"What's the most effective way to go about each Adventure?"

Whatever your pace, your plan should be to read the presentation in this Guidebook first. If you are working with a group, discuss it fully. If you are working alone, you may have to go over it more than once. When you feel comfortable with the ideas set before you, then begin the accompanying Adventure in your Activity Book. (Be sure to complete all of the activities.)

If you're working with a group, you may want to share your answers, or at least some of them, with each other. Discussing a concern or exchanging ideas can be an effective way to help each other grow.

ONE LAST THING

We know you're eager to get started. Just a few final words before you begin.

You may have thought that you have come this way to achieve some specific goal, to make some dramatic overcoming in your life. Not so. The real reason you are here, embarking on *The Quest*, is to know God.

In addition to encountering ideas which reinforce your present beliefs and experiences, you will also be encountering ideas which may be new to you. Please keep an open mind and an open heart. Because of your dissatisfaction with your present situation, you want change, but if you are not willing to change something, nothing can change! All change begins with a change in thinking. All change begins with an open mind.

Secondly, be patient. Don't try to "make things happen." You want evolution, not revolution! When you are consistent and faithful in your quest, good things take place in your life. There is no need to keep checking for results. Results will simply unfold.

Now, when you are ready, pick up your walking

stick, turn the page, and step out to meet your first teaching.

Godspeed on your journey.

the teaching

STARTING OVER | 1

*It is the desire of every
human being to feel he
or she can begin anew.
Do you not feel this
need in your own soul?*

*You can begin again ... and again ...
and again ...*

*"Truly, truly, I say to you, unless one is born
anew, he cannot see the kingdom of God."*
—John 3:3

There comes a time in the evolution of every soul when we "put away childish things" and take on the mantle of spiritual maturity.

The evolution of humankind, the unfolding activity of the entire race, is no longer enough. There is no doubt that this ongoing evolutionary process will force further physical refinements. But the days of being satisfied with changes *only* in our physical form have come to a close.

INNER JOURNEY

This is a new time for us. We are living in the most exciting and expansive era in human history. It is the time of the evolution of the individual, a personal awakening to the *spiritual self.* How far we go is up to each of us. But however far the reaches of this possibility, the journey begins for each one when he or she hears the summons which announces that there is so much more than what is now being expressed.

The feelings of unfulfillment, the yearnings to experience "something more," the emptiness in the soul which nothing seems to satisfy, these are all signposts along the way. They indicate that one has heard the call and reached that point of readiness to enter into the fulfilling process of spiritual evolution.

You yourself would not be embarking on *The Quest* if you had not heard your summons. You know that it is time to shepherd your life into greener, more meaningful pastures. It is time to begin again.

TERRA INCOGNITA

On ancient maps, all uncharted lands were referred to as *terra incognita,* meaning "unknown region." The early cartographers drew dragons and sea monsters in those areas. These frightful creatures were graphic expressions of the mapmaker's own convictions that great dangers awaited those foolish enough to venture into these regions. After all, these were areas as yet unexplored. Nothing was known about them, and so the depiction of monsters was designed to instill fear in the ancient travelers' hearts. At one time virtually all of the "new world"—North and South America—was *terra incognita* to cartographers. But what a wonderful world awaited!

YOUR NEW WORLD

There is a "new world" in you too. It is a world as yet not fully explored. It, too, is rich in resources offering vast stores of happiness, joy, peace, love, and abundance. But the journey into this land is a spiritual quest into the farthest reaches of your soul, for that is where the real riches lie.

As with those ancient travelers, there may be fear of venturing into such an unknown region. Your life may not be perfect now, but at least you are beginning to know where the "dragons" are. If not comfortable with them, at least you are familiar with them, at least they are *your* dragons.

BORN AGAIN

To carve out a new path into the uncharted territory of the soul is to be born again. Being born again may sound like a frightening proposition, but it really isn't, because we are always beginning again. Life is a series of little "deaths" out of which life, in a different form, will always return. We "die" to infancy to be "born again" into childhood. We die to childhood to be born again into adolescence. We die to adolescence to be born again into young adulthood. And so it goes, each "death" leading to a new "birth."

A friend once considered, then decided against, a new birth. "I've been seriously thinking of going back to school, but then I thought, Who wants to hire a fifty-year-old Ph.D.?" Having raised her family, she was thinking of studying for her master's degree in education then continuing on for her Ph.D. But she never did.

Instead, she decided that she did not want to begin again. She constantly lamented that it was "too late to go back to school," that she was "too old to start a new profession," that she was "the wrong sex to get hired at a decent salary." She offered a multitude of reasons to stay where she was. She saw too many dragons on the map.

Yet for some reason, her remarks ignited a smoldering ember in her twin sister who was a single parent of three teenagers and, at that time, was solidly entrenched in a well-paying job which she hated. Yet seven years later, at age fifty-one, her sister was awarded a Ph.D. in psychology. Now a successful child psychologist in a suburban school system, she is very happy to have made the decision she did when she did.

Our friend's sister "died" to her old job, to her old state of consciousness, and was "born" into a new job, into a new state of consciousness. She faced the dragons and found them merely images on someone else's map.

THE TRUE REBIRTH

We are all capable of similar positive changes in our lives. We can all look past our pet "monsters" and decide to explore more of God's good for us. But no matter how much physical or emotional transformation we undergo, no matter how significant our change, *unless it leads to a spiritual rebirth, there can be no lasting growth.* Unless it leads to an awareness of who and what we really are, it is just another dead end.

Spiritual rebirth can take a lifetime to develop, or it can explode into our lives in a split second. It comes with the realization that we are more than our flesh and blood. We are more than our degrees or titles; we are more than our possessions; we are more than our relationships. The new birth of which Jesus spoke takes place in the soul. With it comes the knowledge that "I and the Father are one," that we are part of the great Creative Force which made us and which powers this universe.

GOD MAKES NEW AND BETTER

The ultimate rebirth is an awakening to Spirit, and that rebirth always leads to a better life. It doesn't matter what preceded that awareness. Truth is not obligated to what has been. Think of the evolution of civilization. If we were not able to create anew and to be reborn, we would all still be living in caves. We'd be anchored in the past, repeating our thoughts and actions in an endless loop. What *can be* is not bound by what *is* or what *was*, and that has to be the most freeing concept anyone can imagine!

It is the very nature of God to make "new" and "better." God's desire for you is absolute good! You'll be reading that a lot in *The Quest* because it is the most fundamental truth. God's good is not conditional; it is absolute. It is not earned by what you do or how you act. It is not dependent on what you've experienced in the past or are experiencing now. God's good exists *now* and is available *now*. It is always available in your "now," even if it has never been a part of your past.

God's principle of good for you is not bound by your experience of sickness or lack or poor relationships or whatever negative condition you've experienced in the past. God's principle of good is available at each "new birth" in consciousness.

"POSSIBILITY JUNCTION"

Our friend didn't know this when she thought she couldn't go back to school. She didn't know that exactly where she was all things were possible. Not only did the "givens" exist in her life: female, age forty-four, mother, out of school for a few decades, and so forth, but existing concurrently was a plethora of other possibilities. She was at "Possibility Junction"—the junction of where she *was* and where she *could be*, and it's at Possibility Junction that we always find God's good.

We all live at Possibility Junction. Each "now" moment is another junction, the chance to make another decision. In each now moment, we decide what we want out of life. Often we feel that the easiest decision is no decision at all—just to keep going in the same direction. But life repeatedly teaches us that no decision is still a decision!

Perhaps you feel as our friend did: you're too old or too young or too sick or too poor or too unlovable or too whatever it is you may be identifying with at the moment. But the truth is that you are capable of expressing more good and experiencing more good because you are part of the Creative Energy of this universe which is *all* good.

BEGINNING TO CHANGE

Where does change begin? It begins first of all with the realization that you are worthwhile, that you are not separated from God, that you are *a part of* God not *apart from* God.

Secondly, you make the decision that you want to feel one with God. This is a decision you don't make just once and then that's it forever. It's a choice that must be redecided at each junction of "then" and "now," at each moment of your life.

There may be days ahead when you feel discouraged—when you feel you could have done better. Just when things seem to be going along smoothly—boom!—something blows up in your face. Or the plans that seemed so positive and hopeful in January turn into a mess by April.

These are precisely the times when you must remind yourself that you can begin again. It is not the end. You are allowed an unlimited number of times to pick yourself up and start over. A chalkboard can be erased forever. You can always start fresh with a clean slate. The hero or heroine makes many new beginnings on the journey before attaining the prize.

If you can now say that you want to know more of God and that you want God to be more active in your life, then you've made an important decision. You have set yourself up to accept more good, and that's all that you need to be born again ... and again ... and again.

$\mathcal{M}$ile markers

- The evolution of humankind is now an inner one of spiritual transformation of the individual.
- Life is a series of rebirths out of which life, in a different form, will always return.
- There is no lasting growth without a spiritual rebirth.
- God's desire for you is absolute good.
- God's good for you is not bound by the past. It is a creative process, the nature of which is to make you "new" and "better."
- You are always at Possibility Junction, and you can begin again!

Great Power of this universe, I have heard Your call. I feel You drawing me closer to the realization of Your presence in my life. I hunger to know You more. Thank You for leading me higher ... and for holding me safe as I begin again.

You are now ready to proceed to the Activity Book.
Read the introduction and then move on to Adventure 1.

the teaching

*F*RIENDS | 2

*There is extra power
available by being with
people who support you
in your desire to change.*

Creating your spiritual support group

*"For where two or three are gathered in my name,
there am I in the midst of them."*   —Matthew 18:20

Have you ever repotted a withering plant into a
larger container with more nutritive soil? It immediately begins springing back to life.

This is because it is no longer imprisoned in an
environment which impedes its growth. Those elements that had surrounded it and had been so important to its earlier growth can no longer support any
further progress. In fact, not only can they not assist
further growth, they actually contribute to its withering.

It's often like that with the people who surround
us. Too often they are the elements we look to for our
emotional and, to some degree, our spiritual nourishment. If they don't support our growth, then we are

like the potted plant limited by its surroundings. We need a larger pot, more nutritive soil. Friends, supportive friends, provide a rich environment that allows us the safety and encouragement to grow and to thrive at our own pace.

A SPIRITUAL SEEDLING

You are a spiritual seedling. (Compared to our limitless spiritual potential, we all are.) Because you are, your spiritual quest must be nurtured as one would nurture any tiny plant.

Like a seedling, your growth may need sheltering from the winds of pessimism blown toward you by well-meaning (and not so well-meaning) "friends" and from the droughts of discouragement within yourself. It is crucial that you surround yourself as much as possible with supporters, with people who are not only happy, but eager to help you find the God within you.

Although the inner journey is a solo one, through encouragement, motivation, inspiration, and prayer, the support of caring friends can make it easier for you to achieve your transformation.

As seedlings, we are fragile, easily swayed in any direction and easy to uproot. The more we grow in spiritual awareness, the stronger we become and the more able to resist the events and circumstances that tend to drive us off our chosen path. So from this moment on, our energies should be invested in our growth, in activities which are spiritually rewarding and lead to higher states of consciousness.

Be especially careful not to squander your energy on negative people, people who don't believe in what you are doing or people who disapprove of your quest. Interacting with them can drain and dissipate your energy. Instead, seek those who support you, for they will return increased energy to you.

SPIRITUAL SUPPORT GROUP

Any support group, even an informal one, has great energy because all members share a common goal. A *spiritual* support group has even more creative energy because the goal that everyone seeks is the highest goal that exists.

Captain Eddie Rickenbacker, the famous World War II pilot, crashed into the Pacific after leading a special mission. He and his crew were lost at sea for twenty-one days. He wrote of his experience: "In the beginning many of the men were atheists or agnostics, but at the end of the terrible ordeal each, in his own way, discovered God. Each man found God in the vast empty loneliness of the ocean. Each man found salvation and strength in prayer, and a community of feeling developed which created a liveliness of human fellowship and worship, and a sense of gentle peace."[1]

The community of friends, the crew, that Rickenbacker speaks of was not a group of their choosing. They were thrown together by the vicissitudes of war. Having come together in such calamitous circumstances, they were forced to support each other not only on the level of physical survival, but eventually on the higher level of spiritual growth. Each man, with the blessing and support of the "community," was able to feel safe in exploring his own

1. James S. Hewett, (ed), *Illustrations Unlimited*, Tyndale House Publishers, Inc., Wheaton, Ill., 1988, p. 254.

spiritual values. Each gave the other his blessing of support and the sustenance of his good will. With not enough food or water, each man was forced to face his own life at its fundamental level—that of a spiritual being residing in a physical body—and each felt safe in the spiritual support of others. Gathered together as they were in a spirit of "human fellowship and worship, and a sense of gentle peace," each man found the God in himself.

Jesus said, "For where two or three are gathered in my name, there am I in the midst of them." Let's take Him at His word! Although He may not be physically present, we can interpret this to mean that the spirit which Jesus represents is very much present.

That makes perfect sense, doesn't it? If two or more people come together in a spirit of cooperation, understanding, compassion, joy, peace, love, and mutual blessing, imagine the energy they generate! In such a feeling of good, only good can exist. "There am I in the midst of them." In other words, there are my attributes in the midst of them—love, peace, abundance, wholeness, and all of the other qualities of good—of God.

THE POWER OF A GROUP

Ten college students were individually given a test to measure their intelligence. The average test score was 113, which was a bit above average. A similar test was then given to the same students, but this time they all took the one test collectively as a group. The questions were projected onto a large screen, and then they all would agree to a single "group" answer. The one score for the group was 145.

Why the difference? It's obvious, isn't it? If one

person didn't know an answer in the individual testing, he or she did not get credit. But, in the second test, if one student didn't know an answer, someone else probably did. Each student supplemented the others' knowledge.

In much the same way, a spiritual support group can "supplement" you. There may be times in the months ahead when you feel discouraged. You may feel that you have stopped making progress, that you've gone about as far as you can go. Perhaps, for the moment, you will have. After all, even plants rest between seasons, gathering their energy for the next growing period. But some of the others in your spiritual support group *will* be making progress or will be able to encourage you either by their words or by their examples. The unfailing tide of good will be lifting them and, as any sailor knows, when the tide comes in *all* boats rise.

Also, the group itself takes on an "over-soul," a mind, a power greater than the sum total of all the members of that group. The group generates a power far greater than the sum of its individual members. That's why it is so important to have a carefully chosen spiritual support group. It will be your "booster" when your own enthusiasm sags.

CLIMBING MOUNTAINS

If you were trying to climb a mountain, you wouldn't choose a support group of people afraid of heights! Be careful about surrounding yourself with people fearful of spiritual heights—their own or yours.

Now this doesn't mean that if someone is not on your exact spiritual path, he or she should be dismissed from your life. That's a quick way to become a hermit! Lots of people have husbands, wives, and children who do not share their spiritual aspirations, but they don't divorce them or disown them. Nor do people quit their jobs because their bosses or co-workers don't believe as they do.

Respect your mate's, children's, and co-workers' spiritual beliefs, but don't necessarily look to them to supplement yours. They are scaling a different part of the mountain. Their way will take them toward the top, too, but it may be at a different time and in a different way.

We are all on a path to know God. Eventually, we will all complete the journey toward God-awareness, but *your* time is now. You have chosen this time to journey on your quest. It will be even more rewarding if you can travel the path with spiritual companions.

Hopefully, you will be creating a spiritual support system. (The Activity Book will give you specific help.) Be sure you recruit the right people into your group. Ultimately, all paths eventually lead to God-awareness, but why follow someone who's not sure where to go or how to get there? Why not make the journey with *two or three gathered in (His) name?* There will be the spirit of the Way-Shower in the midst of you.

Please Note: If by choice or circumstance, you do not create a spiritual support system, try to give your energies to people and things which are supportive of your spiritual growth. Alone or with others, the journey lies before you—beckoning. Follow.

M ile markers

- The support of caring friends can make it easier for you to achieve your transformation.
- All of your energies should be invested in your growth.
- A support group generates a power far greater than the sum of its individual members.

Thank You, God, for my supportive friends. I now draw to me the right people with whom I share my journey. I know that their caring support is really an expression of Your great love.

Please proceed to Adventure 2 in the Activity Book.

the teaching

$\mathcal{W}$HAT GOD IS | **3**

You know there is something greater than you. What exactly is this "something" which we call God?

Defining the indefinable

"I thank thee, Father, Lord of heaven and earth, that thou hast hidden these things from the wise and understanding and revealed them to babes."
—Matthew 11:25

In a tiny Italian village stood a most beautiful church. For as long as anyone could remember, people had come from near and far just to see the magnificent fresco called *The Holy Family*, which was painted on one of its walls.

But one unfortunate day during World War II, the village was bombed, and part of the famous fresco was reduced to rubble.

After the war, the church was rebuilt, with the exception of the one wall. Where the beautiful fresco had once been, there now was only little more than half of the work left, sitting side by side with a glaring stretch of new, bare plaster.

The saddened villagers desperately sought to salvage their treasure. Artists and experts from all over the world were brought to the church, in hopes that they could restore the beloved painting. One by one they tried, but none succeeded. No one could capture the style and the colors of the original. It seemed as if the scene were gone forever.

Then one day a very old man walked through the church doorway. He said he had heard about the damaged fresco and felt sure that he could restore it. After some time, he managed to persuade the priest to let him try his hand at restoring the pathetic wall. For two full days, the man worked in silence. The priest was becoming very uneasy, anxious to see some proof of the man's ability.

But at the end of the third day, when the priest made his daily inspection of the work, he could hardly believe his eyes. A small portion of the missing fresco had been restored to its original beauty!

The man was commissioned to complete the work, which he did in a few months. When he finished, the church bells wildly rang out the great news and people everywhere streamed into the church. It was the most special day the tiny village had ever known.

A great celebration was held to honor the artist. Someone asked him how it was that he could accomplish what so many others could not. He smiled and said: "It was I who painted that fresco more than fifty years ago. I created it, and now I have restored it."

And that is what God is like. It is God who created the universe, and it is God who can, will, and does restore it.

Notice we said that "God is like ..." God is so vast and so unknowable in totality that we always end up finding things that God "is like" rather than defining what God "is." You've probably heard the story about the blindfolded people who, after having their hands placed on an elephant, were asked to define the object. Each, of course, could only know the part he was experiencing. "It's a large snake!" exclaimed the man holding the trunk. "No. It's a huge leaf," said the one feeling an ear. "I say it's a solid pillar," added the person with his arms around a leg. "You're all wrong," countered the one holding the tail. "It's a buggy whip."

Each of us can only know the God of his or her own experience. Just as there are as many definitions of an elephant as there are hands on the animal, there are as many definitions of God as there are people on this earth. Each of us sees God in his or her own way.

Like sunlight passing through cut diamonds, each stone defines the sunlight in relation to its individualized facets and interprets the sunlight in its own manner. The sunlight is still the same, but it is being expressed—defined—in countless distinct ways. Michelangelo saw God as a man with a flowing beard in the sky when he painted that figure on the ceiling of the Sistine Chapel. Thomas Carlyle saw the universe as one vast symbol of God.

The artist Vincent van Gogh believed that the best way to know God is to love many things. He was probably right. The more of God's creation we can become aware of and love, the more we become aware of the Creator who brought it all into existence. Yet, even if we were to know and love every person and thing we ever encounter, we still would not really know God. After all, how could we possibly hope to know and understand a Power, a Mind, capable of imagining a universe and then creating it?

MYSTERY IN MELONS

Picture a ripe watermelon seed, black and shiny. It contains the power to draw from the earth and through itself two-hundred thousand times its weight! When you can explain how it takes sunlight from the sky, water from the clouds, and minerals from the earth and turns them into a bright green rind and vivid pink core deliciously enfolding many black seeds just like the one which started the process and each of which is also able to draw through itself two-hundred thousand times its weight—when you can explain the mystery of the watermelon, you will be able to explain the mystery of God.

But don't let that discourage you. Is it really necessary to define God in order to experience the presence of God and the power of God? Not at all. Can you define and explain electricity? No. Even Thomas Edison admitted he could not. But you can see its effects and experience its power and benefits as it lights your home and powers your television set. You can know God as a transforming experience in your life just as you can know electricity: not by what it is but by what it does.

Since God is greater than the sum total of all that is, it is beyond our capacity to know all of the infinite facets of God. Yet we can know some of them. We can know God as love, as peace, as joy, as wholeness. We can know God as all of the transforming principles of good. We can know God because we know ourselves and our families and our friends and all of the wonders of creation that are part of our lives.

If we know God in this way, what does it matter if we cannot define God? When you flip the switch on the wall, the light goes on. You might not be able to explain it, but you can know it as light. When you turn to God, light comes into your life. You don't have to know how it works. All you have to know is that light comes into your life.

Jesus warned that God is not revealed to the "wise and understanding." To attempt to know God through the intellect or by studying or reading *about* God is fruitless. The harder we try to know God by that method, the more elusive our God experience becomes.

It is only when we are open and innocent, with no preconceived notions about sensing the presence of God, that we discover we have made that inner connection with God. Then we find that knowing God is a simple and very natural experience for us.

ATTRIBUTES OF GOD

There are many names for God: Truth, Love, Good, Higher Power, Universal Mind, Peace, Spirit, Substance, Creator, the Presence, Father, Mother, Father-Mother, Divine Mind. These are only a few of them. Whatever way you feel comfortable identifying this Creative Force is right for you. The name is not nearly as important as what it represents in your heart. We believe that *there is only one Presence and one Power in this universe—God, the good.* This truth is at the very heart of *The Quest*.

There is only one Presence. There is only God. Therefore, God is omnipresent. This universal presence is an aspect of God. Since God is all, there can be nothing outside of God. There can be no place where God is not. Everything is part of God. Therefore, God is more than omnipresent; God is Omnipresence!

Let's slow down and really think of that: *everything is part of God, everything.* Think of how that knowledge affects us. Think of how such an abstract statement helps us live better lives. If we embrace the fact that everything is part of God, then we must admit that we are *all* part of God, we are all one with God and one with each other. There can be no quarrels, no conflict, and no wars among people who truly understand that oneness.

And more than that, wherever we are, God is. No matter what problem we are facing, no matter how confused we are, no matter what we are going through, God is with us. How comforting that knowledge is.

God is also omnipotent, all-powerful. This is another aspect of God. Yet even more than being all-powerful, God is Omnipotence, All-Power, the *only* Power there is. And this Power is good!

Not only are there no other powers, there can be no other powers! Since God is in all places, there is no room for any other gods or any other powers. That means the power that is God is always in our lives and always available to us. And we can use this power to the extent that we can recognize and acknowledge it.

Furthermore, God's omnipotence is precisely why

there can be no evil. If God is perfect good, in every "place," and has all power, then there can be no "place" where evil can have power. Just as there can be no fire in a universe of water, so there can be no evil power in a universe of good.

We realize this brings up the very legitimate question of "if there is only one Power operating in and through us and It's good (God), then who or what generates all that we consider to be 'bad'?" The answer is quite simple. While the power in us is most assuredly God's, we have been given the freedom to use it in any way we desire. The power of electricity provides a good analogy. We can use it to light cities, run machines, and make our lives easier. We can also use it to execute people in an electric chair.

Atomic energy is another strong analogy. It can provide power for our homes and light up a city when used for peaceful means or it can annihilate a city when deployed for destructive means. We humans determine how we use it.

And it is we who decide how to allow God's power to express itself in our lives. No matter in which direction we use it, it *still* is the power of God. Sound startling? It just proves the magnitude of our importance to God, that we have been entrusted with such a power as well as the ability to determine its expression in our lives.

Furthermore, since the only power is God, and God's plan for us is only good, we have to assume, and trust, that even when in some areas there appears to be "evil," there is always a larger, higher plan for good. We may not be able to see it, but it's there. (This puzzling question of "evil" will be discussed more fully in Teaching 10.)

God also has universal knowledge. God is omniscient. God knows all things. More correctly, God is Omniscience. God *is* All-Knowledge, which is all knowingness. The mind of God is universal and encompasses all things. How could it be otherwise? How could the ultimate Creative Force not totally embrace all knowledge? It *is* all knowledge. And that's great news, too, because it means there is an answer to every problem, to every challenge in our lives. Here's why: Since we are part of God, our own minds are part of God's mind. God's mind operates through us! This means we have access to all of the intelligence of the universe.

Notice that in listing these attributes of God, we did not just say that God is omnipresent or that God is omnipotent or that God is omniscient and leave it at that. God does not only "have" these attributes. God does not only "possess" these attributes. Rather, God *is* Omnipresence, God *is* Omnipotence, God *is* Omniscience. To have or to possess implies that these are separate aspects which must somehow be acquired when, in fact, they are all part of the totality of what God is.

Omnipresence, Omnipotence, Omniscience—one God. One God, and that God is all, and that God is good.

DIVINE ORDER

We'll be talking later about your role in all of this, but right now let's be concerned with God's role. God's role is to love and protect and guide you every step of your way. You only have to contemplate the miracle of the life within one tiny cell of your body to realize the care and concern which lovingly went into your creation. The wizardry of intelligence in a single cell is a phenomenon no scientist in the world can duplicate.

God's power is within you, available at all times to help you and to bring more good into your life. It is the nature of God to create perfection and to continually make new. Once you accept this basic truth, be prepared for things to get better. It could be that all God wants from us is awareness of the Presence. This simple awareness opens the way for God to be active in our lives, and that means some major transformations are about to take place.

We come to see that there is a "divine order" to our lives, that things are working in a way which feels right. We view each event and person as an integral part of this order and are able to perceive how each is a participant in a grander scheme than just the immediate. The more aware we are of God's presence and power in our lives, the more clearly we recognize that divine order is taking place. We don't "make it happen." It is already established for us. Some people call it luck. We call it God.

A PERSONAL GOD

Surely you have questions which haven't been answered here, but things will become more clear as we progress on the journey. We seem to have come upon a sunlit clearing in the forest, a perfect place to rest awhile on our journey. At this point, we'll leave you with your own abstract thoughts about what God is and what God means to you, something to ponder for a lifetime.

For now it is enough to know that God has created

you and sustains you. As vast and infinite as God is, this Spirit cares for you and responds to you in a personal way. The more you cooperate with It, the happier and easier your life will be.

It is only natural for God to be personally and intimately involved in your life. Never for a moment forget that. You might be tempted to say, "That's ridiculous. How could Something which holds the constellations in their patterns, turns the tides of the giant seas, and brings spring each year ever be concerned with little me?"

How could It not?

*M*ile markers

- You can only know the God of your own experience.
- Knowing God is a very simple and natural experience.
- There is only one Presence and one Power: God, and God is good.
- God is Omnipresence, Omnipotence, and Omniscience.
- God is all.
- We don't make divine order happen. It is already established in our lives.

Thank You, God, for creating me and sustaining me. I know in my heart that You are the only Presence and the only Power in this universe and in my life. You are all there is—and It is good.

Please proceed to Adventure 3 in the Activity Book.

the teaching

WHAT AM I?

4

Have you ever asked yourself what you are, who you are, and from where you came? Once you know those answers, your life can improve dramatically.

How do I fit in?

> *"To you has been given the secret of the kingdom of God."*
> —Mark 4:11

A third-grade class was being led through the Natural History Museum with their teacher. A guide patiently explained each exhibit. "This large creature is a dinosaur. Its real name is *Brontosaurus.* It lived 80 million years ago. In our next display is another dinosaur. It is a two-footed, flesh-eating *Tyrannosaurus.* Next is the largest bird that ever flew ..." Working their way through the museum, the children were in awe of the strange creatures with even stranger names. Finally, they came to a lifelike exhibit depicting early Cro-Magnon men and women dressed in animal skins, sitting around a campfire. One little girl looked at these alien man-ape creatures and saw her own dim reflection superimposed on the glass which separated her from the figures. "What am I?" she asked her teacher.

Have you ever stared into your own eyes in a mirror and looked beyond the reflection of yourself, beyond the circumstances of your life, beyond the details of your birth—your parents, grandparents, ancient ancestors? Have you ever looked past even the clouded reflections of the countless eons that have brought you to where you are now and wondered ... "What am I?"

QUESTIONS LEAD TO QUESTIONS

You are not alone in asking. The Tree of Learning is swarming with people looking for a clue. Climbing up one side are the scientists observing, measuring, weighing, calculating. "Is light a particle or a wave?" "Why is the universe expanding?" "What is the structure of the atom?" Their questions lead to answers which lead to questions which lead to answers which lead to more questions.

Climbing the opposite side of the Tree are the theologians discussing, meditating, thinking, philosophizing. "What is the nature of God?" "Where is God?" "What is Truth?" "Why are we here?" Their questions lead to answers which lead to questions which lead to answers which lead to more questions. The scientists on one side of the Tree and the theologians on the other and everybody in between, including the little third-grader, are looking for the answer that is on the uppermost leaf of the top branch of the highest limb.

The question "What am I?" is the basis of *all* inquiries, from scientific to theological. From Aristotle to Einstein, from the Old Testament writers through the disciple Paul to each individual on the planet, finding the answer to "What am I?" is the unconscious trigger of every action in our daily lives.

IS YOUR "WHO" YOUR "WHAT"?

Notice the question is not "Who am I?" This would be too limiting. "I am the electrician." "I am the office manager." "I'm a nurse." "I'm a surgeon." *Who* I am defines the superficial me: "I am Bill's son Harry." "I am Harry's wife Meg." "I am Nancy, a third-grader on a field trip to a museum." "I am a museum tour guide." Muhammad Ali, the great heavyweight boxing champion proclaimed, "I am the greatest boxer in the world!" So you see that *who* I am can only be a temporary definition.

"Who am I?" attempts to define the sum total of characteristics that make up our earthly "persona," our ever-changing sense of self, our *personality.*

But the answer to *"What am I?"* identifies our *individuality.* It defines us at our nucleus, and that is the "I" we all yearn to know.

Ralph Waldo Emerson said, "Man is a piece of the universe made alive." There is a great degree of truth to that. We are creations of God. That makes us "children" of God, and so we resemble God. This is not to say that we are God. We are not God anymore than a wave is the ocean, but the created reflects the nature of its creator. The wave is born of the ocean—it is a "child" of the ocean, and so while it can never be "the ocean," it is nonetheless one with it.

Not, God!

Like the wave, we are expressions of God's universe. We are indeed "the universe made alive." Each of us is a congregation of inert elements of the physical universe—carbon, hydrogen, nitrogen, iron,

49

sodium, and many others, all of which are no different from the elements in the Earth, the other planets,
and the stars. But we are unique, vital clusters of
those elements, able to walk and talk and dance and
sing and think and love and contemplate our place in
the universe. We are pieces of the universe made
alive! The universe would not be complete without
each one of us.

Yet we are more than complex arrangements of
physical elements. We reflect the nature of God, with
all the secrets of the universe available to us.

GOD'S QUEST

Think of the immense journey that life has taken
evolving to where we are. From the earliest single-
celled forms of life all the way up to complex human
beings, it has been a slow, steady march toward perfection. Throughout the millennia, the Creative
Power of the universe—the Power we call God—has
sought to create the perfect vehicle through which to
express Itself. It has been God's own quest!

So here we are, with all the dreams and ideas and
hopes of God invested in us. An old Kalahari proverb
says that God is dreaming a dream, and we are it!
We are it, the children of God, the beloved creatures
through which the Creator intends to best express
Itself to the universe. We have been chosen—divinely
ordained—to be the hands, the feet, the voice, the
eyes, the ears, the hearts of God.

Although we are the pinnacle of God's creation and
dreams, with all the responsibility which that implies,
we are not created and then left to our own devices.
God is always right here with us, holding our hands—
like an invisible guide on our quest—if only we choose

50

to follow it. Truly, we are the children of God.

PERSONALITY AND INDIVIDUALITY

But what we *really* are and what we *seem* to be
can be as vastly different as a mute eagle egg lying
humbly in its nest and that majestic eagle gracefully
spiraling upwards on a current of warm air far above
us. The difference between the two is in the *awareness* of who and what they are.

Like the yolk of the egg which contains the genetic
code for the eagle, the essence of us, our "yolk," is
our individual oneness with God. We call this our
individuality. It is our real self, our true self. It is
our spiritual identity.

But like the unhatched eagle, we are imprisoned in
shells of our own. Our shells are the hardened, outdated attitudes and behavior which we show to the
world. This is our *personality,* the human part of us,
the external of us. Because our personality can express itself in so many ways, we can have a very difficult time identifying *who* we are.

Our current personality does not define the essential us. Our identity is our individual awareness of
our oneness with God. We are spiritual beings. Just
as it is natural for an eagle egg to become a magnificent bird, so all of the forces of the universe are directed toward nurturing us in our transformations.

If an eagle egg could see, it would gaze in awe at a
soaring eagle, thinking, "I'll never fly like that. Eggs
can't fly!" That's right, eggs cannot fly, and they
never will, but eggs can hatch into eagles.

Right about here, you might be tempted to ask, "So
why don't I hatch?" The answer to that question

emerges once you have an understanding of your three-fold nature: spirit, soul, and body.

THREE-PART HARMONY

In order to proceed on your quest, there must be a constant source of inspiration available to you. Think of it as a well from which you can draw fresh ideas and inspiration. After all, your roots must be constantly nourished if you are to grow. Your spirit is your infinite well of inspiration. Sometimes referred to as *superconscious mind*, it is the source of all you are.

Your spirit is your true *individuality*. It is infinite, unchanging, and indestructible. In the next teaching, it is referred to as your true "Christ center." It can be thought of as that part of you where you "connect" with God. From this "connection" flows all of the good that God wants for you. This flow of divine ideas never ceases. How could it? The Source is infinite.

"Okay. So if there is an unlimited amount of good flowing toward me, why am I not getting it all? What's wrong here?"

If you were to hold an empty cup under a bubbling waterfall, how much water would you come away with? Not more than a cupful, that's for sure. A waterfall may surge gallons and gallons each minute, but you're only able to take with you the amount of water that can fit into your cup or your canteen or your bucket or your tub or your tanker truck ...

Let's think of your spirit as a "waterfall," offering an infinite amount of ideas and inspiration. But you only can utilize the amount which your container can accept, and your container is your soul.

SOUL IS PIVOTAL

The soul, or mind, is your consciousness. It is your thoughts, feelings, and memories. It takes divine ideas from your spirit and molds them into a shape that satisfies its present need. Yet the soul can only use what it can accept. (Remember the cup, bucket, tub, and so forth.) So, for instance, while we know that love is always freely flowing from Spirit, if in your mind you don't feel worthy of love, then you can't experience love in your life. In a sense, you're standing in front of the waterfall with a small, leaky cup.

This is why some people have more love or prosperity or other good things in their lives than others. Their consciousness of love or prosperity is greater. They have taken larger containers to the waterfall.

The soul is the entire mind—both the conscious mind, where thinking and reasoning take place, and the subconscious mind, where feelings and memories reside. And isn't it our thinking, feeling, and remembering that really inhibit our good? "I know I'll inherit this disease, just like my mother." "I'll never be prosperous. No one in my family ever was." "I always have such rotten luck. I'll bet my X rays will be bad."

We also limit our good by the many negative beliefs of society that we adopt as our own: *"It's the flu season*, I'll be getting it soon ..." "Well, there goes my prosperity, down with *the coming recession ...*" "I'll never find anyone special *at my age.*"

Spirit is always giving because Its nature is to protect, guide, and inspire us. But the gifts from Spirit must be allowed to flow unhampered by the fears, worries, habitual thinking, and negative beliefs that too often jam the soul. These filter out much of our good, diluting it to the flavor of our present feelings about ourselves.

We find it helpful to think of the soul as pivotal. It can receive inspiration from one's spirit, or it can receive impressions from the five senses. Such impressions could come from reading that a sickness is "incurable" or hearing "you don't have enough education to find a good job" or thinking "I'll never find another friend like that."

The soul possesses the awesome ability to look to the spirit within or to the world without. Just think! Every moment of your life you are making the decision either to be fed by what God offers or by what the world offers!

It doesn't take much figuring to realize that if there's a change to be made in any area of your life, it has to begin with a change in your soul. This is where your transformation takes place. Since your spirit is perfect and unalterable, and your body and outer affairs merely reflect what's going on in your thoughts and feelings (your soul), that leaves the soul (or mind) as the place where the work must be done. Everything that you will be accomplishing in our journey together will be accomplished inside of you—in your soul, in your consciousness. That's why we keep referring to *The Quest* as a journey of the soul.

BODY BUILDING

We now come to the third aspect of what we are: the body.

Michelangelo's *David* did not begin as the magnificent statue which stands today in the Academy of Fine Arts in Florence. Before Michelangelo ever

54

picked up a chisel, an infinite number of Davids existed in the raw marble. But to Michelangelo's consciousness, there was only one unique *David* in that stone. The *David* that he created perfectly mirrors his consciousness at the time he did it. It reflects the thoughts, feelings, memories, impressions, and collective ideas of the human race which he held. Thus, Michelangelo is the soul of *David*. It was he, using the character of his own thoughts, expressing his own consciousness, who formed the "body" *David* to mirror those thoughts and that consciousness.

In much the same way, the soul "sculptures" a body (and affairs) which mirrors its own consciousness. Our bodies, as well as the state of affairs of our lives, are reflections of our minds. They are thoughts transmuted into cells, tissues, and circumstances.

To the extent that the soul utilizes divine ideas from spirit, the body and outer affairs move toward perfection in the same way as scrupulously following a perfect set of blueprints would give you a perfect house. But when the soul redirects its attention away from spirit, you're on your own. ("God, not Your will but *mine* be done!") It's like throwing dice and taking your chances!

"WHAT AM I?"

So what are you? You are composed of spirit (the divine you), soul (the mental and emotional you), and body (the physical you). Your spirit is your true identity because you are a God-being—a perfect idea in the mind of God. The more you identify with your spiritual self, the closer you are to answering "What am I?"

"Who" you are is what you are expressing right

now. "Who am I?" is up to you to decide every moment of every day. "What am I?" was decided by God a long time ago.

Somewhere in the past we may have forgotten. We no longer remember what we are. Like Sleeping Beauty, we lie numbly waiting for the handsome prince to awaken us. But once we hear the call to venture forth upon our quest, our souls stir. We are awake. And we remember.

Mile markers

- As a wave is part of the ocean, you are part of God.
- You have been created to be the hands, the feet, the voice, the eyes, the ears, the heart of God.
- You are spirit (the divine part of you), soul (the mental and emotional you), and body (the physical you).
- Your spirit (the Christ within you) is your true identity.
- The soul is where you do the work, where you make the changes.
- The soul is pivotal and can look within as well as to the outer.
- The conditions of your life mirror the condition of your soul.

Thank You, God, for the awareness of who and what I am. I am awake to the realization that You have created me to express You. I make the commitment today to be Your hands, Your feet, Your voice, Your eyes, Your ears, Your heart. Live Your life through me, God, fully and completely.

Please proceed to Adventure 4 in the Activity Book.

Do you know the difference between Jesus and Christ? Understanding this difference will provide you with a wonderful key to yourself.

The man and the Christ

"I am the light of the world; he who follows me will not walk in darkness, but will have the light of life." —John 8:12

When Benjamin Franklin wanted to introduce street lighting to the people of colonial Philadelphia, he did not lobby politicians, he did not publish editorials, he did not argue with those who disagreed with him. Instead, he simply hung a brilliant lantern on a long bracket in front of his own house.

Every evening, as dusk approached, he faithfully lit the wick. People out in the dark night could see Franklin's streetlight from blocks away and were grateful to walk in its friendly glow.

Soon Franklin's neighbors started putting lanterns on brackets in front of their own homes, and it wasn't long before the entire city was illuminated each night with street lamps.

A BRIGHTER LIGHT

This is pretty much the way Jesus has influenced humankind, by example, by showing us what to do and how to do it. By letting His own light shine, He not only lighted the way for us but gave us the idea that we, too, have lights that should be shining.

Who is this Jesus, and why has He had more of an impact on humanity than any other person who ever lived? He wrote no great books and created no important works of art. He was not an international financier. He never commanded a powerful army, and He never ruled so much as a tiny nation. His death caused scarcely a ripple, other than among the relatively few followers He had attracted during His short public life.

If a time machine could take us back to the hills of Nazareth at the time of Jesus' childhood, we imagine that we would see a young boy who looked and acted the same as any other boy His age. He ate, drank, laughed, and cried. It's likely that He caught colds, had stomachaches, played hard, got angry, worried about his studies, and thought about girls. He probably attended Hebrew school in His hometown with all the other boys.

However, no matter where or what He studied, His *real* learning came not by tuition but by *intuition*—not from any outer reading or lectures but from an inner knowing. At some point, a great revelation came to this seemingly ordinary youth. He may not have grasped it totally at first, but there came a time in His spiritual growth when He was aware of the extraordinary Power within *Him*.

This was the true beginning of The Age of Christ.

At that moment, Jesus of Nazareth, the carpenter's son, began His quest for Jesus, "the anointed One," Jesus "the Christ."

A STAR TO FOLLOW

The Quest is based on the *teachings* of Jesus, on the life-transforming discoveries He made. Why? Because when we study Jesus' *life* (instead of worshiping Jesus the man), we see a perfect example for us to follow. After all, was there ever anyone more spiritually centered? Was there ever anyone whose words and actions so exuded love? Was there ever anyone more at peace with Himself and with His life than Jesus? That is why His life and teachings are the examples we can learn from in the quest for the transformation of our own lives.

Business students study the lives of great entrepreneurs so they can emulate their successful careers. Actors study other great actors to find more creative techniques. Writers read other great writers to improve their own writing skills. It is only natural that many on a spiritual quest turn to the study of Jesus' life and teachings. Many of these people call themselves Christians, but the word "Christian" is not important. The objective is to reconnect with the divinity within—to find God. The divine relationship between us and God is the only thing that counts.

TWO MINISTRIES

Jesus had two ministries. First were the healings and works He performed while on Earth. The second is a ministry which is only now being acknowledged and understood. It is for today. It is the deeper level of His teachings. You will find they are more applicable, more meaningful, in the twenty-first century than they were when they were first presented. They reveal that Jesus is not some God from the past. He is a living force whose teachings, if deeply understood, can show us how to eliminate unnecessary suffering from our lives today.

The essence of this second ministry is the assurance that our ultimate purpose is to experience the presence of God daily. If we can do that, then no matter what's going on in our lives, *everything* will be all right.

It's important to note that throughout His earthly ministry, Jesus never put the focus on Himself. At one point a man knelt to Him and said, "Good Teacher, what must I do to inherit eternal life?" Jesus quickly admonished him, saying, "Why do you call me good? No one is good but God alone" (Mk. 10:17-18).

This was not any false humility on Jesus' part. This was simply an acknowledgment of His humanness, His admission that He relied totally on God, for in fact, He repeatedly claimed He was helpless without God. "The Son can do nothing of his own accord, but only what he sees the Father doing" (Jn. 5:19).

JESUS THE MAN

So much attention has been paid to Jesus' divinity that we have overlooked His humanity. He was born fully human, just like the rest of us. He was fully a man. He was tested in the same ways that all of us are tested, but He transcended His humanness and opened the way to self-mastery, to a oneness with God.

Evidence seems to suggest that this self-mastery was a progressive unfoldment, always growing, always expanding. One can see it in His reluctance to begin His ministry at the marriage feast at Cana (Jn. 2:4), and in His working through His anger in the temple (Mt. 21:12), and in His initial snub of the Canaanite woman who asked help for her daughter (Mt. 15:22-28).

It is apparent that Jesus was always working to identify and experience His own spirituality. His teachings and healings are ample testimony to the continual expansion of His consciousness.

FREE WILL

There is an incident where Jesus returned to the synagogue in Nazareth. He knew the ancient prophecy of a messiah in The Book of Isaiah and He read it aloud in the temple: "The Spirit of the Lord is upon me, because he has anointed me to preach good news to the poor. He has sent me to proclaim release to the captives and recovering of sight to the blind." Then He closed the book, sat down and said, "Today this scripture has been fulfilled in your hearing" (Lk. 4:18, 21).

Many theologians point to this passage in Isaiah as a prophecy of the coming of Jesus and claim that this scene in the temple proves the prophecy was fulfilled in Him.

It seems more likely the ancient prophets, rather than anticipating a specific messiah, had an intuitive awareness of the Christ principle—that divine spark latent in all humanity. They created a template, a model. In a sense, it was a "job description"! It called for someone who could find the Christ in himself and who would lead others to the Christ within themselves. They knew that this was achievable and that someone would eventually appear who would be able to do it.

So, when Jesus read Isaiah's prophecy, it was as if He were announcing, "This job description fits me. I volunteer; I will take the position. I will be the one. I will do all that I have to do to allow the Christ *in* me to express *as* me. And by my example, I will show others how to do it."

It seems obvious that Jesus made a conscious choice here. And it was *His* decision alone to make. This was Jesus, exercising His own free will, making a self-motivated decision for Himself. He was not forced into it, nor was it predestined that He step into this role.

What *was* predestined was the inevitable discovery of the divinity of humankind by someone, but it was not predestined that Jesus be that someone. How can we know? Because where there is predestination, there is no free will, and Jesus, being fully human like you and like all people, had freedom of choice.

To help explain this concept of predestination versus predisposition, we can say that it was predestined that the law of gravity would be discovered, but that doesn't mean Isaac Newton was predestined to do it. True, his scientific background and his temperament lent him a strong *predisposition* to make the discovery—but he was not preordained.

It was predestined that someone would someday break the four-minute mile barrier, but it was not predetermined that Roger Bannister be the one. Yes, because of his motivation and training, he was *predisposed* to do it, but so were many others.

Or how about this? We can say it was predestined that humans would someday fly. The laws of aerodynamics always existed, so it was inevitable that someone would eventually discover them. But the Wright Brothers were certainly not *predestined* to be the way-showers in flight. Yes, they had a strong predisposition, but they were not preordained.

In the same way, Jesus was not predestined but rather predisposed to achieve total mastery of Himself, to find God within, and to become the Christ. But it was *His* decision to make. He could have given up at any time. He could have failed!

WHY THE STRUGGLE

This is important, so let's explore this further. If Jesus had been predestined to be the Messiah, if there were no free will involved, why the desperate inner struggle in Gethsemane? (Because this is reported in three of the four Gospels, there is good indication that something of this nature took place.) After thirty-three years on His quest, He was the closest He had ever been to the goal of complete self-mastery. Yet, in a last holdout of human resistance, it seems He was tempted to go off and live a normal life, perhaps to get married and have children and live the life of a simple carpenter. Who knows? In the end, He won the struggle by *totally* surrendering: "Nevertheless not my will, but thine, be done" (Lk. 22:42).

"Nevertheless"! Nevertheless what? Doesn't this imply that He considered doing something else? "Not *my* will ..."! What was His will? Obviously different from God's will. Yes, He won the struggle, that's true.

64

He made the right choice between God's will and His will. *But He could have failed to choose God's will!* The fact that He did not fail doesn't prove that He *could* not fail. It proves that He, Jesus, decided He *would* not fail. It was always *His* choice.

Also, what about those earlier temptations in the wilderness? Let's not forget them and the fact that He *overcame* them. That implies that there was an overcoming to be made, and overcomings are made by humans, not God.

Consider this: If Jesus were "God incarnate," and He had that much trouble with temptations, what hope could there ever be for us? If He is God, that automatically deprives us of any ability to identify with Him. There is no lesson to learn—only a God of which to be in awe.

WE CAN DO IT TOO

Fortunately, that is not the case. Jesus audaciously insisted that whatever He had done, each of us could do. "He who believes in me will also do the works that I do; and greater works than these will he do" (Jn. 14:12).

That's a crucial statement, absolutely central to your transformation, because it tells you that you can experience the same spiritual insights that Jesus had. He is promising you conscious communion with God, if you will search the spiritual depths within yourself as He did.

Jesus is saying to follow His way and discover the secrets of your inner Self—the Christ in you—as He has discovered the Christ in Himself.

JESUS THE "CHRIST"

This seems like a good point at which to stop and get clear on what "Christ" means.

"Christ" is not Jesus' last name. The word *Christ* comes from the Greek word *Christos*, meaning "the anointed." "Christ" is a title reserved for anyone who becomes aware of and fully realizes the depths of his or her divine possibilities as Jesus did.

Even more importantly, Christ is God individualized in each of us. It is the name of the divinity within us. It is our pattern for perfection. "Christ" is not the name of someone born in Bethlehem 2000 years ago. (That was Jesus.) The Christ is an aspect of God. It has existed since the beginning of time. It is the identification of our highest degree of spiritual potential. The "real" you is your Christ self—your spirit.

Jesus was so aware of this presence of God in Him that He became one with It: "I and the Father are one" (Jn. 10:30), and so we call Him Jesus the Christ or Jesus Christ. He was not God made man. He was man becoming more Godlike.

When we talk about Jesus, we are talking about a soul so highly evolved that He became the perfect example of the God potential in each of us. That is what Jesus was, and is, all about: finding unity with God and thereby discovering the Christ power within. That's what you are all about too. That is what *The Quest* is all about.

THE MISSING LINK

So much has been written about Jesus. The Gospels are filled with stories about His life. Yet we miss a major point if we believe that the Gospel stories are stories about God acting as a man. Where is the learning experience for us in that? Can we identify with the way God acts? Can we learn lessons from watching what God does? If we believe that Jesus was God, then the Gospels become interesting stories but with little that we can relate to in our own lives.

The Gospel stories are chock-full of messages and help for us because they are about one *man*—Jesus—on the quest. This is the key to understanding Jesus. If we don't approach Him from this perspective, we may have merely erected another monument to a god.

Christianity has lost sight of this human aspect of Jesus through worshiping *Him*! That is decidedly *not* what Jesus wanted. Remember, Jesus never put the focus on Himself. It was always—*always*—on God.

The principles that He revealed are a true missing link between God and us. We had always separated ourselves from God. We talked *about* God. We asked *of* God. We prayed *to* God. Prayers were answered *from* God. God was always a fearsome Being "up there." We were always fear-filled beings "down here."

But Jesus realized that the kingdom of God was not somewhere separate and removed from us. It was to be found within the hearts of all people. But instead of looking there, most of us have been looking at Him!

When Jesus asked us to come unto Him, He was inviting us to journey with Him and view the reality of life from a new perspective—a perspective He Himself had discovered. He was saying, in effect, "Don't worship Me, look within."

Don't you see His message? It means that we can

all do what He did when, and only when, *we make His discovery for ourselves.*

A MESSAGE FOR TODAY

The great discovery that Jesus made 2000 years ago is still relevant. It has everything to do with us and with our lives today. He is telling us that the same Infinite Mind that is in Himself is in us. Just as Jesus tapped this resource in Himself, we also can tap the limitless Power in us. We can all have a first-hand and immediate experience of God, and we can do it by following the example of Jesus because He is a *real* example. He is an example of a person, like you, who had the experience. He did it, so you know it can be done. If God, acting as a person, had been the first to climb Mt. Everest, it would still seem un-reachable. But one *real person* climbed it, which means it can be climbed by other people.

Yes, Jesus Christ was special, but as special as He was, we are all that special *in potential.* Note well that phrase *in potential.* Although we begin as the same "seed" as Jesus, He worked at becoming the perfect flowering of that seed and, in fact, became perfect man. He recognized the divine potential within Himself and expressed that divinity in His lifetime. This took Him from Jesus, the son of Jo-seph, to Jesus the Christ—Jesus "the anointed One." There was no longer any distinction between Jesus the man and His Christ self. They had merged as one.

A commitment to the inner Christ must be one of the first steps in your spiritual journey. What Jesus attained is no more than is expected of each of us. He found unity with God. Aren't we all striving for this unity? When we realize that the human part of us can't solve our problems, we will find ourselves seeking that same inner power that He sought—and found.

SECOND COMING

No doubt you've heard people speak of the second coming of Christ. What exactly is this second coming? Will Jesus come back to Earth at some future time to complete unfinished business? If so, when will it happen?

Jesus does not have to come back. Through His teachings and His example, He has already given us more than enough to take us as far as He went—or as far as we want to go.

So the second coming of Christ is not some historical event in the future. The second coming is an awareness—a person's recognition of the Christ presence within him or her. In other words, when the awareness of the Christ within "dawns" on a soul, the second coming has taken place. We say that the Christ is born in that individual. Rather than an incident to take place at some future time, the second coming is a possibility in each present moment—a possibility in each one of us.

We are all potential Christs. When we completely give ourselves to God as Jesus did, then we, too, are anointed. We, too, become "the Christ, the only Begotten." And when we do, we will experience the abundance of peace, prosperity, and love that God has in store for us. Jesus did it. He said that we could do it. That's why we follow His teachings. They are maps to show us the way back to our divine Source. And they are the most important maps on our quest.

$\mathcal{M}$ile markers

- Jesus is a living force whose teachings can show you how to eliminate unnecessary suffering from your life today.

- Jesus repeatedly claimed He was helpless without God.

- Jesus is the man. Christ is the divine essence of each individual.

- Jesus was not God made man. He is a man who became Godlike.

- Jesus acknowledged His oneness with God and lived from His Christ essence.

- You have the same potential as Jesus.

The Christ presence within me is the same presence which shone in Jesus. I let my own light shine, so that I, too, may be a blessing to this world. Thank You, God, for Your truth as revealed to me through Jesus Christ.

Please proceed to Adventure 5 in the Activity Book.

*The Bible is your story
and is filled with lessons
for today's world. Learn
how to discover its exciting messages for you.*

A new look at an old book

*"Then he opened their minds to understand
the scriptures."*   —Luke 24:45

Reading the Bible is like dining at a sumptuous
buffet. No matter the time of day or the mood you're
in, if you are hungry, you can always find something
that will appeal to you.

Who wrote the Bible? When was it written? Is it
the Word of God or of human beings or of both?
Should we take the Bible literally? As the best-selling
book in the history of the world, virtually everyone
who has read it has an opinion. Some argue for the
inerrancy of the Bible, stating that it is God's Word
and therefore should be taken literally in *every* detail.
Others see it merely as a harmless collection of interesting and historical moral anecdotes. In light of all
of the speculation surrounding it, does it have any

value? Or is it passé?

WHAT DOES PROVING IT PROVE?

All of the conjecture as to biblical fact and fiction, no matter how scholarly and profound, is only an intellectual assessment of this great work. Even if we did know the authors, even if we did know exactly when it was written, even if all of the questions of biblical scholarship were answered, what would we have gained? Would this knowledge bring us any closer to knowing God as a living Presence expressing through us? In viewing it merely intellectually, we miss the Bible's greatest messages: those metaphysical lessons that lie camouflaged in its characters, events, and symbols.

A mere intellectual understanding of the Bible is not the purpose, nor the extraordinary value, of this spiritual masterpiece. (Our Teacher, Jesus Christ, condemned the Pharisees for teaching the *letter* of the Scriptures and neglecting its *spirit*. They were more interested in scrupulously following the Mosaic law of how to cleanse their cups, for example, than in showing love and mercy to a neighbor!) The Bible, when seen past its "letter," when understood metaphysically, takes on a special meaning—one which we can use *directly* in our daily lives. That is why it is part of your *Quest* experience. As you trod the unfamiliar path ahead of you, you will be able to reach into the Bible for sustenance, much as you would reach into your knapsack for food.

BEYOND THE OBVIOUS

The word *metaphysical* is taken from two Greek words: *meta* meaning "above, beyond, or over" and *physika* meaning "physics." Metaphysical literally means "beyond the physical." So when we interpret the Bible metaphysically, we find personal meanings beyond the words. Underneath the obvious lesson, there is always the hidden meaning for each of us. If we study the Bible as religious history only, the living inner reality is lost. We fail to see it as an idealistic portrayal of our own spiritual development. Clearly, for those of us willing to look past the words, the Bible is a story of our own personal evolution. It is a story of our own spiritual unfoldment and growth. In allegory, story, and parable, it details how we were created with divine potential, how we have misplaced our divine heritage and, most importantly, how we can find it again. Because the Bible was written by people with spiritually illumined minds, we can see that unfoldment only to the extent that we allow Spirit to illumine our own minds.

We're going to take an overview of the Bible now, to get a feel for how it represents the spiritual evolution of humanity. Then we will look at a few specific stories to show you how you can discover their personal meanings for you.*

LIGHT THE WAY

The wonderful phrase, "Let there be light," found in the first chapter of Genesis, sets the tone for the entire Bible. In order to discover the layers of meanings of the Bible, we have to bring some light to them. Spiritual ideas can only be discerned spiritually, just as television signals can only be discerned with television receivers. We can learn our lessons only when

*The Revised Standard Version of the Bible is used for all references.

we allow ourselves to tune in to those lessons.

In Genesis, humanity is conceived and brought forth in innocence, unaware of its divine nature. In life we, too, are conceived and brought forth in innocence, unaware of our divine nature. The Garden of Eden in which Adam and Eve were placed represents all of God's unconditional good. We, too, are in a garden of divine ideas. And like Adam and Eve, we can choose to fall from innocence, disregard God's way and go our own way. Thus the double-edged sword of free will is born.

Much of the rest of the Old Testament is the story of the children of Israel, symbolic of us, in their struggle to find the Promised Land. Breaking their bondage to the Egyptians is our story as we struggle to break our bondage to our human shortcomings so that we can begin our journey into spirit. As did the Israelites, we, too, have wandered in the desert looking for our home. Our desert is the barren wasteland of dead-end thinking which we stumble through as we look to reconnect with God.

The Old Testament prophets? Surely they are our spiritual thoughts warning us, teaching us, directing us. The Israelites' constant disregard of the prophets' revelations perfectly reflects us each time we turn our backs on that still, small voice that so often speaks to us. Every story, event, character, and symbol in the Bible represents a state of consciousness in us as we, too, look for the promised land—as we, too, look to reunite with our spiritual home.

The Old Testament represents a state of consciousness that you have already experienced. It is the state of mind that told you if you *do* a certain thing, you can have good in your life. Your good is conditional. It depends on what you do and do not do. It depends on how you act.

The Ten Commandments are the cornerstone of the Old Testament and represent its consciousness. Immutably carved in stone, they imply that if you do certain things (love God, honor your parents, keep the Sabbath holy) and don't do other things (kill, steal, covet) this will make you worthy of God's good. In other words, if you do something in the outer, you change your inner self and become a better person.

NEW TESTAMENT, NEW CONSCIOUSNESS

The New Testament is different. It assumes that you have graduated from that elementary school of spiritual awareness. Don't you really know by now that it's wrong to kill, to steal, to commit adultery, to covet what is not yours? Of course. And because you know that, you're ready to take the next step in consciousness. The New Testament shows a new way. Rather than *doing* something, the New Testament says to *be* something. "You, therefore, must be perfect, as your heavenly Father is perfect" (Mt. 5:48).

Like some primitive amphibian lurking on the edge of a muddy tidewater and sensing it is time to continue its evolution in the land of air and sunlight, the entire New Testament is a triumphal march from our dim suspicion of the divinity within us to a glorious expression of that divinity. Jesus represents the Christ awareness in each of us as we allow it to become more and more active in our lives.

Jesus' life represents spiritual humanity in expression, the person each of us is destined to become. The saga of Jesus is the saga of your own soul, not necessarily where it's been but where it is capable of going. His birth to a virgin represents the birth of the Christ in you, capable of being conceived only by God. Jesus was born of Mary, a woman. A woman in the Scriptures usually symbolizes your feeling, emotional, and intuitive nature. The realization of the Christ in you is born in your feeling nature. It can't be intellectualized or analyzed. It can only be brought forth on an intuitive level.

(Whereas female characters in the Bible usually represent our feeling nature, male characters in the Bible usually represent our intellectual nature. They symbolize that part of each of us which looks only to facts and logic for answers. The scribes and Pharisees are the perfect biblical examples of this exclusively intellectual leaning. Their entire emphasis was on the letter of the law, and Jesus constantly chastised them for their intellectual bullying. It becomes obvious when reading the Bible that a balance of our male and female qualities, a judicious blend of the intellectual and feeling natures, serves us best.)

LOTS OF LESSONS

It's time, now, to metaphysically interpret some of the specific stories in the Bible. Keep in mind that every character, place, and event represents an aspect of *your* own self. What it means to *you* is the only important meaning it has. It may mean something entirely different to someone else. There can be no "right" and "wrong" metaphysical interpretations, because we each find a meaning relative to our specific life challenge and growth. Let's begin with a couple of examples from the Old Testament.

The story of Lot's wife is a good one (Gen. 19:15-26). On the surface, we see a stern and wrathful God punishing someone for what would seem to be a rather minor transgression—sneaking a glance backwards. After all, who hasn't done that? The obvious lesson: Obey God or you'll suffer the consequences.

As with all Bible stories, there are layers and layers to this story. Letting each character, location, and event represent a part of you, let's take a deeper look at the story of Lot's wife—this time from a metaphysical viewpoint. This is what it might mean to *you*.

Couldn't Lot's wife represent your feminine, feeling nature? Lot and his wife and family were on the road leaving Sodom, a city of sin that was being destroyed. They were instructed not to look back, but Lot's wife glanced back and was immediately turned into a pillar of salt.

Have you ever, like Lot's wife, looked back on a calamitous time of your life, a disastrous relationship or an early dysfunctional family life or a serious sickness or any negative happening in your past? To the degree that you involve your feeling nature (Lot's wife) in this retrospection, you are frozen in your spiritual growth. You are figuratively turned into a lifeless "pillar of salt." It doesn't matter that intellectually you concentrate on staying on the path. (Lot plodded on, never looking back, even after his wife was immobilized.) If your emotions are invested in something negative from your past, these negative feelings will restrict your growth.

The woman who suffers abuse as a child cannot grow into her full potential until she forgives and works through her painful feelings about that part of her past. Constantly looking back freezes her where she is. It inhibits any further growth. She is unable to grow past her feelings of unforgiveness. A man, constantly told as a young boy that he was worthless, cannot feel worthwhile until he stops looking back and investing his feelings in that early message.

Aren't the metaphysical lessons of this story much more subtle and rich than the surface one of obeying God? You already know you should do that. What you want to know now is how you can apply this story to your life to help you with your specific problem today! Isn't one of the messages for you in this story to stop looking back at a troubled time? (Actually, whatever your past, "good" or "bad," it has to be released before you can move ahead.)

THE CASE OF THE POOR WIDOW

In another story, a poverty-stricken widow complains to Elisha that she is broke. He asks her what she has, and she grumbles that all she has is one jar of oil. He tells her to go outside and borrow empty vessels. In other words, go outside of your present consciousness, which sees only lack. Empty your mind of poverty thoughts.

Then the woman is told to pour what oil she does have into the empty vessels, which she does. And what happens? The oil keeps flowing until her son (a male, representing the intellect, that analytical part of us that deals with "facts") tells her "there is not another" empty vessel! "Then the oil stopped flowing" (2 Kings 4:3-6). When your consciousness can't accept any more of your good, your good stops flowing. If you think you are only worth minimum wages, then that's all you will ever earn.

This story is a blueprint for prosperity, but that's only one of its lessons. There are layers more.

Let's move on to the New Testament. The Gospels are filled with vignettes of Jesus' "miracles." Each one gives us insight into the powers latent within ourselves. Let's look at a few specific stories.

There was that incident when Jesus was asleep in a boat and winds and waves threatened to overturn it (Mk. 4:35-41). Might not this mean that when the realization of the Christ in you is "asleep," all sorts of storm and turmoil appear in your life? All you have to do is to "wake up" to the Christ within and, speaking from this center, address your problems with the same command Jesus used: "Peace! Be still!"

In the story of the loaves and fishes, Jesus is faced with precious little to feed thousands. Instead of looking at what He didn't have, He "looked up to heaven" (Mt. 14:15-21). Looking up represents raising one's gaze, raising one's consciousness. If you keep looking at the problem, you stay in the problem. But if you look up, you are seeing above the problem into the solution.

In Jesus' resurrection of His friend Lazarus, He *hears* that Lazarus is dead; He *sees* that Lazarus is dead; He even *smells* that Lazarus is dead. All of His senses, all of the "facts," tell Him that this is a hopeless situation. (If being dead for four days is not hopeless, then nothing is!) Yet what did He do? "Jesus lifted up his eyes and said, 'Father, I thank thee that thou hast heard me.'" Again, He looked above the problem, He looked past the "facts." He commanded in a loud voice, "Lazarus, come out," and Lazarus came out bound in bandages from head to foot. Jesus said, "Unbind him, and let him go" (Jn. 11:1-44).

Your message? No situation that you face is "hopeless" if you face it with God. If you look "up," if you raise your consciousness above what you see or hear or read, then you, too, can command in a loud voice, "Problem, get lost."

On His way to Lazarus, Jesus told His disciples, "Our friend Lazarus has fallen asleep, but I go to awake him out of sleep." What a perfect way to put it. Jesus, who represents the Christ in you, "awakens" a memory that is dead. It is when you are asleep to your potential that you become bound up in your problems. It is only the recognition of the Christ within that has the power to unbind you and let you go.

In story after story in the New Testament, we are shown the possibilities in us when we operate from our Christ center. The death and resurrection of Jesus are the final lessons. It shows us not only the goal, complete oneness with God, but also that we must "die" to our human sense of separation before we can reach that goal.

THE LAST WORD

So the Bible takes us from Adam to Jesus, from unenlightened human consciousness to enlightened Christ consciousness. Viewed this way, the Bible itself is one great epic quest. It is the evolution of a soul—a journey we all must make, and the Scriptures tell us how to do it.

Now you see how the Bible can help you. It is a recital of what was and is taking place in the consciousness of humanity. It is what is taking place in you. It gives you insights that can help you solve your problems today. Let it be a rich and practical source of sustenance to you on your journey.

If you cannot use the Bible to improve your life, to help you find your oneness with God, then it becomes just another good book. But the Bible, both the Old and New Testaments, is more than a "Good Book." It is the ultimate "How-To" manual.

Mile markers

- Metaphysical lessons lie camouflaged in the characters, events, and symbols of the Bible.
- Underneath the obvious lesson there is always the hidden meaning for you, personally.
- The Bible is the story of your own spiritual unfoldment and growth.

Thank You, God, for Your living truth as it speaks to me in unmistakable ways.

Please proceed to Adventure 6 in the Activity Book.

*The concept of oneness
will show you that you
are not your brother's
keeper—you are your
brother.*

You make the universe complete

"I and the Father are one." —John 10:30

An emaciated beggar stopped Count Leo Tolstoy, who was out for an evening stroll. The great author, perceiving that the man was hungry, groped through his pockets for some money to give him, but found not a single cent.

Tolstoy was distraught at his inability to help the man. He took the beggar's worn and dirty hands in his, lamenting, "Forgive me, brother. I have nothing with me to give you."

The pale, tired face of the beggar lit up. "Oh, but you have just given me a great gift," he smiled. "You called me brother."

UNIQUELY THE SAME!

On the surface, we may seem very different from one another. After all, we are different races, have different politics, different religions, different philosophies, different beliefs, different nationalities, different opinions, different values. One of us may be a scraggly beggar while the other is an educated writer. But are we really that dissimilar? Too frequently we may notice our superficial differences while overlooking our incredible oneness.

We have already learned that the essence of us, our individuality, is the unique way in which God exists in each of us. (Just to recap, we also call this the Christ or the individual spirit. Remember?) This is not dependent on our race or religion or nationality or sex. It doesn't depend on how we look, how we act, what we believe, or what is believed about us. It is our connection to God, to the omnipresent Creator of all that is.

It may help you to think again of an ocean wave. Each wave, at its core is, was, and always will be ocean. It cannot help it. It may churn and seethe and foam in trying to be different, but that doesn't affect what it is at heart. Let's not confuse how something expresses itself with what it is. The ocean wave rumbles and froths hugely and menacingly in response to the wind. It becomes calm and serene in response to the warm sun. We can call one ocean wave a Catholic, another we can call a Jew, another a Hindu. We can label certain waves female and others male. We can identify some waves as Democrats and others as Republicans. That does not affect in any way the wave's oneness with ocean and, in that oneness, its unity with other waves.

The very circumstance which makes each of us so completely unique also makes us so absolutely the same! At a level far beyond our surface personalities lives the Christ, and this divine Presence is exactly the same in everyone. Its *workings* in each person's life are unique in that person, without doubt, but Its *presence* is identical throughout all humanity. No matter how each wave looks, it will always be ocean.

NO BOUNDARIES

Of what importance is that to you? It means that at your most spiritual level there is no boundary that marks where you leave off and someone else begins. Is there a boundary between one drop of water and another in the vast sea? No. And neither can you separate yourself (your "true" self) from the rest of the universe.

The word *universe* means "turned into one, a whole." Quite literally, the universe would not be complete without you. A whole needs *all* its component parts, and no one part is any more important than another.

At this early stage in your quest, begin viewing things from the perception of oneness. See the interrelatedness of *everything*. Why? Because in spite of what you may infer from the news headlines, which take great pains to exaggerate our differences, oneness is the natural state of humankind and the urge toward oneness is the natural tendency of the universe. Scientific literature is teeming with examples of how various cycles and rhythms in nature are synchronized. This tendency of things to synchronize with the rhythm of the universe can be found everywhere. In human beings, it begins at conception, when the fetal heartbeat, respiration, and general life rhythms soon attune themselves to those of the mother. It is obvious during breast-feeding when the heart rate and respiration of mother and baby synchronize. It has been known for years that women in college dorms will, without conscious effort, tend to synchronize their menstrual cycles.

One of the most dramatic examples of this movement toward oneness is the phenomenon that takes place when individual heart cells are put into a nutritive solution. Initially, each microscopic cell is pulsing, beating, to its own internal rhythm. (One is reminded of little Christmas lights which twinkle at different tempos.) But soon a most curious thing happens. Two of the tiny cells will come together and immediately begin to beat as one! Then two others will join and beat as one. And then two more. Everywhere in the small dish single heart cells will seek each other and unite as one. Soon the newly formed duos will begin linking with other duos, and *they* will beat as one. Then these quadruplets will merge with other quadruplets and so on, until at last there is only one single group of heart cells, all beating as one!

RECOGNIZING OUR ONENESS

There is something in these tiny cells which not only remembers what they were individually, but which also recognizes their oneness with each other. In acknowledging that oneness, each is driven, inexorably, toward achieving that oneness.

Heart cells are not alone in their impulse toward unity. There is an insatiable urge within every segment of the universe to become one with the One, one with the Whole. From the tiniest cell in a far-off corner of the cosmos to the complex being that you call "me," there is a yearning to return, like the Prodigal Son to the Father's house. It is the eternal pull of the Creator, ever drawing Its creations nearer.

Jesus spoke often of this phenomenon of oneness. "I and the Father are one," He maintained and, indeed, He did become one with the Father. The wave returned to the ocean.

Maybe you are not interested in all of the scientific evidence of this oneness, but once you open yourself to the idea, you'll begin seeing evidence of oneness everywhere and in everything. You will begin to experience an urge to "reconnect" with who and what you really are. You will know that you are part of the great creative Presence called God.

Once the idea of oneness is comprehended, the quest becomes so much easier, so much more meaningful. When you cannot only recognize but actually celebrate your oneness with God, with the universe, with the world, with everyone else, there is no longer any competition! There is no need to get ahead of someone. There is no fear of being left behind. There is no concern about "getting my share." What's more, you realize that every member of the human race is also on a quest. We all have the same dreams, the same fears, the same longings. The journey of a single soul is really the journey of all souls. We can see this if we just stop ... and listen ... and care.

Your very personal and special awareness of oneness is the exhilarating feeling that comes with knowing you are exactly where you belong—with God. You are on *The Quest* because you want to come home.

$\mathcal{M}$ ile markers

- Too frequently we notice our superficial differences while overlooking our incredible oneness.

- The presence of the Christ is in everyone.

- At your most spiritual level, there is no boundary that marks where you leave off and someone else begins.

- The urge toward oneness is the natural urge of the universe.

- Once you comprehend the idea of oneness, there is no longer any competition, no fear of being left behind.

I feel my connection with every living thing. My heart is open to the oneness of the universe. My eyes and ears behold the unity of all people. Their joy is my joy, their pain is my pain, because we are part of each other. Thank You, God, for these feelings of oneness which so touch and move my soul.

Please proceed to Adventure 7 in the Activity Book.

the teaching

CAUSE AND EFFECT | *8*

*The law which governs
the universe is abso-
lutely reliable and un-
breakable. Learning
how it works is crucial to
your success.*

The law that never lies

*"Judge not, that you be not judged. For with the
judgment you pronounce you will be judged, and
the measure you give will be the measure you get."*
—Matthew 7:1-2

It was the late 1800s and an important Member of
the British Parliament was hurrying through the rain
and fog of the bleak Scottish countryside to deliver a
crucial speech. Still miles from his destination, his
carriage was forced off the road, its wheels plunging
axle deep in mud. Try as they might, the horse and
driver could not move the carriage. So important was
his speech that even the aristocratic Englishman, in
his formal attire, gave a hand. But it was no use.
The carriage would not budge.

A young Scottish farm boy happened to be driving
a team of horses past the distraught parliamentarian

and volunteered to help pull the carriage loose. After much effort and considerable exertion, the carriage was finally pulled free. When the boy steadfastly refused to take any money for his help or for his clothes which were torn and dirty from the ordeal, the Englishman asked him what he wanted to be when he grew up.

"A doctor, sir. I want to be a doctor," was the reply. The gentleman was so impressed with the boy and so grateful for his kindness that he said, "Well, I want to help." And surely enough, he kept his word. Through his generosity, he made it possible for the young lad to attend the university.

More than fifty years later Winston Churchill became dangerously ill with pneumonia while in Morocco. His life was saved by a new wonder drug called penicillin, which had been discovered a few years earlier by a Scottish-born physician, Sir Alexander Fleming.

Fleming was the farm boy who helped the Member of Parliament on that dark and rainy night in Scotland half a century before. The Member of Parliament? None other than Winston Churchill's father, Randolph.

ALWAYS A BALANCE

"As you give, you get." ... "What goes around comes around." ... "The measure you give will be the measure you get."

Scientists put it into more analytical terms: Every action causes an equal and opposite reaction. (Anyone who has ever hit a tennis ball knows that.) No matter how it's said, it all means the same thing.

You probably already have a fairly good idea of this law. Every example of it may not be as dramatic and colorful as the opening story, but you can utterly rely on the fact that for every effect there is a cause. Conversely, for every cause there has to be an effect. This is the basic law of the universe, and so it is usually referred to as (what else?) the law of cause and effect.

Let's slow our pace for a moment so that you really get the impact of this law. Because the universe is based on it, your journey will be much simpler once you comprehend it. We come to it early in *The Quest* because you will need to take the understanding of this law with you. It will serve to get you through any rough parts of the trail.

Let's go back to our opening story. Alexander Fleming, as a boy, performed the selfless act of helping a stranger out of the mud. In response to this kindness (not to mention time and effort), Randolph Churchill set up funds so that the boy could go to the university and later become a physician. In this case, the effect came directly out of the cause. Boy helped man, man helped boy.

In the second part of the story, Winston Churchill's life was saved as a result of the kindness and generosity his father had shown a Scottish farm boy half a century earlier. This time the law was still at work, even if it took some fifty years to complete itself. Man helped boy, boy helped man by saving his son.

This story illustrates the law of cause and effect in its most simple-to-understand operation. What was initially set into motion as a cause eventually came to harvest as an effect. As you sow, so shall you reap, Jesus taught. Whatever seed you plant will one day come to flower.

IT EXPLAINS A LOT

It is imperative that we understand this law of cause and effect, because it explains so much. Our lives, and all life—the whole universe—at any given moment are rife with the results (the effects) of causes which were set into motion previously. And, concurrently, at any given moment we are setting into motion the causes which will be reaped by us in the future.

Some effects are immediate: touch a hot stove and you have a burned hand, knock a vase off a shelf and you have a broken vase, help a man out of the mud and he offers to pay for your education. Some effects take longer to blossom: abuse harmful drugs while you are pregnant and have a drug-addicted child in nine months, plant an acorn today and have an oak tree in several years, pay for a farm boy's education and have your son's life saved half a century later.

NO EXCEPTIONS

What it boils down to is this: Every thought, feeling, word, and action—*without exception*—is a cause which sets into motion an eventual effect. The law is immutable. The cause can be as small as a fleeting sense of anxiety over a physical symptom, in which case the effect is a fleeting change in the body, releasing negative and destructive chemicals. Or the cause can be as gargantuan as a national leader's decision to drop a hydrogen bomb, in which case the effect is the death and mutilation of millions of people.

There's no way to get around this law. When we set a cause into motion, we have to be prepared to reap the effect.

But there is a very interesting twist to this law of cause and effect, something we have to appreciate or life won't make much sense at times. *We do not always reap where we sow!* What does that mean? Simply this: The cause that you set into motion in one area of your life may come to fruition (have its effect) in an entirely different area of your life. In the case of Fleming and Churchill, the reaping was easily identified with the sowing. It's not always that clear.

A woman was wonderfully patient and loving with her stepson, only to have him steal her money and her car and run away from home. But the patience and love which the woman had set into motion was a cause which had to result in an effect somehow and somewhere. Where was the harvest? Not in the stepson's relationship with her, obviously, but in a seemingly unrelated area. (Actually, there are no "unrelated areas.") Soon after the stepson ran away, her relationship with her husband—a disaster when the boy lived with them—became much more loving.

Here's another example. A social worker spent many hours a week volunteering his time without much thought (or chance!) of financial remuneration. He sowed the seeds, put the cause into motion with his counseling, but his harvest, his effect, took place in another field. His grandfather, deciding to go into a retirement home, sold his dairy farm and gave most of the proceeds to his favorite grandson, the social worker. The social worker had done the good work and, knowing that good is always rewarded, knew his reward would come from somewhere. And it did.

Here's an exceptional example of the law that happened to some friends of ours. They had contracted to do a segment of a weekend seminar for $800. However, when they arrived early to set up for the day, they were told that they would receive only half of the agreed-upon amount. Since the seminar was sold out and the people attending were not involved in the disagreement between them and the sponsor of the seminar, they decided to go ahead with the weekend. At first they were angry at being cheated out of $400 but, after praying about it, decided not only to do the seminar but to do the very best seminar they had ever done. They knew that if they proceeded with this attitude, their reward, somehow and in some way, would automatically be commensurate with their loving efforts. So they put it out of their minds. They spent a full day presenting their seminar and even stayed long after it was over to answer individual questions.

Upon returning home, they stopped to pick up some brochures they were having printed. When the printer saw them, he remarked, "You two are such nice people, and you've given me so much business over the last two years that this one's on me." They looked at the invoice lying on the counter. The amount was $400.07. (God does have a sense of humor!)

What goes around comes around. "As ya gives, ya gits." The law is not usually that obvious or immediate, and it's seldom that blatant, but for every cause there *must* be an effect.

STOP ONE, START ANOTHER

While it's true that every cause you have set into

motion will eventuate in a corresponding effect, don't start looking over your shoulder for your past to catch up with you! Know why? *Because you can always put a new cause into motion.* That should be a comforting thought, considering all of the foolish things you may have done in the past.

Life is more like a sailboat race than a bowling game. Once thrown, a bowling ball heads inexorably toward exactly where you've directed it. The effect, the number of pins you knock down, is directly traceable to the cause: the way you threw the ball. After the ball is thrown, you can no longer affect its path, no matter how much you wiggle and squirm and coax as it travels down the alley. But in a sailboat race, you are constantly jibbing and tacking in response to changes in wind and wave. You are constantly changing course.

If your actions in the past have been the cause of an effect you don't like, *put a new cause into motion.* A husband's constant nagging at his wife led her to separate from him and take their two children with her. He was devastated, but honest feedback from his peers in group counseling showed him that his constant negative comments were the cause of his wife's leaving. He asked her for a reconciliation and, this time, concentrated on giving her and their children loving comments. He put a new cause into motion and of course was rewarded with a new effect, a positive one this time. The family is now back together.

If you are dissatisfied with a part of your life, know that it is the effect of a cause that you have put into motion and that at any time you can start again.

Your new cause will bring a new effect. "The measure you give will be the measure you get."

YOU ALWAYS REAP SOMEWHERE

One final point before we leave this all-important law. While you don't always reap *where* you sow, you always reap *what* you sow. If you plant radish seeds, there are no prayers or words or actions that can make them grow into anything other than radish plants.

A radish seed can never become a tomato plant, an acorn will never become a birch tree, a porpoise embryo can never result in a giraffe, a resentment can never bring peace. The infallible law is that you reap what you sow—maybe not always *where* you sow, but always *what*.

To those who don't understand it, this law of cause and effect can seem almost cruel in its impersonal and unbending manner. To those who do understand it, the law of cause and effect is the fairest, most rational of all laws because it guarantees that no capricious force can harm us or make us do something we don't want to do. When God gave us the gift of free will, we were also given the law of cause and effect to guarantee it would work. This law is a most trustworthy ally, always reliable and totally predictable.

Once you're aware of the causes you are setting into motion, you have the comfort and trust of expecting a like result—somewhere ... sometime. It's a law that never fails.

*M*ile markers

- Every thought, feeling, word, and action, whether large or small, is a cause which sets into motion an eventual corresponding effect.
- You don't always reap *where* you sow, but you always reap *what* you sow.
- You can always, at any moment, put a new cause into motion.
- The law of cause and effect is your trustworthy ally, always reliable and totally predictable.

I make the commitment today to let all of my thoughts, feelings, words, and actions go forth to produce good effects in the world. Thank You, God, for the comfort and the assurance of Your unfailing law.

Please proceed to Adventure 8 in the Activity Book.

*Do heaven and hell
really exist? Yes, but
perhaps not in the way
you originally thought.*

Where are they and how do I get there?

*"Behold, the kingdom of God is in the midst of
you."* —Luke 17:21

During his first campaign for Congress, Abraham Lincoln attended a church service conducted by a fiery evangelist. The congregation was asked to stand and sing a series of stirring hymns. After the songs were finished and while they were all still standing, the preacher commanded, "Anyone who wants to go to heaven, sit down!" There was immediately the thunderous sound of bottoms slapping pews. Everyone sat ... except Lincoln, who stood tall and straight amidst turning heads and hushed whispers. Somewhat puzzled, the preacher pressed further, "Anyone who doesn't want to go to hell, sit down." Still Lincoln remained standing like a lanky lighthouse in the middle of whispering waves of chatter.

"Mr. Lincoln, if you're not going to heaven and you don't want to escape hell, just where do you want to go?" thundered the evangelist.

Amid excruciating silence, all eyes turned to Lincoln. A broad smile came to his face. "I'm going to Congress," he said.

NOT ON ANY MAPS

Could be that Abe Lincoln knew a thing or two about heaven and hell that the preacher and the rest of the congregation did not know, namely, that heaven and hell are not places to go or to avoid. Heaven and hell are states of mind.

There is no geographical location where the streets are paved with gold, people play harps, and Saint Peter stands sentinel at a pair of pearly gates, arbitrarily deciding who may enter. Nor is there a geographical location ruled by a red-garbed being with horns, tail, and pitchfork, where people scream in agony and are tortured endlessly in eternal flames.

The notions of this kind of heaven and hell have been popular for centuries. If you happen to have been brought up in a traditional Christian home, chances are these ideas were passed on to you, too, and at a very early age. If they were, and if they are still your dominant impressions of heaven and hell, perhaps you can suspend this belief for a bit and stay open to what may be a new idea to you. The truth is that the idea itself is actually an *old* idea. It has its origins with Jesus, your Leader on *The Quest*.

HEAVEN

One of Jesus' primary teachings is that the kingdom of God is within. Not somewhere in the sky out there beyond our visual perception, but right inside of us. "For behold, the kingdom of God is in the midst of you." Jesus spent much time spinning parables and weaving metaphors about heaven. Yet there is not one word in the more than one hundred references that He made to heaven where Jesus describes it as a physical place "out there." Rather He said, "The kingdom of God is near" (Lk. 21:31). He would continually state what the kingdom of God is like ... And when He was pressed to get more specific, He would compare it to a grain of mustard seed (Mt. 13:31), or leaven (Mt. 13:33), or a treasure hidden in a field (Mt. 13:44), or many other comparisons.

Heaven is a state of mind. When you live in the awareness of God as a presence and a power in your life, when no matter what happens in the outer world the "real" of you is unchanging, peace-filled and expectant of good, heaven will indeed be in the midst of you, heaven will indeed be near.

It seems that while most of us have moments when we experience this heaven, for some reason or other we have trouble sustaining it, and so we move in and out of heaven helter-skelter. Is that the way with you too?

Although you may not stay in this state of heaven full-time, even a "short vacation" in it is enough to convince you that it's there and that you can return again anytime you wish. Your aim—the aim of *The Quest*—is to take up permanent residence in this state of mind called heaven.

By the way, nowhere is it written that being in this kind of heaven means not being playful or having fun. Some astute observer of the human condition once joked, "I don't mind going to heaven if I can go to hell every Saturday night." A funny comment, and like anything funny, there is at least a bit of truth to it. The "truth" it holds up to us reflects society's belief that "evil" things are often fun and "good" things are mostly a bore. Yet one of God's greatest gifts to us is a sense of humor and the ability to laugh. Heaven can be all that you want it to be and much, so very much, more.

HELL

Now what about hell? What about the myth of a devil and his dreadful abode? While merely a myth that is easily explained, myths die hard, especially if they are engraved in our souls when we are children.

The famous French priest, Abbé Arthur Mugnier, was asked if he believed in hell. "Yes," he hesitatingly replied, "because it is a dogma of the church, but I don't believe anyone is in it."

Well, the Abbé was right. People are not languishing in some physical location of hellfire and damnation. This doesn't mean people don't suffer in hell. They go there many times.

HAVE YOU BEEN THERE?

Have you ever been in hell? We have a friend, Sally, who is a former drug addict. She describes the time she was using drugs as "sheer hell." As a result of her addiction, she lost her job, her house, her husband, and nearly her life! Her children were taken from her by the courts and placed in foster homes. She hung out in the streets, sleeping in abandoned cars and flophouses. She was beaten and abused by the men she chose to be with, and she describes her self-esteem at that time as "lower than flat feet." Finally, she was sent to jail and, as part of her probation, had to attend a rehabilitation program. This was the beginning of her ascent out of "hell." Now, with over two years of drug-free living and with a good job and her children back with her, she uses such heartfelt, poetic words to convey the supreme joy of her recovery: "I thought that God had opened the gates of heaven and let me in, but I had opened the gates of hell and let myself out."

Hell is a state of mind. It, like heaven, is within. Yet if that's true, then where did we get the idea of eternal fire at a specific geographical location? It must have come from somewhere, and indeed it did.

THE HISTORY OF HELL

The word *hell* is not a correct translation from the original language of the New Testament, which was Greek. (Although Jesus and the people in His area spoke Aramaic, the New Testament was originally transcribed into Greek.) The "hell" referred to in The Gospels represents the word *Gehenna*, which was in a valley southwest of Jerusalem, where the refuse and filth of the city was burned. It was actually the city dump. There was no Environmental Protection Agency and so the consuming fires burned continually. In Jesus' day, it was a smoky, smelly, gruesome place.

Centuries earlier it had been even worse! Certain idol-worshiping kings of Israel had practiced appalling religious rites in this same place, sacrificing children in the fires. The region was called the Valley of Hinnom, which means groans and anguish. A perfect name for such a grisly site!

So Gehenna, located in the Valley of Hinnom

southwest of Jerusalem, became legendary as a place of human suffering and eternal fire. When Jesus and his contemporaries spoke of what we are now calling "hell," they were not referring to some underworld of eternal fire. They were referring to that infamous valley, using it as a metaphor for what happens inside of us, in our souls, when we go through our inner torments.

FIRE CAN BE GOOD

Fire is also a purifier, and we have to know that when we go through the "fires of hell," we need not come out frazzled and destroyed. We can come out changed for the better—transformed. There might even be some fires for you to encounter in your quest for your spiritual identity, but if there are, they will be only within yourself, not in some afterlife damnation. Furthermore, like tempered steel, you will emerge stronger, more resilient than ever before. No one has to stay in hell. Like our friend Sally, you can open the gates and let yourself out.

USE YOUR OWN JUDGMENT

Along with heaven and hell, we usually hear the term *judgment day*. That's the day we supposedly will all be taken before God, who will render the final judgment as to whether we go "up" or "down." Is there a judgment day? You bet there is. But it's not where, what, or when most people think it is.

Judgment day takes place each time you set a cause into motion. If you are responsible for some wrong action of any kind, you are "punished" *by* the deed itself. Your own thoughts and deeds are continually setting up their results, their judgments, and are "taking action" for or against you. No one escapes the day of judgment, because it is taking place every moment of our lives. (This will be expanded upon in later lessons.)

So, we see how heaven and hell and judgment day are not places or experiences waiting to pounce on us if we leave this earthly existence. Each of those concepts is a part of us right now. They are within.

It is we who determine the outcome of each judgment day, and it is we who make our own heaven and hell.

$\mathcal{M}$ile markers

- Heaven and hell are states of mind.
- The kingdom of heaven is within you.
- You create your own heaven or hell.
- The anguish of a personal hell can serve to strengthen you if you will let it.
- Judgment day takes place every moment of your life.

Thank You, God, for Your ever-present sanctuary of love and joy and peace within me. I know that all strength, all comfort, all wholeness are already mine when I enter the kingdom of heaven which you have established for me. I claim that kingdom now.

Please proceed to Adventure 9 in the Activity Book.

GOOD AND EVIL | 10

*Are there two powers in
this universe, one good
and one bad? Is there a
Satan?*

If God is good, why is there bad?

*"Get behind me, Satan! You are a hindrance to
me; for you are not on the side of God, but of
men."*   —Matthew 16:23

The ancient Greeks worshiped Athena as a god-
dess. Her greatest shrine, the Parthenon (Temple of
Athena), completed in 438 B.C., was classic Greek
architecture at its highest. Its beauty can still be
experienced today as it stands on the Acropolis, overlooking the city of Athens. The ancient city's most
outstanding sculpture is also a tribute to Athena. It
is the statue *Athena Parthenos*, by the master sculptor Phidias. Created to stand in the Parthenon, it
would become the very symbol of Athenian civilization.

The work on the statue of Athena created great
excitement in Athens. Every day Phidias found himself surrounded by the curious. One day, as he was

105

tediously perfecting one of the strands of hair on the back of the head of Athena, the sculptor was challenged by an onlooker: "That figure is to stand a hundred feet high, with its back to the marble wall. Who will ever know what details you are putting behind there?"

Without pausing, Phidias replied, "I will know."

BUILT-IN GAUGE

Phidias could have gotten away with less attention to detail. He knew that. But he honored an inner mandate which transcended the work itself: the need for excellence, of doing a thing right, of giving one's best. Doing it not for someone else's approval but simply because it feels right.

You have the same mandate that Phidias had. We all do. It goes beyond popular approval, man-made laws, moral codes, and religious injunctions. It's a built-in gauge which tells you the difference between walking the high road and taking a lower path, even when taking a lower path might not matter to anyone else or be known by anyone else.

But it matters to you. *You* would know it. Even if known by only you and only in a secret place in your heart, missing the mark, taking less than the high road, muddies your spiritual path and slows you down.

If you are honest with yourself, you will probably have to admit that you instinctively know when you've missed the mark, when you've fallen short of doing or being your best. You know it without anyone's having to tell you. How do you know? You know because you have the Christ within you, always nudging you toward higher and better. That is Its nature. It is your built-in gauge, which measures your spiritual heights.

YOU AND THE LIGHT

Your spirit within you, the "real" of you, identifies itself *only* with the "Light" (just another name for God) and with what might traditionally be called "good." It really doesn't know anything else. So, every time you heed this instinct, every time you follow the Light, you are experiencing as well as expressing God's good.

Actually, it is not so much following the Light as allowing the Light to shine through you. The less resistant you are to the Creator's expressing Itself through you, the more you will experience and express that same Light, that same good, that is God.

Each day you encounter unexpected events and situations as you journey along the path. Every time you come upon one, you have a decision to make. You can decide to heed the good, or you can decide to ignore it. It's a soul choice. (Recall how the soul is pivotal, how it can turn and listen to the clamor of negativity and fear in a noisy outer world, or turn and listen to the spirit within.) If you decide you want to heed the good, to listen to your spirit and allow God to live freely through you and as you, be advised that your spirit can only be found on the high road. It *is* the high road, so that is where you're going to have to travel if you want to be in contact with it.

WHAT ABOUT EVIL?

The fact is that God is good, only good. If God is the only Presence and the only Power, where does evil fit in? As a matter of fact, it *doesn't*. God does not, *cannot*, create evil or darkness.

You might say, "Are you trying to tell me that there's no evil in this world?"

Of course not. We all experience darkness at times, and often people don't behave in Christlike ways. There have been enough robberies, rapes, murders, and wars to prove that. It may even seem that there is some sinister force at work in your own life. But how can there be? There is only one ultimate force, and that's God.

There is no dark power in this world which exists as a wholly self-contained entity. First of all, where could it get its energy to keep existing? Secondly, if there were an evil power that existed apart from God, then God wouldn't be much of a God! No, there cannot be two separate and distinct powers, good and evil. There can only be one: good.

The dark aspects of humanity? They are simply humanity acting separately from God, humanity acting not as *a part of* God, but *apart from* God. What people call Satan is nothing more than the product of our human thinking, selfishly trying to keep us off the high road when we really know better. It is the part of us which must wither as our spiritual awareness grows.

Let's think back to the temptation of Jesus in the desert. We saw that the so-called "Satan" which challenged and tempted Him was actually aspects of His own psyche trying to assert themselves. This was what Carl Jung, the Swiss psychiatrist, referred to as the "shadow." It is that primitive, destructive side of the self which is kept in check, according to Jung, by the ego and the persona but most of all by consciousness itself. It is responsible for our conception of original sin and, when projected outward, of the devil. Jung said it consisted of the animal instincts that humans inherited in their evolution from lower forms of life and the shadow, according to Jung, typifies the animal side of human nature.

The devil is *never* anything other than one's own devilish thoughts and feelings and these, no matter how devilish, can be changed. That is not to imply that it is always an easy task to do. While sometimes changes happen in the twinkling of an eye, more often they take months or even years of diligent attention. But either way, if you desire to change, you will. Just as in the desert Jesus confronted His "shadow" and overcame it, so can you confront and overcome yours.

Let's face it, there can be plenty of dark thoughts and feelings. You've experienced them and so have we. Everyone has. To be rid of them, you have to deny that they have an existence of their own. They don't exist on their own—they can't. Acknowledge them as part of yourself. Once you've done this, you have begun the process of releasing them. You'll be absolutely astonished at how the shadows scurry away when you turn on the light. There were no monsters under the bed after all! As we journey on *The Quest*, we begin to see that the trail ahead is growing safer with each passing day.

TIME TO "LIGHTEN UP"

We've been talking about darkness. Let's talk about light. This is the age of light. Light is breaking through everywhere. Don't you find that it can no longer be suppressed in your own life? You are thinking thoughts and feeling feelings now which are higher, brighter, more illumined than at any other time in your life. (The very fact that you are traveling on *The Quest* is proof enough of that.) This is the part of you which is starting to identify with your spiritual nature. Like a rising sun after a moonless night, that spiritual nature is emerging more and more. Eventually, if you allow it to, it will become like the noonday sun, replacing any darkness and becoming the dominant part of you.

KEEP YOUR SUNNY SIDE UP

Darkness and light, good and evil. When you turn from the light, you have darkness. When you turn from the positive, you experience the negative. When you turn from God, you experience ... perhaps whatever pain you might be experiencing right now.

God is Light. That Light will illumine whatever It shines upon. It is shining in you right now. If you are seeing shadows in your life, they are your own because, in some way, you have turned your back to the Light.

CHAIN REACTION

A little word of caution seems in order here. You have no doubt observed what seem to be shadows haunting the lives of friends and loved ones. In your concern, you may think you can switch on their light for them. This is an easy trap to fall into, and we've all done it. But these are *their* shadows, *their* negativities. You cannot change their decisions to stay in the dark, no matter how much you "know what's best" for them. Only they can change themselves.

What you can change is yourself. When you allow

your Light to shine, some amazing things begin to happen. You see more and more of the Light in others. This becomes a chain reaction and they, in turn, see more of the Light in themselves. Light is not selective. It shines in all directions.

DARKNESS DOES A DISAPPEARING ACT

If you want to get rid of an "evil" in your world, you don't have to blame it on a devil or some force other than God, because there is only God. If you want to get rid of "evil," you can only get rid of it in yourself. Surprisingly, this is really easier to do than you might expect. Don't let the darkness cause you to feel overwhelmed. Your journey on *The Quest*, if traveled with dedication and enthusiasm, is leading you inevitably to the Light.

Darkness has no existence of its own. It is totally at the mercy of light. Like a bug on a kitchen floor, it will only come around when the light goes out. As soon as there is light, the bug takes flight! Darkness, too, vanishes immediately when a light is turned on. Where does it go? Nowhere, because it never really existed to begin with. It was merely the absence of light. Allow the power to flow into the bulb and the darkest corners of the room are illuminated.

It will be like that for you. Make the choice to move up to the high road, into the "light," and the "bad" in your life automatically starts falling away and eventually leaves you.

Curiously, once the old destructive feelings of resentment, anger, fear or whatever begin dispersing into nothingness, they never return with quite the same passion as before. It's as if they had never existed with such intensity. Somehow they are watered down. And each time they come back, they will return with lesser intensity and will be that much easier to release again. As release follows release, they are weakened even more. Until, finally, they disappear. The process is not necessarily instantaneous, but it is certain. You are not so much getting rid of the darkness as you are remembering the light.

THINKING ABOUT THINKING

Why not begin thinking about your thoughts from now on, not analyzing them but merely observing them? Am I cooperating with God? Am I turning on the light? Your quest provides you with ample opportunities for making right choices.

Although this process may not be as instantaneous as turning on a light, as you *diligently* practice making right choices, you'll begin to take command of your thoughts as Jesus did: "Get behind me, Satan! You are a hindrance to me; for you are not on the side of God, but of men." Maybe you won't be saying it in the same words, but if the thought is the same, the effect will be the same.

God is the only power and the only presence, always there, waiting to be experienced. What are "good" and "evil"? Good is anything which helps you feel your connection with God. Evil is anything which moves you away from a sense of the presence of God. You don't need anyone or any law to tell you which is which.

Mile markers

- The Christ within you is your built-in gauge which measures your spiritual heights.
- You must travel the high road if you want to experience the Christ.
- The dark aspects of humanity are only our thoughts and feelings. This is the only Satan there is.
- Darkness has no existence of its own. Shine light on it and it soon vanishes.
- Good is anything which helps you feel your connection with God. Evil is anything which moves you away from a sense of the presence of God.

*Thank You, God, for the daily reminders
to stay on the high road. Thank You
for Your light within me, clearing the
shadows and filling me with peace.*

Please proceed to Adventure 10 in the Activity Book.

*Prayer is the experience
of speaking to God.
There are appropriate
ways of doing this.*

$\mathcal{H}ow$ to talk to God

*"Hitherto you have asked nothing in my name;
ask, and you will receive, that your joy may be
full."* —John 16:24

Far, far into the Arabian Desert, so far that few
have seen it or even know of its existence, stands a
small fortress. In silence and isolation, it rises out of
the timeless sands, ready to offer safety and provisions to anyone who might come upon it.

It is said that Thomas Edward Lawrence, better
known as "Lawrence of Arabia," found refuge and
sustenance in the little fortress on numerous occasions. When under attack, often at overwhelming
odds, he could make his way to the tiny bastion,
finding strength within its walls. It would become his
life-support, sustaining him through the perilous
siege. This remote desert hideaway provided him

with food, water, safety, and the opportunity to re-group, so that when he was ready, he could face the world again.

INNER FORTRESS

We have our own fortress, always ready, always waiting. It is the safety, the protection, the comfort we experience when we enter into conscious communication with our Creator. It is that unmistakable sense of security which Martin Luther must have felt so many centuries ago when he wrote the moving hymn "A Mighty Fortress Is Our God."

It is prayer that opens the door through which we enter this citadel of strength and safety, protection and renewal. Times of prayer, of conscious contact with the Power which powers this universe, provide us with sustenance and renewed vigor so that when we are ready we can face the world again, lifted and refreshed, armed with a new sense of the all-right-ness of things.

HOW DO I PRAY?

Prayer is such a misunderstood phenomenon. Virtually, every religion has some form of prayer, and followers of each religion are told to pray. But seldom are they taught how to pray, and so most people are troubled by doubts as to whether they have been praying correctly.

What exactly is the right method of prayer? There is none. There are as many different methods of praying as there are people to pray! Prayer is simply speaking to God, aloud or silently, in whatever language, style, manner, or words that feel comfortable.

More important than the method of praying is the

reason for praying. Prayers are not to impress God. They are to impress us, to raise us to the level of consciousness where we realize that, because we are one with God, every good for us already exists.

LIFE IS A PRAYER

Our whole life is a prayer. This is crucial information for anyone on *The Quest*. Every thought and every emotion and every act is a message to the great Universal Mind of God as to what we are claiming for ourselves, what we want to see established in our lives.

Let's get specific. Jesus taught that if we ask, we receive, that true prayer is always answered. But the problem arises when we try to use our will to force God-ordained universal laws to work. We start thinking that our words alone are enough to change things, that our prayers alone are enough to "make us deserving." But, as you'll see, it doesn't work that way.

A man we know was orphaned at an early age, had almost no education, and has never attended a religious service. We doubt he has ever uttered what most people would call a "formal" prayer. Yet this man lives a life of joy and thanksgiving. He loves and blesses all of the plants in the nursery he owns. He projects that same feeling of love to all of his customers, to his friends, and to his family. You only have to be in his presence a few moments before you pick up his enthusiasm and appreciation for the wonder of life. You feel good just being around him. He is happy in his work, has many loyal friends, and no one can ever recall a time when he was not in good health. It is quite obvious how the general tenor of his life is a constant prayer which is continuously being answered.

We know (*knew*, actually) another man. He routinely and dedicatedly spent fifteen minutes each morning and each evening in "formal" prayer. He prayed with great passion for the healing of his lungs. For thirty minutes out of every twenty-four hours, he fervently affirmed healthy lungs, asking God to restore his diseased tissues to wholeness. But the other twenty-three and a half hours—what of them? They, unfortunately, were a different story. The man continued his lifelong habit of smoking. Against his physician's warnings and contrary to his own common sense, he smoked until the day before he died, leaving this earthly plane a bitter man who cursed God for not answering his prayers.

Yet perhaps his prayers really *were* answered because his "life-prayer" was the message he sent twenty-three and a half hours of every day. If this sounds harsh, just remember the idea of our entire lives being a prayer. What was the overall message of that man's life? *That* was his true prayer.

What is the overall message of your life? We each have to ask that question of ourselves, for the answer shows us what our *true* prayer is.

THE TWENTY-FOUR-HOUR PRAYER

Our intentions are transmitted every moment of our lives, not just during those special times when we "pray." True prayer, the twenty-four-hour kind is always answered. And if your thoughts, feelings, and actions are in agreement with your formal prayers, you have great power at your fingertips and can expect seeming miracles. Your "joy will be full," for you will be experiencing the unimaginable wonder of God's will expressing through your life.

Before we go any further, let's back up to the phrase "seeming miracles." If by miracle, we mean an event or a condition outside of universal laws, we are wrong, because there can *never* be anything outside of the cosmic laws that God set up. However, sometimes things happen which are so far beyond what we would expect, that we call them miracles. They happen when we get ourselves out of the way so that God can work freely. It's like removing the dam in a brook so that the water can tumble and flow where it will. What miracles really are, then, are natural outworkings of the law. Even when they take place "instantaneously," they still have gone through the entire process of that law. (We'll talk more about this in the future.)

If we believe that we need a miracle in order to attain our good—whether it be healing, prosperity, concern for another, whatever—if we feel that only a miracle can help, then we are automatically limiting the power of our prayer. In focusing too specifically, we are ignoring the fact that God's desire for us is total good. No miracles are needed to bring that good to us. The very nature of God is wholeness, abundance, and love. As part of God's creation, we are inheritors of all that. To tap into those attributes is natural, not miraculous.

THE STRONGEST PRAYERS

Here's a simple rule. When your thoughts, emotions, words, and actions are all "in sync," are all congruent—saying the same thing—and when you sincerely feel that you are voicing God's will for you,

you have your strongest prayer. Rest assured your good will come to you. For example, if you are praying to God for strength to stop drinking, regularly attending Alcoholics Anonymous meetings, keeping in touch with your AA sponsor, scrupulously applying the Twelve Steps of the AA program to your life, staying away from your old "haunts" filled with people and patterns which had been destructive to you, expecting things to work out in a positive way, and lovingly helping others to stay sober, now that's a *prayer*! The wishes of your heart (in this case for sobriety) are reflected in every aspect of your life. Your thoughts and actions agree with your words, making for a powerful "life-prayer."

Remember, living our prayers produces the highest results. We can't expect a ten-dollar answer from a ten-cent prayer. Apathetic, indifferent, ungrateful, ego-centered lives generate similar results. Creative, dedicated, grateful, God-filled lives result in more of the same. And so it goes.

2 + 2 = ?

Still, the question most of us ask is, "If prayer works, how come my prayers aren't answered?" The explanations range from "it's God's will" to "it's punishment for your sins" to "pray harder!" But there's something that even God cannot do, and that is to work in opposition to universal laws—laws instituted by none other than God. This needs some explanation.

Is there any way that your prayers can make two plus two equal five? That would be foolish praying, wouldn't you say? How about combining two parts of hydrogen and one part of oxygen, and then praying for gold? No deal. H_2O is water, and no amount of praying can change it.

True prayer is not asking God to change universal laws to suit you, nor is prayer begging God to give you something you want or to take away something you don't want. Does that mean you can never ask for things? After all, didn't Jesus tell us to ask, *believing,* and we would receive? You would hardly be human if you had a sick child and didn't pray for his or her health. And what's wrong with praying for help when you're starting a new job or a new relationship?

In fact, there's nothing wrong with praying for such things *if you feel in your heart that it is God's will for you.* The only valid prayer request is for what you feel is God's will. This precludes praying for someone's harm or praying for you to get something at the expense of someone else. If it is God's will, then everyone wins.

So, if you are going to pray for something, a good tag to put at the end is "this or something better." What this means is that you are praying for God's will *as you see it.* We can never be absolutely sure what God's will is, but don't worry. If you are really sincere in wanting God's will but your prayer is somewhat off base, clear signposts will soon pop up along the way to lead you in the direction that God wants you to go. The key is to desire God's will.

MISGUIDED PRAYERS

Remember, the purpose of prayer is to raise yourself to the level of consciousness where you are aware that God's good for you already exists. If your prayers don't come from an awareness of your oneness with God, they are misdirected and will only take you further from God-consciousness. "In praying do not heap up empty phrases" (Mt. 6:7).

For example, aren't prayers of supplication, "O God, please, please, I beg of You," really meant to soften a stern and wrathful God? If I grovel enough, perhaps God will feel sorry for me and grant my wish.

Or how about prayers of flattery? "God, You are so great, so good, so wonderful. Grant me this wish ..." Aren't these uttered in hopes of appealing to the ego of some vain and arrogant God?

Or how about contractual prayers? "God, I'll do this if you do that," as if God is a merchant, selling favors to the highest bidder.

Then there are the times when we repeat the same prayer again and again and again, not for the legitimate reason of enriching our own inner consciousness, but rather to get a "busy" God's attention. Doesn't this ascribe human qualities to Spirit? These are not prayers so much as attempts at manipulation. Our prayers cannot influence God to be more Godlike or less Godlike! To believe they can is to be like the rooster who thinks it is his crowing that makes the sun rise every day.

What's more, would you really want a God that you (and everybody else) could manipulate and influence? Imagine the chaos! Whoever begged the loudest, prayed the longest, spoke in the most flattering terms, or struck the best deal would have his or her prayers answered. But that is not the purpose of prayer. If we have been trying to change God's mind by choosing certain words, we are entirely missing the point of prayer.

Since mind is the connecting link between God's desire for us (absolute good) and our wish to experience that good, we only have to change *our* minds! That is what true prayer does. It convinces us of the legitimacy of our claim to God's gifts. It enables us to see the universal storehouse of divine ideas and to make ourselves available to the contents of that storehouse.

ANNOUNCE YOUR INTENTIONS

Let's get practical about prayer. Look at it this way. Prayer is a connection *you* establish between you and God. In a sense, you are the transmitter, God the receiver. What exactly is it that you transmit to God? Anything. Really, anything! Your thoughts, your feelings, your concerns ... whatever. Prayer, you see, is talking to God. It is communication from your individual mind to the Universal Mind of God, a plugging-into the Source of all life.

The highest use of prayer is to announce your intention of opening yourself to God's will and God's good. It is your endeavor to link up with and accept all of the qualities of God. It is a sincere invitation to allow God's life to be lived through you. It is making a conscious alignment with the good which comes with this. No need to beg God, because you already have access to it all. Prayer is the way to express your thanks for your life and its blessings, those you have and those still to come. This is called "affirmative prayer." It declares the truth that God's good is already yours.

ONE ROOM DOES NOT A MANSION MAKE

Consider this. If you are praying specifically for

more prosperity, you may get it, but that is asking for only part of your good. You are limiting all the rest—health, love, joy, peace, and the teeming font of absolute good that already is yours.

It's like the eccentric British millionaire who lived in only one room of his sixty-room mansion. This was the room where he kept all of his money in stacks of gold coins. He never left this room. He never allowed himself the pleasure of the other rooms or of the beautiful woods and streams and ponds of his luxurious country estate.

The man's inheritance from his father included the land, the home, the livestock, the money, the books in the library, the automobiles, the exquisite works of art, and much more. His father had left him all that he had. It was his father's good pleasure to give him his entire estate.

The father could not force his son to take and use all that he bequeathed to him. The son had to claim it. That's *all* he had to do, but he didn't have the consciousness for the wealth and abundance which his father desired for him. In his mind, he never got past that one room and the money in it, so he never enjoyed all of the benefits and pleasures of his own estate.

You can't pray to make God give you your good. God *is* the good within you now. God is life and love and prosperity and health and joy and peace and all good things. How do you realize these things? By allowing prayer to raise your consciousness to the level where you can accept them, knowing that they are yours because you are the child of God.

PRACTICING THE PRESENCE

Prayer is also the deliberate activity of recognizing our oneness with God. Brother Lawrence, a medieval French monk who worked in the abbey kitchen, revealed that he felt closer to God, that he "practiced the Presence" more fully amid the clatter of pots and pans than he did in the chapel during formal prayer.

Of one thing we can be sure: God longs for us to practice the Presence, to express our willingness to be guided and protected. Therefore, our prayer should be to inform God of this willingness. *"Here I am, God. Use me. Live Your life through me."*

It's been said that prayer doesn't change things; prayer changes people, and people change things. This is perfectly true. Prayer changes us by expanding our consciousness, and in this expanded consciousness, we can accept more of what God wants for us.

Prayer puts us in the God-mode. It is a reminder to us of what we are and what God is and how good our lives really can be if we will just allow God to take charge. If this is what we truly desire, then prayer is a way of letting our intentions be known.

A MUST-DO ADVENTURE

Finally, let's consider this. The idea of speaking to an invisible force, a force of such magnitude that we are incapable of comprehending it, seems whimsical, deluded, and futile to some. Nevertheless, all true prayer is not only perceived but responded to as well. God did not create us only to abandon us like some great cosmic joke. The Creator cares about, sustains, maintains, and expresses Itself through the created.

If in the past your attitude toward prayer has been less than enthusiastic, your quest requires that you take a new look at it. In fact, prayer is one of your staples for survival in the valleys as well as the heights.

Talk to God. The results will surprise you. This is one adventure you cannot afford to miss.

$\mathcal{M}$ile markers

- Times of prayer provide you with sustenance and renewed strength.
- The reason for praying is more important than the method.
- Your whole life is a prayer, and life-prayers are always answered.
- "Miracles" are natural outworkings of the law.
- Having your thoughts, feelings, words, and actions all "in sync" is your strongest prayer.
- Prayer is talking to God.
- The highest use of prayer is the announcing of your intention to open yourself to God's will.
- Prayer is a way to express your thanks for past, present, and future blessings.
- Prayer is not to change God. It is to change you.
- Prayer puts you in the God-mode.

God, I want to know You more. I want to serve You more. I want to love You more. I am willing to let You take charge of my life. Show me Your will and Your way, God. I am ready.

Please proceed to Adventure 11 in the Activity Book.

$\mathcal{T}$HE SILENCE

Sometimes you have to get completely still so that you can hear what God wants you to know. It is the most important part of your day.

Connecting with your inner power

"But when you pray, go into your room and shut the door and pray to your Father who is in secret; and your Father who sees in secret will reward you." —Matthew 6:6

The damp north wind was blowing a chill off the moors. It would be good to be inside on an evening like this. The American drew his coat collar tighter as he made his way to the home of his Scottish friend.

Ralph Waldo Emerson and Thomas Carlyle had enjoyed a strong friendship through correspondence for many years before they actually met. Now, after all that time, Emerson had finally come to Europe, making a special journey to Scotland, so that he could at last meet the renowned essayist and historian face-to-face.

When Emerson arrived for the momentous occasion, Carlyle greeted him warmly, offered him a pipe, and then lighted one for himself. The great men then sat together in virtual silence until it was time to retire for the night. At that point the two warmly shook hands and praised each other for the fruitful evening they had shared together.

A SECRET PLACE

There are times when feelings are too deep, too special, too moving for words. Perhaps you have felt such a closeness with another human being or maybe you experienced it alone in nature. Times like these call for silence, so that we can perceive their full meaning, savor the sweetness, and listen with an inner ear for the message inherent in the stillness. It is in the silence that we meet God.

Jesus left us specific instructions about this silence. He made quite an issue out of entering a secret place when you want to connect with God. Go into a room and close the door, He said. Go into a place where there is only you—you and your God—and shut out all of the clamor of outer things, including your own thoughts.

The secret place of silence that Jesus told us to enter is not just a quiet room in your house or a deserted strip of beach or anywhere else that you might go for solitude. It is more than that. It is an inner space, an internal and very personal place of total silence, which no one else can ever enter or disturb. It is that perfect, unchanging part of you which waits like a safe harbor, a friendly port, to welcome you in calm or storm, in peace or in distress. It is, in a sense, where you "connect" with God.

A TIME TO LISTEN

This teaching of *The Quest* will introduce you to "the silence" and how to benefit from it. What we are calling "the silence" (some call it meditation) is very important to your journey because it is here, in the silence, that you find your peace and your strength.

Spending some time each day in the secret place of stillness may be the most rewarding thing you can do to further yourself on *The Quest*. It will give you a chance to consolidate your gains, and it will enable you to cope more successfully with any dragons or demons which might happen to stray (or pounce!) onto your path.

It's well and good to know about your spiritual nature—to talk about it and learn about it—but that in itself is not enough. The object is to *experience* your spirituality, to *feel* your oneness with the one God, to *sense* the comfort and the healing and, yes, the guidance which God offers you. However, all of this is impossible if you are too busy, too anxiety-ridden, too stressed, too noisy to listen. It's like eating a nutritious meal while stressed: unless there is peacefulness during and after the meal, there can be no proper digestion and assimilation.

How many times have you had the frustrating experience of trying to communicate with someone who would not stop talking? As you've discovered, it is impossible to get your point across if the person won't be quiet.

This holds true with God too. God is forever ready to communicate with you. All the guidance and inspiration and divine ideas that you could ever possibly want or need are there for you. They are ready to transfer from universal God-Mind to your own sub-conscious mind so that you can draw upon them as you need them, but in order to receive divine ideas, you have to be in a receptive mood, quiet and still.

LISTENING TO GOD

You already know that prayer is talking to God. Meditation is just the opposite—it is *listening* to God. There is nothing mysterious about the process; anyone can do it. Your quiet times become an open door through which you walk into a broader light, a larger sense of yourself and your world. Things just automatically fall into better perspective after you sit still and listen.

The Activity Book will give you practical assistance with entering the silence so that you can begin to connect with the Source of all good within you. In the stillness of the silence, you will be able to move beyond the intellectual mind into the realm of spiritual "knowing." Since the intellectual mind is incapable of entering into this realm, you will find yourself immersed solely in the perfection of God.

There may be segments of the path which are rocky and difficult to walk. There could be sharp cliffs or dark stretches of forest. Yet it doesn't matter what the landscape of your outer world might look like, because you carry within you a safe haven—an unchangeable refuge of safety and tranquillity.

"HOLY COMMUNION"

The silence is a holy time within the body temple, a time of worship, joy, and thanksgiving deep within your living sanctuary. It is a time of lying down in green pastures, being led beside the still waters, and having the soul restored. You will come away from it renewed in body and mind—harmonized, revitalized, illumined, and at peace with yourself and with your world.

The Life-Force (God) is always waiting to hold communion with you. It is during the silence that the contact is made.

$\mathcal{M}$ile markers

- It is in the silence that you meet God.
- The silence (meditation) is listening to God.
- In the stillness, you move beyond the intellect into the realm of spiritual *knowing*.

I still my body. I still my mind. I relax completely. I surrender my spirit, soul, and body to You, God. Fill me with Your presence as I sit and I listen ... in the silence ... in the silence.

Please proceed to Adventure 12 in the Activity Book.

$\mathcal{A}$ RANDOM WALK

Let's rest. Lay down your walking stick and relax while we tell you about our tree.

After living in Florida for a few years, we decided it was time to buy our first orange tree. A local nursery was having a sale, so over we went.

The orange trees were all young, and we were told they wouldn't bear fruit for a year or so, but we noticed one small tree which had a magnificent huge navel orange hanging from it. The orange was so heavy it seemed as if it were going to break the branch. We couldn't resist.

We planted the tree and took special care of it and its precious single fruit, watering it every day. When it came time to pick the orange, it was sublime— sweet, meaty, and juicy.

In a month or two, our little tree had developed at least fifty orange blossoms. We were ecstatic. The first orange had been so exquisite that we eagerly anticipated more like it. We watched as the flowers fell off and tiny green fruit, the size of small marbles, started developing. Our tree would soon be crowded with bright orange fruit.

MESSAGE FROM A YOUNG TREE

Then a most curious thing happened. A month later there wasn't one bud, one flower, or one orange on the tree, just leaves! What happened? We went back to the nursery and questioned the man in charge.

"A young tree can't sustain so many oranges. It's not developed enough," he explained. "It expends so much energy trying to feed all the oranges that none gets fed well, and the tree itself doesn't even have enough energy left to grow." He added that with a tree that young we should have cut off the new buds except one or two so that the tree could use its energy to strengthen and grow. When it eventually got strong enough, it would easily sustain hundreds of oranges.

His explanation turned out to be a lesson in Truth as well as botany.

In an effort to improve our lives, we often read many books, listen to many tapes, and attend many inspirational lectures. Each new technique we want to immediately incorporate into our lives. We can't wait to begin.

Yet each idea, each technique, is a tiny bud. Each technique needs energy to be nurtured and developed, just like a blossom. If we are going to concentrate on five or ten ideas at a time, none will develop properly.

However, if we take one idea, just one idea at a time, and put *all* of our effort into mastering it, that one idea will lead to more quality growth than many ideas used slightly.

We will always remember that first orange. It was the only one on the tree, but it was sweet, meaty, and juicy. It had received the full attention and nurturing of the tree, and so it was everything an orange should be.

TIME FOR A BREAK

The past twelve teachings have presented you with many "buds." Hopefully, you have been concentrating on them one at a time. Hopefully you have stayed on one teaching until you have felt comfortable enough with it to go on to the next. If not, then this is a gentle reminder to do so. In fact, allowing time for these teachings to take root is so important that we have scheduled a breather.

This the perfect time for a little break in *The Quest*, a time for a random walk on your journey to allow you to go wherever you wish. Having now traveled one-quarter of the journey, you might want simply to "lie down in green pastures" and refresh your soul. Use this time in any way you wish. It is your short vacation from *The Quest*. We are not suggesting that you forget all of the teachings you've learned or incorporated into your life. We're merely suggesting that you rest. Do anything you like, but put *The Quest* aside for a time.

How long a recess should you take? A week should be enough to help you digest this first quarter of *The Quest*. If you feel you need more time, by all means, take it. You'll find that when you pick up your walking stick again, you will resume your journey with fresh enthusiasm, energy, and excitement.

See you when you get back.

WELCOME BACK!

How was your vacation?

We trust it was enjoyable and that you are ready to get back on the trail, refreshed and enthusiastic.

Many new opportunities for spiritual growth lie just ahead. So, if you will pick up your walking stick, we'll move on.

GOD'S WILL | *13*

Why do we insist on having things our way, when God's way is so much better?

Why can't I do it my way?

"My Father, if it be possible, let this cup pass from me; nevertheless, not as I will, but as thou wilt."
—Matthew 26:39

The symphony orchestra was on stage, absorbed in their final tune-up and last minute practicing of the intricate passages they would soon be playing. Violinists noisily sawed on their strings while walking their fingers up and down the necks of their graceful instruments. Behind them, the woodwinds gently purred their mellow sounds. Seated behind the woodwinds were the trumpets, blaring in staccato confusion. In the rear, percussionists banged away, tuning their timpani. It was a grand cacophony.

The conductor stood poised on his podium, patiently waiting for the right moment. At last he took his baton and gently tapped on the music stand in front of him. Immediately the din subsided, the musicians came to attention. A hush enveloped the hall. The concert was about to begin.

If you've ever attended a symphony concert, you may have asked yourself, "How can musicians, in the midst of such a discordant confusion of sounds, hear the quiet tapping of one thin stick?" Easily. They are expecting it! They are listening for it!

HOW GOD SPEAKS TO US

In the same quiet way, God speaks to you. Forget the movie version where God's will is made known in a beautiful, booming, basso profundo, English-accented, echo-chambered voice. Truthfully, God's will for you comes more as a never-changing murmur that laps gently upon your consciousness like ripples on the shore of a peaceful lake. God speaks to you in a still, small voice like the tapping of the conductor's baton. It is a gentle tapping, a sweet nudging in the direction of your good.

You will never know God's will by intellectualizing and conjecturing what that will is. God doesn't speak in words. God speaks to you in feelings, in dreams, in intuitive perceptions, through the words of others, through the love of others, in an inspiring story, in a beautiful scene, in the gaze of a loved one, in the face of a child, and in dozens of other gentle ways. You cannot know God's will intellectually. Only by becoming aware of life, of living—only by being awake—can you hear it.

God's will for you is absolute good. How can it be otherwise? If you believe that God is pure and perfect Good and that creation is the "offspring" of God, then how could God envision anything "bad" for any of those offspring? Jesus said, "What man of you, if his son asks him for bread, will give him a stone?... How much more will your Father ... give good things to those who ask him!" (Mt. 7:9, 11) You want such wonderful things for your children, don't you? Then how could God want less for you?

It seems clear that God's will for you is absolute good. That fact must be woven into the very fabric of your thoughts and your feelings. It must be the basis of all decisions concerning you and everyone in your life.

The divinity within you is within everyone. It is there regardless of whether you are aware of it. To fully let this divinity have its way with you is what God's will is all about, for when you let God's will be done, all things in your life become good. No, much more than that, they become wonderful beyond your fondest dreams.

OKAY, BUT ... WHAT DO I DO NOW?

The more pressing question for most of us is not what God's overall or long-term will is for us. (Even those whose concept of God is that of a stern and wrathful Deity believe that the Creator ultimately wants good for everyone. It is just that, to many people, it is a conditional good, based on their completing a fear-filled walk along a very narrow path. Any slip forebodes eternal damnation.) The more pressing question regarding God's will is for more specific instructions: What should I do now?

I'm having so much trouble taking care of my sick mother, but I feel guilty about putting her in a nursing home. What is God's will?

I have an offer for a much better job, but it requires relocating and my children don't want to go. What is

God's will?

I've had my home for sale for a year and can't sell it. What is God's will?

I've been in this relationship for two years, and I want to get married, but she doesn't. What is God's will?

My son just got a divorce and is begging to move back home with me, and I'm not so sure I want him. What is God's will?

These are our daily challenging questions, the decisions that face us every day and that beg to be addressed. It seems when we reach our wit's end, when our thinking and reasoning can't take us any further, then we want to know *God's* will. *"And, God, please don't give me vague generalities. Tell me what to do! And tell me in a loud voice, so I can hear it."*

But, ask yourself seriously, even if God did tell you in a loud voice what to do, would you listen? Would you always follow instructions? "God, what can I do? My neighbor is driving me crazy every day." What would you do if God boomed out the answer in stereophonic sound: "Love your neighbor as yourself"?

INSIDE ANSWERS

So often we look for outside answers to inside problems. Remember, there is a divinity within you. No matter what your problem appears to be, the *real* problem is seldom the problem you see. The real problem is your inability or unwillingness to allow this divinity to unfold its plan through you.

It is human nature to see the problem as something "out there" that is interfering with your happiness, with your desire to be rich or not to be poor, to be respected or not to be scorned, to be loved or not to be hated, to be ... or not to be.

You find yourself asking your friends, your neighbors, and your loved ones for answers. You may even seek professional counseling if your pain is severe enough. "What do you think I should do?" You can end up getting all kinds of advice but still not answering the question, "Is this the best thing for me?" Without God's being involved in the decision, you are taking a chance, a *big* chance.

It may seem scary at first, but in the long run, it is infinitely easier to turn your life over to Spirit, to allow God to make all of the decisions, because when God shapes your life, the changes are appropriate and automatic. We must always be aware that there is a higher, broader plan of perfect divine order. We cannot fully understand this plan, but it is enough to know it exists and that all life—no matter what the appearance—seeks to establish divine order.

DOES IT HAVE TO BE OUR WAY?

This all sounds very nice, very pat, doesn't it? "Turn our lives over to Spirit ... allow God to make the decisions." Trouble is, we sometimes talk a good game but when it comes down to actually letting God take over, that's a different story. We want what God wants for us, as long as God wants what *we* want!

It often turns out, however, that God's idea of what is good for us is not at all what we had in mind. Yet we humans do love to think we know what's good for us and find it very difficult to let go and let God. It can be frightening; it's venturing into that *terra incognita* again.

Once you try living this way, you'll look back and

see how right it was, how it brought you to a higher place faster and more easily than you could have done yourself, even if you could have figured it all out. God's will is always for your highest good.

IN THE BEST OF COMPANY

You are not alone in wanting things to work out *your* way. Did you read the quotation from Jesus at the opening of this teaching? (If not, go back and look at it now.) It was uttered, agonizingly, in the garden of Gethsemane prior to His arrest and was recorded in the Gospels of Matthew, Mark, and Luke.

Picture the scene: Jesus, even at that late date in His life, was torn between His will and God's will. He sensed what lay ahead for Him. It must have been extremely tempting to run away and live a "normal" life. "Let this cup pass from me." (I don't want to do this ... why me, Lord?)

But then He remembered: He remembered what He was to show us. Most of all, He remembered that when we let God's will be done, it always works out to be the very best—the highest and finest it can be—if only we trust enough to let that happen. So Jesus remembered, and He trusted. "Nevertheless, not as I will, but as thou wilt." (I'm okay again, God. I'm back on the trail. I lost it there for a bit, but everything's all right now.)

Because He let God be God in Him, Jesus went through the resurrection process. Had the human will prevailed on that dark night in Gethsemane, the world would never have heard of Jesus Christ or His transformative teachings.

THE QUESTION YOU'VE BEEN WANTING TO ASK

How can you know if something is God's will? No one can tell you absolutely for sure because it requires an inner knowing on your part, but here are some guidelines which can help you:

1. If it results in a winning situation for everyone involved, chances are it's God's will.

2. If things are going effortlessly, without force or manipulation, chances are it's God's will.

3. As long as there's a green light or an open door, proceed ahead. Go through it. Chances are it's God's will.

Life is an ongoing adventure. There is always another door to go through, another phase of the journey just ahead.

God is always speaking to us—always—but when do we listen? Like the musicians in the orchestra, we are constantly plucking and bowing our strings, banging our drums, and blowing our horns, waiting to find out what tune to play. But unlike the musicians, we may not really listen for the Conductor, who wants to lead us in a symphony of absolute good.

If you really want to know God's will for you, listen for it. Expect it. And when you hear it, let it unfold your life. Go with it, wherever it leads, because God's will for you is absolute good.

*M*ile markers

- God's will for you is absolute good.
- When you let God's will be done, all things in your life become good.
- All problems reflect your inability or unwillingness to let God's divine plan unfold through you.
- When God shapes your life, the changes are appropriate and automatic.
- Chances are it is God's will if:
  —Everyone wins.
  —Things go effortlessly.
  —There are green lights and open doors.

Your will is my will, God. Wherever You lead, I will follow. My road is easy and marked by unexpected joy. Help me see the green lights and open doors and glorify You each step of the way.

Please proceed to Adventure 13 in the Activity Book.

*Putting God first puts
your good first. And
all else "comes with
the territory."*

God first ... details to follow

*"But seek first his kingdom and his righteousness,
and all these things shall be yours as well."*
—Matthew 6:33

Grazing cattle do not become angry or distressed if
their pasture changes. Fish do not grow resentful as
the mighty currents change their water. The cows
will have grass to eat, and the fish still have a home.
Animals, it seems, accept change as a fact of life.

If only we humans could do as well! How shock-
ingly easy it is for us to jump off the path, only to
chase down one blind alley after another in desperate
pursuit of something—anything—which waves a seductive promise of fulfillment and satisfaction. But
one by one, each alley leads to the same deadend:
another alluring mirage which grows dim, disappears,
and disappoints.

And so the days of our lives spin by as we quicken

our pace to get more ... more ... more. Or to do more ... more ... more. Or to be more ... more ... more. And the more we get, the more we want. The more we do, the more that needs to be done. The more we become, the more we want to be. Finally, in a frenzy of getting and doing and becoming, we exhaust ourselves, despairing of our hollowness and echoing Maxwell Anderson's chilling words in the song "Lost in the Stars":[1]

> *Sometimes it seems as if God's gone away,*
> *Forgetting the promise that we heard Him*
> *say,*
> *And we're lost out here in the stars.*
> *Little stars—big stars—blowing through the*
> *night.*
> *And we're lost out here in the stars.*

If you've ever looked into the night sky, undimmed by city lights so that you can see all the stars, you know the feeling of insignificance which can overtake you. You can feel swept away by the incomprehensible magnitude of outer space. Yes, we are "out here in the stars." We are in and of the stars, but we are not lost! Right where you stand is the hub of the universe, and *you* are the star of a cosmic extravaganza even more vast and grand than outer space. It is your own *inner space.* When you discover *that* universe, it becomes quite natural to live each day putting God first.

HOW DO I DO IT?

What does putting God first mean? It means being

1. Maxwell Anderson, words, and Kurt Weill, music, "Lost in the Stars," Hampshire House Publishing Corp., Chappel & Co., New York, 1944.

true to the Presence which made you. It means thinking and acting from your highest level and always being open to God's will as it seeks to unfold itself through you. It means, to use the farmer's metaphor, putting your hand to the plow and furrowing straight ahead rather than in meaningless circles, eyes neither to the left nor right but always fixed on God. Then the healing, the prosperity, the peace, or the whatever you have been hoping for will take root in your life.

When you place God first in your life, everything else easily sprouts and grows naturally. This is simply another way of phrasing Jesus' "But seek first his kingdom and his righteousness, and all these things shall be yours as well."

AIM FOR THE CENTER

What a freeing concept this is. It implies that we don't have to concern ourselves with each aspect of our lives. We don't have to fret about our health. We don't have to worry about our prosperity. We needn't be anxious about our relationships. Our responsibility is to seek the kingdom of God and put God first in our lives. The promise is that when we do this, everything we need to make us happy and complete will be provided for us.

The degree to which you place God first in your life is directly proportional to the amount of ease and joy in your life. Putting God first lets your life experience flow out of your relationship with God rather than trying to use God to change your life experience.

The idea, therefore, is to aim not for healing or prosperity or any of the other "things" (noble or deserved as they may be), since they are merely symptoms of a deeper problem—a separation from God. Rather, aim for the experience of the presence of God, be "tunnel-visioned" toward God, one might say. This means release anything that blocks you from such an experience. In this way, what you seek is able to seek you. The healing, the love, the prosperity, "all these things shall be yours as well."

WORKING OUT THE DETAILS

It's so heartening to know that with God first in your life, you don't have to concern yourself with the details of how things are going to work out. The need to manipulate other people and the pressure to control events disappear. Changes can take place all around you, and they will merely be experiences to learn or grow from or to accept or to ignore. The pastures may be relocated or the water changed, but that which counts the most and means the most can *never* change—the presence of God within you. The more you allow it free rein in your life, the less crucial the "pastures" and "water" become.

Perhaps you are already discovering this for yourself. Your concern over the details of life wane as your desire for something more, something greater, increases. The further you travel in your spiritual journey, the more you need and feel God.

Remember, the Power within you has infinite patience and comes forward only when It is called. As you enter this leg of your journey, do so with a joyful shout. Let your voice ring out through the primeval forests of your inner world: "O, Lord of my being, live Your life through me."

Mile markers

- Right where you stand is the hub of the universe.
- When you discover the spirit within you, it is natural to live each day putting God first.
- With God first in your life, you need not concern yourself with the details of how things are going to work out.
- As you put God first, all you need for happiness and completion is provided for you.

I decide right now to place You first in my life, God. I am filled with Your Presence. I release all concerns. O, Lord of my being, live Your life through me.

Please proceed to Adventure 14 in the Activity Book.

PERSONAL POWERLESSNESS | *15*

You have already tried everything humanly possible and found it doesn't work. Now is the time to admit it.

Why do I feel so helpless?

"What is impossible with men is possible with God."
—Luke 18:27

Our journey here grows perilous. The path is strewn with boulders of enormous size, and cliffs drop off steeply on both sides. We have to watch our steps, because it is too easy to stumble over the dangerous need to control.

The human need to control is a blueprint for disaster. We try to control the events in our lives and the people in our lives so we can feel secure. Yet no matter how hard we try, if we are relying solely on our human resources, we will surely fail.

The only safe way to get through this segment of your journey, crisscrossed as it is with such dangerous crags, is to stop, stand still, and admit that you are powerless *on a human level* to create a life that really works. "I admit *personal* powerlessness to improve my life."

TO "BEE" OR NOT TO "BEE"

A bee flew into our car one day while we were stopped at a traffic light. Try as we might to get it out through an open window, it insisted on buzzing blindly into the windshield.

When we got home, we tried again to get it to leave, but this only made it buzz angrily against the rear window. Again and again, we attempted to direct it outside, yet each time it evaded us. Afraid of injuring the bee if we continued trying, we left the car in the driveway with the windows open next to our flowering bougainvillea vine, hoping this would entice the bee to freedom. But, alas, the next morning we found the little creature dead on the back seat, mortally exhausted from its desperate efforts.

This poor bee was so sure it had the answer to its dilemma: "I'll just keep doing what I'm doing—but with more energy," and so it buzzed with greater and greater intensity into the window. It stubbornly maintained that it could solve its own problem, when the truth was that the bee's way got it nowhere.

It may sound silly when applied to an insect, but all the bee had to do to reach the flowers was admit its personal helplessness. Its "bee-ness" was not capable of supplying the answer. "I admit *personal* powerlessness to get out of here," would have led to its salvation, because with that realization it would have stopped its futile struggle. At that point, we could have taken it gently from the midst of its predicament to the sweetness of freedom.

We couldn't help but see a little of ourselves in the

bee. How often do we try to solve a problem on its own level, even when we see it's getting us nowhere? How often do we look for a solution from a human perspective when it was our human efforts which got us there in the first place? It is rather sobering to realize that whatever predicament we are now facing, it was our best thinking that got us there! It is also sobering to realize that our best thinking is keeping us there!

YEARNING FOR MORE

You are on *The Quest* because you want to improve your life, you want help in dealing with all of the things that must be dealt with. If your life were absolutely perfect, you would not be willing to do all that *The Quest* entails. But here you are, exerting the effort, because you're dissatisfied with something. You are yearning for more.

Are you having trouble controlling a person or a circumstance in your life? Do you need physical healing or the healing of a relationship or prosperity or a better self-image or even more of an awareness of your spirituality?

We often seek secrets for change so we may live the same old ways with less pain. This is a major pitfall. Let's be on the lookout for it. We believe we can keep doing *exactly* what we've always done, yet somehow obtain different results. But the secret is that change just in your outer world will not make you happy. You can't control "out there." You can't impose your will on anything "out there."

Come to think of it, could you *ever* control anything? Can you control the dog or cat you own? Who walks whom? Or how about the parakeet? Who changes whose paper on the bottom of the cage? Or what about your children? Can you really control them? Could you ever, even when they were infants? Just who was changing whose diaper? And yourself? Can you always control what you eat or drink or smoke? Can you always control your temper? Can you always respond to others positively? Can you change the uncomfortable situation in which you might now be involved? Can you change the person whom you find annoying? Can you change the healing need you have now? No, you really cannot do any of these things.

All of this is what most people would call bad news. You simply cannot produce permanent changes in anything "out there."

BAD NEWS IS GOOD NEWS

But the "bad news" really is the good news! If controlling your outer world were the only way for you to be happy, you would be completely stressed out trying! Imagine being in charge of everyone's actions and reactions. Imagine trying to control and modify natural phenomena like having to stop the rain for your picnic and then start it for your garden. Directing the world is a full-time job, and the qualifications for the job are humanly impossible to fill. Instead, God is in charge! In God's infinite wisdom, no human is appointed to do it. What a relief! The fact that we can't control our outer world is not bad news at all. It is fabulously good news.

There's even better news. Your outer world doesn't have to change in order for you to feel good. There *is* something you can control after all, something that *only* you can control, and that is your mind—your thoughts and feelings. You have a choice no matter what is going on around you. The secret is in changing your inner world, in changing yourself. When you change "inside," whatever is going on "outside" doesn't matter.

Researchers in a diving bell can go hundreds of feet under the ocean (depths that would normally kill them) and survive. Yet their only concern is their immediate environment, the diving bell. The icy temperature of the water, the enormous pressure, the predatory fish, all these variables are not only uncontrollable, they are immaterial. The same holds true with astronauts in their space suits. The environment around them doesn't matter, as long as the environment inside the space suit supports them.

When you regulate your inner world (your thoughts and feelings), your outer world doesn't have to change. It doesn't matter what happens *to* you. It only matters what happens *through* you.

A HUMAN ADMISSION

Inner peace is a vital need. We all want to feel that tide of absolute tranquillity sweeping through us, lifting us above all disorder and struggle. Inner peace begins with an admission of *personal* powerlessness. There are no ifs, ands, or buts. "I admit *personal* powerlessness to improve my life." In stressing the word *personal*, you are saying that the personal you (your personality, your intelligence, your knowledge, your strength, your courage, your ideas, in other words, your *human* resources) is not enough to solve the problem or problems facing you. On a human level, the problem is winning. On a *human* level, you are powerless to make your life work.

158

It takes courage to pull back and admit: "I can't do it. I need help." Sometimes the words want to stick in the throat. Yet it's true, for if your human resources were enough, you would have already overcome the challenge you are facing.

This is not in any way saying that the human part of you is worthless. This is decidedly not the case. The human part of you must be accepted. You must honor its existence, but at the same time, you must realize that your humanness alone is *not enough* to bring you to the high level of life you are seeking. For that, it is necessary to go to another level.

WE ALL DO IT

Before you start feeling self-conscious or guilty about your "limitations," remind yourself that we all admit personal helplessness almost every day.

If your car won't start, and you call a mechanic, aren't you admitting personal helplessness? In fact, it's not until you admit personal powerlessness that you can begin to solve the problem. How far would you get if, when the car didn't start, you opened the hood and kept staring at the engine? It is only when you realize that your resources (in this case your knowledge of automobile engines, your mechanical skills, the accessibility of the proper tools, and so forth) are not enough to get the car going that the solution is on its way. In effect, you are saying, "I admit *personal* powerlessness to get my car started." In a case like this, admitting personal helplessness is relatively easy.

Think of the time your sink drain was clogged. After working up a sweat with a plunger and getting nowhere, wasn't it obvious that you had to call a plumber? But before you did, you had to admit personal powerlessness over the problem. You didn't say it out loud or probably even think about it, but you did come to the conclusion that you were personally helpless to fix your drain, or else you would never have made the call.

The electricity occasionally goes out in our homes in a severe storm. After we check the circuit breaker and find nothing blown, we must admit our personal powerlessness. Only then will we seek help from the electric company so the current can flow again.

LET GO AND LET GOD

When we admit our personal powerlessness, we stop fighting. This frees us from the obsession with another person or place or circumstance. It permits us to be human, to accept our humanity instead of struggling with it or looking to it for the ultimate solution. When we do this, we become more comfortable with our lives because a great burden is lifted. We don't have to work alone. Things don't have to be left entirely in our hands. We are *personally* powerless. This is when we can begin to find the true power and, along with it, the solution.

In order to find the help to make meaningful, lasting changes, it is necessary to let God take charge of your life. "Let go and let God." *But first let go.* Letting go is absolutely essential if you want to bring order out of any chaos in your world. Your admission that you are personally powerless—that you cannot control other people, that you cannot change circumstances—allows you to stop fighting with the problem and get on to living with the solution.

"I admit *personal* powerlessness to improve my

life." When you can say that *and mean it*, life will change, because this first step is a giant leap toward the overcoming of any personal troubles you may have. This admission gets you out of the problem and into the solution, because as soon as you realize you are humanly powerless, you will begin to look to where the power *really* is. And the Power is God.

Mile markers

- The human need to control is a blueprint for disaster.
- You cannot solve a problem on its own level.
- You can't change anything in the outer world to make you happy.
- Your outer world doesn't have to change in order for you to feel good.
- The only thing you can control is your mind—your thoughts and feelings.
- Admitting your personal powerlessness allows you to stop struggling.
- The real power, the only power, is God, and God knows how to work things out.

I admit personal powerlessness to transform my life. I know that I need Your help, God. You are the solution. You are the power. You are the way.

Please proceed to Adventure 15 in the Activity Book.

*You will be amazed at
how easy things become
when you turn them over
to God. It saves so much
time and effort.*

Letting God solve the problem

> *"Take my yoke upon you ... and you will find rest
> for your souls. For my yoke is easy, and my
> burden is light."* —Matthew 11:29-30

Karen was only fourteen when her mother died.
Less than a year later her father met and married
Jean.

Right from the start, the stepmother-stepdaughter
relationship was a disaster. As hard as Jean tried,
her efforts were fruitless. Karen was overtly hostile to
her stepmother and took every opportunity to sabo-
tage the marriage. She belittled Jean at home and in
public. She screamed at her for inconsequential
matters. She "accidentally" broke some of Jean's
most treasured possessions. No matter how Jean
tried to make things better, they only got worse. In
one year's time, Karen's behavior was so bad that
Jean was ready to leave the marriage.

At the end of her rope, Jean sought spiritual counseling. She was told the obvious: she was powerless over Karen and would have to surrender the situation to God. For some reason these words impressed her. On an intuitive level, she knew they were true and was able to completely let go of the situation. At that moment of surrender, she experienced "a transcendent happiness." These are her own words:

"After I made the decision to let go, I immediately felt such a tremendous release. I had finally surrendered the problem that was consuming my whole life, and I felt a *transcendent happiness*. I didn't know what was going to happen with Karen or Bob or this whole mess. All I knew was that I was going to be okay.

"Karen came home a few hours later and must have been puzzled by how happy I was. But it didn't stop her from starting in right where we had left off that morning. She yelled and cursed me for going into her bedroom to get her sheets. She was enraged. But, for the first time, I was able to see the hurt little girl in her. She reminded me of a wounded animal. Her world had fallen apart. Her mother had died just a few years before, and she had been forced to share her daddy with someone else. For the first time, I understood her pain.

"I suddenly felt such love for her that I was compelled to hug her. So I did. She stiffened up but it didn't matter, I couldn't let go of her. She began sobbing quietly, trying to cover it up, but then the dam broke. She grabbed onto me and cried and cried and cried. We both did. When she stopped, we sat and talked for five solid hours. We even missed dinner. When Bob came home, we sent him out to eat.

(He sensed something important was happening so he didn't mind.)

"Now Karen and I are both working hard at building a very special relationship. Oh, we still have our moments, but there is an underlying love and respect with none of that bitterness and resentment from before. We're not quite mother and daughter, but we're so much more than just friends. In my wildest imagination, I never could have envisioned this.

"I'll be eternally grateful for finding out about surrendering and turning over problems to God. Things worked out better than I could ever have hoped. And with such miraculous ease! I still have to pinch myself to prove this is not just a beautiful dream."

GOD IS ALWAYS READY

Through the simple act of surrender, Jean's life turned from nightmare to "beautiful dream." All she had to do was allow God to work things out. God is always ready, but Jean herself had been in the way. All of her efforts had sunk her deeper into the problem.

Only when she turned the problem over to God was Jean's happiness possible. When she turned it over to God, *she* stopped trying to change things. Rather than acting from her human self (which would have continued to react to Karen's anger), she rose above the situation. Acting from her Christ center, she naturally treated Karen with love.

Although Karen, Jean, and Bob are not their real names, these are real people. If you are unfamiliar with the act of surrendering and the life-transforming power it holds, their story may sound impossible. If you *do* understand the miracle-working power of surrender, you probably have a similar story to tell.

SURRENDERING IS NOT QUITTING

Letting go doesn't mean giving up. Surrendering is not quitting. Think of the car analogy in the last teaching. As soon as you know you can't start your car, you admit helplessness. However, that's only the beginning of the solution. If you want to get your car going again, you call a mechanic, and when the mechanic comes, you cooperate to the extent that you can. You haven't quit. In this case, quitting would mean getting another ride or walking to work or sitting in your house and pouting! Instead of quitting, you have merely given a "higher power" (one who knows more about the problem than you do) control of the situation. There is a vast difference between surrendering and quitting.

Most people think of surrender as "bad." Patrick Henry challenged, "Give me liberty or give me death!" An American general asserted, "No surrender, no retreat." Surrender has traditionally been looked upon as an admission of weakness—of giving up, buckling under, capitulating.

Contrary to popular belief, surrender can be a positive decision, a positive act. All of nature surrenders. The caterpillar surrenders and becomes a butterfly. The hawk egg surrenders to its "eggness" and becomes a hawk.

Nothing new can happen until the old loses power. When we surrender, we don't sacrifice anything. We only lose whatever is keeping us the same. Actually, we don't lose anything. We gain *everything*.

ADMITTING AN OBVIOUS FACT

Having lived near the beach, we saw many people encountering the ocean for the first time. They didn't realize the power of large waves, so as one approached, they would stand tall and brace themselves. Invariably the wave knocked them down and rolled right over them, but this didn't dissuade them. As the next wave approached, they would try again to challenge it and the results were the same. Finally, the people accepted the fact that the wave was more powerful than they were. They quickly learned that the way to deal with a large wave is merely to dive under it.

Surrendering to a power greater than yourself is really like an admission of an obvious fact. If your life is "broken" and you call on God to help you, isn't this merely admitting the truth: that God in you knows your needs more than you personally do and will help you improve your life?

Let's go back for a moment to the previous teaching and the example of the electricity going out in our home. You'll recall that as soon as we check the circuit breaker and find nothing blown, we've done all we can to get the lights on. At that point we admit our personal powerlessness, but it doesn't end there. The next step is to "surrender" and ask the electric company for help. Until we surrender to the electric company, we are part of the problem. As soon as we surrender and call them, we are part of the solution.

LETTING GO THE RIGHT WAY

How can we surrender and still be involved with the solution? We can because letting go does not mean letting go of our involvement. (Can we leave a stalled car in the garage and expect God to fix it?) Letting go means letting go of the outcome! Letting go is the release of all concerns about the results. If you have really let go and given it to God, you know the outcome will be what is best for you. The immediate outcome really doesn't matter because the *final* outcome will be good. Why? Because God's desire for us is absolute good.

Immediately upon surrendering, we begin to grow and things begin to change. Immediately upon surrendering, solutions become available. Our two dogs are constantly on "squirrel patrol" in our backyard. One day they were staring up at a squirrel making its way across a utility wire. They were so wrapped up with the problem of how to get this "meal" which was crossing their path that they were oblivious to the food we had put in front of them.

If we haven't surrendered, we are still fighting the problem. Surrender allows us to free ourselves from the obsession with the problem. When we do this, we are able to place our full sights on the solution. As soon as the dogs gave up their obsession with the squirrel, they were able to see the solution right in front of them.

We can't move forward in our spiritual development until the battle we are fighting on the human level is either won or we have surrendered. If you have been fighting a battle and are not winning, know this, you can never win alone. In the past you may have been saying to yourself, "God, Your will *and* my will." When you admit your helplessness and then surrender to God, you are saying, "God, Your will *is* my will."

DON'T BE AFRAID

Yes, admitting powerlessness is scary! You feel vulnerable. If you are powerless, you are defenseless, unprotected. A vacuum has been created. But keep in mind that admitting powerlessness is only the first step. The next step is the one that Jean took, the step of surrender, and it's an obvious step. After all, (1) you want the problem solved and (2) you don't have the resources to solve it yourself. You must turn elsewhere for help, and you can only get help from a Higher Power, one which transcends the human level of the problem.

As you let go of your anxiety, you automatically become open to new ideas and new attitudes. Now your energy can go into *creative* living rather than *defensive* living.

When you turn your problem over to God, when you really surrender, you know that all will be okay. You know deep inside that since you are one with God, all will be right in your life. God will take care of it.

Letting go of your human struggling, admitting your personal powerlessness, brings a rush of help from God. Like a miraculous rain flooding into a parched desert, God's power creates an oasis of joy and contentment where no change was ever thought possible.

This is surrender!

$\mathcal{M}$ile markers

- Letting go does not mean giving up.
- Surrender can be a positive act.
- In surrender, we lose nothing but gain the potential for everything.
- Until you surrender, you are part of the problem. After you surrender, you are part of the solution.
- Once you turn things over to God, you *know* the outcome will be what is best for you.

I turn my life over to You, God. As I surrender myself to You, I feel enfolded in peace and comfort. I know that You are making the crooked places straight and that everything is going to be okay. Thank You, God, for Your perfection as it moves through me now.

Please proceed to Adventure 16 in the Activity Book.

Making inner changes is
your greatest assignment
during this lifetime. Why
put it off any longer?

Making new wineskins

> *"And no one puts a piece of unshrunk cloth on an*
> *old garment, for the patch tears away from the*
> *garment, and a worse tear is made. Neither is*
> *new wine put into old wineskins; if it is, the skins*
> *burst, and the wine is spilled, and the skins are*
> *destroyed; but new wine is put into fresh*
> *wineskins, and so both are preserved."*
> —Matthew 9:16-17

"Oh, I'm so glad you're home!" Our friend's voice
was choked with emotion at the other end of the
phone line.

She immediately began telling us of a very trau-
matic incident she had just experienced. "I was driving along Shore Lane when I came upon a woman
crying hysterically along the side of the road. Her
dog, a large black Labrador, had just been struck by
a hit-and-run driver. I stopped my car and ran over

to the pitiful pair. The poor dog seemed mortally injured, writhing in pain and obviously in shock. Without even thinking, I put my hand on the woman's shoulder to comfort her. Then she and I tried to lift the animal into my car, but it was no use. The dog was in such pain and clearly on the verge of death. I stayed while he died in the woman's arms. After it was over, I couldn't help hugging her."

Our friend sighed when she finished the story. There were several seconds of silence before her trembling voice confided, "A year ago I would have just kept on driving."

NEW WINE, OLD WINESKINS

What happens to people that makes them act in new ways? What kind of changes have to take place for us to live different lives—to be, in effect, different people?

We change our residences to new locations, often believing that the farther the move, the bigger the change. We change jobs. We change outer appearances, have a "make-over" and get a new look with a new wardrobe. We even change spouses. Many of us have tried some or all of these, sometimes several times!

We've found, however, it doesn't work. It is sewing a patch of new material on an old cloth, or pouring new wine into an old wineskin. Eventually the old cloth and the old wineskin win out, and the new are weakened and rendered ineffectual. Unless the original is different, is changed, the new is worthless. No matter where we move, what job we take, how we style and clothe ourselves, or whom we marry, we still take the "old us" along. Only the outer has changed.

An acquaintance of ours had always hated his hometown, blaming it for all of his troubles, which included being expelled from high school for constant fighting, to a stint in jail for embezzlement, to multiple divorces. He had always wanted to move to San Francisco because, "I know if I can just move out of this rotten town, everything will change."

At the time we met him he was involved with a woman who verbally and emotionally abused him to the extent that no one wanted to be in their company when they were together. He was deeply in debt because of his profligate spending habits and had just been fired from his fourth job. He was always complaining and lamenting the fact that he couldn't decide what to do for a living. "But if I can just get to San Francisco, things will be different."

The man did move to San Francisco. One day he just up and left his northeast home. After all, wasn't that the cause of all of his problems? Yet in only eight months, he perfectly re-created in San Francisco all of the circumstances that had been in his life back East: the same woman with a different name and different face, the same debts in differing amounts and owed to different people, the same inability to keep a job, the same ambivalence about his life.

This man tried to sew a new patch (San Francisco) on old cloth (his unchanged consciousness). The "new wine" of his changed setting was not compatible with the "old wineskin" of his unaltered attitudes and beliefs and actions. He had attempted a geographic cure for his troubles, thinking that if he moved, they would not follow him. They did.

NEW CONSCIOUSNESS

The old cloth and the old wineskin symbolize our consciousness. Our old consciousness follows us wherever we go. We always take it with us. We can't hide from it, and we can't cover it over. How could we? It is our thoughts, our feelings, our memories. It is the basis of all of our actions. We can move away from our present circumstances, but if our consciousness hasn't changed, we will inevitably re-create the same circumstances because our consciousness will have supplied the only blueprint it knows.

However, the good news is that we can change it. When we sincerely want to change and when we are making spiritual discoveries and putting all of these discoveries into practice in our everyday world, we have to be sure we are working on the inner levels as well. In this way, we can accommodate the wonderful outer changes, and our inner and outer worlds will become congruent. Otherwise, it's only more new patches on old cloth, more new wine in old wineskins.

CHEMICALIZATION

Sometimes we try to take in too much new truth too fast. Excited and enthused by our new discoveries, we try to force the natural order of change by cramming in too much that is too different from the old. And, once again, we have those new patches on old cloth, new wine in old wineskins. The result is disharmony and disorder, and once in a while we can even seem to end up worse than when we started!

This is sometimes referred to as "chemicalization," because it is a reaction akin to mixing two incompatible chemicals. They fizz, sputter, churn and seethe. Occasionally, they even explode! And so can our lives if we don't *proceed at a peaceful and orderly pace, allowing time for new spiritual discoveries to become properly integrated into our consciousness.* It's almost like eating a rich meal. We need time to digest what we have eaten before going back to the banquet table. If we don't, the stomachache we may experience is not because the food is bad. It's because we haven't given ourselves enough time to digest the food.

In a sense, one who is experiencing chemicalization is experiencing withdrawal symptoms. He or she is really breaking an addiction! In this case, it is breaking an addiction to an old way of thinking, but the effects can be similar to breaking an addiction to a drug. If you have ever tried to stop smoking or drinking alcohol or using any other addictive drugs, you have a sense of how any change of thinking can affect your life.

Yes, all change brings change. However, because of the deliberate pace of *The Quest,* you may not experience any dramatic chemicalization. If you do, it should be taken strictly as a positive sign: the new is replacing the old. Unfortunately, the old thoughts and feelings don't give up without a struggle, so just when things seem their worst is exactly when you have to hold fast to the truth and stand your ground. You have to give the new a chance to establish itself, to become rooted. Many people mistakenly interpret this state as negative, as a return of the old, and so they give up at the very moment when they are on the brink of a tremendous breakthrough.

Since you are on *The Quest,* you are evolving at an orderly pace, one which builds on a solid footing and asks for only small changes each day. You probably will not have any experience with chemicalization and needn't concern yourself with it. If you do experience it, however, slow your pace and let all of these new ideas settle in before proceeding.

LIKE A CORN SEED

A friend of ours eloquently describes her childhood days on a farm. She remembers how her father tested seeds to find which variety would grow best. He had a gray woolen sock in which he would place several kinds of dried corn kernels. The seeds would sprout in secret, in the darkness of the sock. No light was ever permitted to touch the sprouting life, for if it did, the seeds would not grow. They had to develop their own inner light. The change—the growth—was taking place inside.

Our friend explained that this transformation from a seed to a plant was a most fragile process, and had to be shielded from the outer forces in order for the sprout to gain its own strength.

This is a perfect parallel to our own spiritual growth. Transformation is an inner process and has to begin in secret where it can call upon its own light and strength, just like the sprouting seed. We, too, diminish and cease to grow if we are subjected to too much of the outer at this fragile time.

YOUR ONLY OPTION

No matter what it is that you want to see happen in your life, it can only take place through inner change. No amount of change in the outer gives you permanent joy or peace, health or prosperity or, most importantly, a sense of the presence of God. Whatever your present situation in life, it is only altered by surrendering yourself and allowing change to happen from within out.

Inner change is taking place in you right now. Draw upon your own spiritual strength, the Power within you, to nurture and sustain you.

The transformation process is an inside job. When you heard your call, the process was no longer a voluntary one for you, it was mandatory. Once you heeded the call, a surrender to inner change became your only option.

Inner change is really the reason you are traveling *The Quest*, discovering the Teachings, entering into the Adventures, and completing your Activities. You are weaving new cloth, pouring new wine into new wineskins.

New thoughts, new beliefs, new feelings, and new discoveries of our spiritual nature bring on inner change and make us act in new ways. That is the kind of change which allows us to live different lives—to be, in effect, different people.

$\mathcal{M}$ile markers

- Many people are willing to rearrange the outer things in their lives, but few are willing to rearrange the priorities of their inner worlds.
- If your consciousness doesn't change, you will continually re-create the same old circumstances.
- Changes in the outer occur only after changes from within. Transformation is an inside job.

I am willing to be transformed at depth. Help me, God, to change whatever must be changed, so that I can express my true self.

Please proceed to Adventure 17 in the Activity Book.

*As immense and immea-
surable as the mind of
God is, it is small enough
to fit into the heart of
each one of us.*

One God, one mind

*"The words that I say to you I do not speak on my
own authority; but the Father who dwells in me
does his works."*　　　　　　　　　—John 14:10

Oh, the mystery and the incomprehensibility of a
mind that can think up a universe and then bring
forth that universe into existence! Such is the mind
of God.

God ... Mind ... Primal Cause, the one original
Mind out of which all creation is born. God is present
everywhere in the universe as intelligence, and this
universal Intelligence, the mind of God, creates with
thoughts and ideas. We can say these thoughts are
the movement of God's creative power out into the
universe.

God is actually thinking the universe into existence this very moment, writing the script, so to

speak. Everything we see around us is part of the handwriting of God. God is "writing" creation in an unceasing unfoldment of some divine grand scheme of things.

The concept of such a Mind is too vast, too complex, too mysterious for us to grasp. When we consider the magnitude of the universe—the stars, the flowers, human life—the greatness of it overwhelms. The Mind that envisions this is greater than all that is. It is beyond our knowing.

This is a Mind which creates the magic of life, which places and holds the mighty constellations in their familiar patterns, which turns the tides two times each day, and brings spring back to us each year.

Yet, as immeasurable as the greatness of this Absolute Being is, It places Itself in the heart of every human being. We can know God in the smallness of ourselves, for the presence of God-Mind is in our own minds.

OUR MINDS ARE PART OF GOD'S MIND

The presence of the mind of God within us can never be taught or described, only experienced. To begin to know the mystery of God, we have to begin to get a feel for what it is to be part of God-Mind. We can only do this through our own human minds, which are capable of contemplating the mind of our Creator. It is through our own minds that we attain access to God-Mind. Can we possibly comprehend what that means? It is the nature of God-Mind to impart an infinity of divine ideas to our individual minds.

The mind of God implants Its own faculties into

the mind of humanity: life, order, faith, love, will, strength, judgment, imagination, understanding, enthusiasm, power, and release. Each of us has these attributes of God-Mind in his or her own mind. With them, we design and bring forth our worlds. These attributes of God-Mind are given to us to use as we wish. They are freely given gifts, with no strings attached by the Giver.

THE ONLY BEGOTTEN

Like an alpine stream gushing forth a torrent of water, Divine Mind is always delivering a steady supply of ideas to us. The fact that we do not always use these ideas, or even recognize them, doesn't stop the supply. But it is when we open ourselves to and use divine ideas that we are being true to our Christ nature. This ability of the individual mind to incorporate ideas from Divine Mind into its own makes each of us a very special and unique creation, the "only begotten" of God. We ... *we* are the only begotten! Because we are the highest of all God's creations, made in the very image and likeness of God, we have been given the power to express in our individual ways all that God is.

Those last three sentences pack quite a punch, and they bring up an obvious question. Why, if we are creatures of Divine Mind and therefore possess all of Its attributes, aren't we automatically conscious of Its presence? And why don't we automatically live our lives in a constant state of perfection?

The answer lies in one of our greatest gifts. Part of our divine inheritance is free will, our ability to choose and create with our own minds. Given this gift of free will we, over the timeless millennia, have

gotten into the habit of "creating our own worlds."
Too often these are worlds of seeming separation from
God-Mind.

All of creation is held in the mind of God, and can
be produced in an infinite number of varieties of
form. When our human minds unite with God-Mind,
things take the right form in the right order. As a
result, we experience joy, health, prosperity, peace,
and unwavering contentment.

THE TRINITY

When discussing the idea of God-Mind, it seems
natural to address the concept of the Trinity, since it
is so familiar (even if not clearly understood) to so
many of us.

The idea of a triune God, which traditional Christianity has espoused, and which is also found in some
non-Christian religions, can actually best be explained in terms of God-Mind.

God—the one Presence and the one Power—has
three aspects or roles: *mind, idea,* and *expression.*
The Trinity can be looked at as the creative process of
God. Mind is the source, the origin, the parent—the
Father/Mother. The mind gives birth to ideas or
thoughts. Expression is the manifestation or out-
working of those ideas. Expression is, in a sense, the
working arm of God and is commonly referred to as
the Holy Spirit. This aspect of God does the work in
our lives.

Mind, idea, expression—three roles of the one God.
Yet they are not separate, anymore than one can
separate an artist from his or her work. We could say
the artist is the mind, the vision for a painting is the

idea, and the actual finished work is the expression. Three aspects, but all part of the one.

AS WITH GOD, SO WITH US

We humans follow the same creative process as God-Mind. We begin with the beingness of our own minds. Our minds give birth to ideas, and then those ideas go on to become manifest in our lives.

We already used the example of an artist, but anything else you can think of will follow the same process. Even something as mundane as a shopping list is an example. You are the mind which gives birth to the idea of what you need at the store. Then those thoughts are expressed on paper as your list.

Architect, idea, blueprint. Poet, inspiration, poem. Tailor, pattern, suit. Cook, recipe, dinner. The list goes on forever.

The process also applies to less tangible or material things. If a person's mind gives rise to a steady stream of fear thoughts, they will eventually be expressed as some undesirable condition or situation in the person's life.

Mind, idea, expression. The same creative process as God, except that our human ideas are not as perfect as God's.

Once we comprehend the perfection, the rightness, of the ideas of God, we have to conform to those ideas. By conforming, we discover that God's will is perfect in every way. There is no need, therefore, to ever pray or beg for God's will to change to suit us. We discover that It is already working on our best behalf.

THE PUSH FOR PERFECTION

God-Mind is continually urging us higher and higher because the most superb way in which God can express is through us—through human creation. Your Christ essence is God's perfect idea of humanity *in you*—perpetually longing to unfold itself. In you! You allow this to happen by thinking of yourself as God thinks of you.

In spite of all of the diverse (and perverse) ways we have used the power of our minds to construct our lives, God has never—*can* never—relinquish the vision of perfection for humankind. We can only imagine that God must have an insatiable yearning for us, the "only begotten," to fulfill the perfection of that vision.

$\mathcal{M}$ile markers

- God is present everywhere in the universe as intelligence.
- The presence of God-Mind is in your own mind.
- It is through your own mind that you attain access to all of God-Mind.
- You have all the attributes of God-Mind.
- When your human mind unites with God-Mind, things take the right form in the right order.
- The Trinity is mind, idea, and expression, the creative process of God.
- You follow the same creative process as God-Mind.
- Human creation is the highest way in which God can express.

O great mind of God, Creator of this universe, express Yourself through me. I am open to Your ideas, Your will. Help me to know You in the midst of my human self as I unite my mind with Yours.

Please proceed to Adventure 18 in the Activity Book.

LAW OF MIND ACTION | *19*

Your thoughts are the most powerful part of you. They actually create your world.

How to control your life

> *"Go; be it done for you as you have believed."*
> —Matthew 8:13

What a piece of work we are! We can create glorious symphonies and magnificent works of art, develop the most imaginative instruments to investigate our universe and ourselves, invent ingenious machines that vastly improve our quality of life, and selflessly devote our lives to helping others.

On the other hand, we are capable of creating weapons of mass destruction, plundering and pillaging whole countries, and selfishly stepping on others to "get to the top."

Think of all the wonderful as well as terrible creations of humankind. From one end of the spectrum to the other, they have one thing in common: each began as an idea, a thought.

The first wheel was a thought before it moved a cart. Leonardo's fresco of *The Last Supper* was painted in his mind before he ever picked up a brush. Attila the Hun's rampage through Europe started out as a campaign in his mind. Albert Schweitzer's great humanitarian work in Africa first lived as a yearning inside of him. The reign of terror which Jack the Ripper inflicted on London began with the horrors of his own thoughts. The founding of the United States of America was an idea before any words were ever put on paper. And the present state of your life? It, too, began as thoughts.

LIVING BRICKS

There is nothing, *nothing*, that did not begin as a thought. The universe was brought forth from an idea in God-Mind. You and everything else in this universe began as an idea. All that is and all that has been and all that ever will be, began or will begin with a thought.

Thoughts are the power of the world. They are the very blueprints for our lives. And just as God brought forth the world with a thought, we bring forth our world with our thoughts. God creates people, and people create their conditions. There is a cooperation between God and each of us as we create our world. But whereas in God-Mind all ideas are for our good, we take these ideas from God-Mind and filter them through our minds to create our world. That can be a marvelous thing, except when our minds are choked with perceived limitations and false beliefs.

It is from our thoughts that we systematically draw the people, places, and circumstances into our lives that eventually become our reality. Each thought is a living "brick" that, piled one on another, constructs our future. True, it is action which shapes our material world, but actions are nothing more than three-dimensional thoughts. It is through our thoughts that we give life to our world. To us has been given the power to create and to destroy.

SCANNING THE BLUEPRINT

We move in the direction of our thoughts. Where we are looking is where we are heading. We do this automatically when we are walking, running, bicycling, or driving a car. Where we put our vision, where we put our attention, is where we eventually end up. We are always scanning the blueprints of our thoughts, scrupulously following the plans to create an exact outer replica of the inner idea. We don't always do this consciously, of course, but we do it.

"Thoughts held in mind produce after their kind" is a more contemporary version of the biblical Proverb: "As he thinketh in his heart, so is he" (Prov. 23:7 KJV). Said either way, it is the law of mind action. What it means is that our bodies and our life circumstances are faithful renditions of the consistent and persistent ideas in our minds. The thoughts that we hold are the types of circumstances that we will produce. As we think in our hearts, so we will become. That's why as you travel *The Quest*, you will repeatedly come upon this signpost: "Change your thoughts and you change your world."

THE GATEKEEPER

When we are talking about thoughts and ideas in the mind, we're talking specifically of the subconscious mind, the level of the mind which automatically carries out the orders given to it. Who or what gives these orders to the subconscious mind? We do, with our conscious, directed thinking.

We program our subconscious minds with what we accept unchallenged from television, for instance, and the world in general. "Now that you're 35, you have tired blood." "If you don't use this deodorant, you won't be as popular." "We're in a recession; times are bad." It is the responsibility of the conscious, rational mind to decide what it accepts, retains, and dwells upon. It's an immense responsibility.

We hit a snag here, however, because too often we abrogate the responsibility of our conscious minds. We let all kinds of negative, destructive, erroneous ideas come flooding in unchallenged. It's as if the conscious mind were a gatekeeper, or a filter, but we indiscriminately open it up to whatever flotsam and jetsam come floating by! All of the stale beliefs of the human race about age, the false idea that wars bring peace, the negativity spouted all around us by people who don't know its destructive power ... things like these can come pouring into us if we don't keep our filters in place.

Whatever the conscious mind allows in goes directly to the subconscious. If we are constantly and persistently letting in and entertaining destructive ideas, how can our actions be constructive? The subconscious is where the power lies. Whatever is consistently and persistently held there goes on to become expressed in our lives.

Jesus understood how the subconscious mind works when He taught that whatsoever you desire, when you pray, believe you have received it. It is in the subconscious that our real beliefs and emotions reside. Although He taught the law of mind action two thousand years ago, Jesus' teaching is timeless (as are all of His teachings). What He said was that it is the *belief* that creates the pattern by which the subconscious mind brings forth visible form and structure. In other words, what has been consistently and persistently held in mind so that it has taken root and has an emotion attached to it, that is what's created.

TRANSFORMATIVE KNOWLEDGE

The power of the subconscious mind is a phenomenon which cannot be overemphasized. Every deep-seated conviction, expectation, and emotion is going to eventually translate itself into the tangible world. At this point in our human understanding, we may not yet be fully cognizant of how this process works, but we do know that it does work. For example, through the study of psychoneuroimmunology, it has been documented that strong thoughts and emotions metamorphose directly into hormones and chemicals in the body. These chemicals directly influence our health. Thoughts and emotions determine not only our physical health, they establish our total life experience. We can use our thoughts to make changes in our lives.

This is transformative knowledge, because it means if you take on new beliefs and new ideas and new *feelings* about things, they cannot help but be reflected in your life. You have been given a free will. You have been bestowed with the God-given ability to affect your own life experience. Your thoughts are the generators of such changes. And *that* has to be absolutely sensational news!

LIKE MAGNETS

Before we move on to the Adventure in the Activity Book, there are a couple of points that have to be covered. The first could very well be in answer to a question you're asking: "If my thoughts and feelings make my world, does that mean I had been thinking 'car crash' before I had that accident?" Or, "Does this mean I've been dwelling on cancer?" Or, "Could *my* thoughts and feelings have caused my son's death?"

The answer to each of those questions is "yes" and "no." No, we don't necessarily draw specific events into our lives although, yes, it can happen with enough focus and concentration. However, through the power of our thinking, we are continuously drawing *kinds* of events into our lives. In a sense, our thinking creates the framework. The *types* of ideas and feelings attract similar types of experiences. In fact, not only do we attract them, we create them.

REACTION = SEED

Fortunately, once things do come into our lives, we have absolute control over our reactions to them. How important that we understand this. We constantly are creating our world through how we deal with our world. Each action or reaction is another thought. Each action or reaction is the seed of a future circumstance.

Nevertheless, don't feel you have to invest a lot of time and energy into figuring out what specific thoughts and feelings caused specific circumstances in your life. If you are lost and stop at a gas station to ask directions, you don't have to know how you got to the gas station. All you have to know is how to get from where you are to where you want to go.

If there are things in your life which need a new direction, know that you are creating your tomorrow with the thoughts and emotions of today and proceed from the present.

THE WINNING COMBINATION

The second point we want to make is a major one. You've surely noticed that, along with thoughts and ideas, emotions and feelings have been regarded as generators of mind action.

Your mind (or soul) is made up of your thoughts *and* feelings, and feelings are strong dictators. In fact, whenever you pit a strong feeling against a thought, the feeling will win 100 percent of the time. (People running out of a burning building have not stopped to think. They are acting strictly out of an emotion, in this case fear.) We are driven by our emotions. We won't even get up off a chair and cross the room unless our emotions prompt us. If we "just don't feel like it," we won't do it.

But attach an emotion to the thought of crossing the room and off we will go. It could be the emotion of fear that our child will touch an electric outlet, or the emotion of love that urges us to get up and hug a friend. The thought of getting off the chair and crossing the room is not enough. It must be attached to an emotion.

Yet emotions are really thoughts, a complex mix of sensory perceptions and judgments, that have formed strong patterns. In a sense, they are thoughts given

192

the power of hormones, thoughts that have reached a critical mass and been transmuted to a level that prompts us into action. Unlike thoughts, emotions take place entirely in the unconscious.

With that in mind, you can appreciate the potential of a thought-emotion combination. Often our thoughts say one thing and our feelings another. "Yes, I know prayer can help, but it's really no use. I'll never be healed." Thought going in one direction; emotion going the opposite way.

When a thought and a feeling are synchronized and both are going in the same direction, however, you are wielding the most powerful tool in your possession. It leads inexorably toward life-transforming action. "Joe saved his life with prayer, and I *know* I can do it too." *That* is the kind of empowerment Jesus had in mind when He declared it as "done for you as you have believed."

The human mind, with its thoughts and feelings, is the mightiest and most wondrous creation in all creation. When linked with God-Mind, your human mind has no limits in its ability to alter the world, your personal world.

As we journey further, we will come upon discoveries which will shed more light on the process of changing one's thoughts and feelings. For now, as we begin this adventure, bring with you the conviction that "as he thinketh in his heart, so is he." Also add this to your belongings: Thoughts held in mind produce after their kind.

Here it is in a nutshell: Like attracts like. It always has and it always will. It is an unbreakable universal law. It is the law of mind action.

Mile markers

- Everything begins with an idea.
- Your thoughts are the blueprint for your life.
- Your thoughts today create your world of tomorrow.
- Change your thoughts and you will change your world.
- Through the power of your thinking, you are continuously drawing *kinds* of events into your life.
- You have absolute control over your *reactions*.

Thank You, God, for the transforming power of Your Divine Mind as I allow it to express through me. My will is Your will. I desire to celebrate You in all that I do and in all that I say and in all that I am. With You as my Partner, I create my world in a new and more positive way.

Please proceed to Adventure 19 in the Activity Book.

$\mathcal{T}$HE POWER OF THE SPOKEN WORD | $\mathit{20}$

Every time you speak,
you influence your world.
You are either building it
up or tearing it down.

Words can kill or cure

"By your words you will be justified, and by your
words you will be condemned." —Matthew 12:37

Our small, green planet turns on its axis and another day is born in our hemisphere. The land and the sea stretch hungrily for the warm rays of the sun, which had been waiting for their arrival. The sun's rays are utterly universal in their radiance. They beam out in all directions, flooding anything in their path, lighting up the entire outdoors.

Light bulbs are like that too. Their rays travel in all directions at once, indiscriminately lighting the whole area. Even a tiny match struck in the dark will send its flickering rays in all directions.

So it is with any conventional light. The only way to direct such randomly diffused light is with shades and mirrors and prisms, but even then, light particles still want to go off in all directions. That is why even the most focused spotlight will still light up areas nearby, and the light will spread out noticeably the further it extends from its source.

Laser light is different. The light from a laser is "coherent light." Rather than scattering in all directions, the light particles are in phase with each other; they are all going in exactly the same direction. This increases their power enormously. Light from such a coherent source is powerful enough to burn a hole through a piece of steel! No wonder lasers are so extensively used in industry.

The laser can also be made "tame" enough for use in delicate surgery, to reattach the retina of a human eye, for example.

Laser light is extraordinary, incredibly precise in its focus and singularly powerful in its effect.

THE CUTTING EDGE OF WORDS

Words are the lasers of human thought. Rather than scattering in all directions, thoughts, when they are expressed as words, are in phase with each other. They are all going in the same direction, and this increases their power almost beyond belief.

Words, in fact, are random thoughts which have been brought together to become "coherent thought." Before we can *speak* the thoughts we have, they must be made more cohesive, more coherent. (How many times have you heard someone say or said yourself, "I'm trying to get my thoughts together"?) In joining thoughts together, they take on additional power. Like the laser, but with even greater potential, our words can create or destroy.

It is true that thoughts are supreme as the molders of our world. Thoughts are initiatory to all changes. But something else happens when we put our thoughts into sentences, when we speak the word. It sets up potent vibrations in our bodies. Speaking and hearing and feeling our thoughts impress them more fully on us than merely thinking them. Words move us into action. When we declare our thoughts, when we speak, every atom of our bodies responds to the sound of our voices. Not only do we *hear* what we say, we actually *feel* what we say.

Every word, therefore, has an effect. The intensity of the effect depends on the intensity of the thought and feeling behind it and the way the word is spoken.

An obvious and very basic example of this is the fact that soothing words create the release of "soothing" chemicals in the body. This is true not only for the speaker of the words but also for the listener. Angry words, on the other hand, cause the release of harmful "fight or flight" chemicals. Again, this happens not only in the person speaking the angry words but in the one spoken to as well. This is proven, measurable, scientific fact.

Still, even without the scientific proof, we already know this to be true. If you have ever spoken soothing words to a frightened child or remember hearing such words spoken to you, you know the power of loving thoughts put into words. Conversely, if you have ever spoken harshly or been spoken to harshly, you know the power of angry thoughts put into words.

It is common knowledge that speaking soothing

words of love and encouragement to plants makes them grow faster and better. Harsh, hateful words spoken with vehemence tend to make them wither. If our words can have such an impact on plants, imagine the impact we have on ourselves!

Every word we speak is saturated with energy that will create or destroy. We are accountable for "every idle word" we speak, for it brings forth after its kind. In a very real way, the word becomes flesh and dwells among us and in us and as us. We cannot help becoming what we say we are. The more resolutely and intensely we speak the word of who and what we are, the more surely we move toward becoming what we say. If we happen to accept the words directed to us by others, if we make their words our own, then we will move in that direction as well.

LIKE AN OLD CART HORSE

There is no doubt that all words affect us, but it is our own words which affect us the most. Whether we make our statements kiddingly or seriously, our words have impact. The subconscious has no sense of humor. It doesn't know the difference between your jokingly referring to yourself as "such a dope" and your actually thinking that you are a dope. The subconscious is like an old cart horse, to which a "giddy-up" means "get going." The horse doesn't know if it is said kiddingly or seriously. All it knows is that when it hears those words, it is time to obey.

WORDS ARE MIRRORS

The words you use reflect your state of consciousness, but they are more than that. They are the very cause of the maintaining of that consciousness. So, if you tell yourself, "You messed up again. You really are worthless," you are not only affirming your present sense of worth, you are setting the parameters of your worth for the future: Today's words become tomorrow's reality.

To constantly lament, for example, in the midst of an economic recession: "I'm really worried about my money. I just know I'm going to get laid off and lose everything" is to dwell on lack and fear. Such words crystallize your negative thoughts, but even more than that, since you are a cocreator with God, the words you speak direct the creative power of Infinite Mind.

God has no hands or feet or vocal cords or eyes or ears, but you do, and you manipulate your physical world with these attributes. However, God works with you. Having given you free will, God is willing to carry out whatever plan you have for yourself. Therefore, you are cocreator with God. You cocreate your own world by linking your mind with Divine Mind. That link comes through your words. Your words tell God, the Ultimate Creative Intelligence, just what it is that you want.

If you want prosperity and abundance in your world, speak only words of prosperity and abundance. If you want peace in your world, speak only words of peace. If you want love in your world, speak only words of love. (The power of the laser is in its coherence—all light particles are in phase—all are traveling in exactly the same direction!)

This is not a denial of the fact that there is less than abundance and peace and love in your world. On the contrary, it is simply declaring to the universe and to yourself just what it is that you want.

SOLO VERSUS SYMPHONY

Knowing the mighty potential locked up in every spoken word, you can surmise the even greater potential intrinsic in words spoken in concert, words spoken together by groups.

Just as performing a beautiful violin piece gives it more power than merely thinking about it, words become more empowered when spoken aloud. We hear them and feel them, whether violin solo or words, and become emotionally invested in them.

How much more emotion, more power, when the violin is joined by a full symphony orchestra! And how much more emotion and power when we speak the word with others, when a like-minded group affirms a statement of truth with passion and intensity. A new and even greater dimension of energy and power is generated as the group speaks together as one great soul. What a phenomenal force is created. It is as if a group of lasers got together and became one great laser beam. Words spoken like this can have astounding effects.

As a group, we can speak words of healing, comfort, strength, peace, harmony or whatever we desire—for an individual in the group, for the group as a whole, or for an individual or group in some other place. (Time and space are not factors when we speak positive words for others. The spoken word is so powerful that it cuts right through distance and time in a way which science cannot yet fully explain.)

YOUR WORDS, YOUR LIFE

There is a wonderful story about a wise teacher of truth who was walking through the woods with his students when they came upon the partially decomposed carcass of a dead deer. The students, in an attempt to protect their teacher from seeing such a repulsive sight, tried to steer him around it. But the teacher would not alter his direction. When he came upon the deer, he looked it over carefully and said, "My, what beautiful antlers."

He chose to look past the obvious and express the beautiful. He didn't dwell on the decomposed flesh but rather on the noble antlers, so his words were not of repulsion but of loveliness.

We can do the same with our lives. Certainly we can find enough ugliness around us if we care to look for it, but there is also an abundance of beauty. Which do you want in your world? The words you speak determine which it will be.

Mile markers

- Your words have power to create or destroy.
- The spoken word sets up potent vibrations in the body, resulting in measurable physiological changes.
- Your subconscious mind automatically obeys your heartfelt words.
- Words spoken together by a group have even greater effect than those spoken by an individual.

God, let my words serve to glorify You. May they heal and comfort and harmonize my life and the lives of those around me. I speak the right words now so that my world becomes transformed.

Please proceed to Adventure 20 in the Activity Book.

The two tiny words I am *are the biggest in the world. Few people realize their full impact.*

The only name you have

"*I am the way, and the truth, and the life.*"
—John 14:6

"My true nature is fear."

"The very essence of me is sick and tired."

"Poverty is God's will for me."

"Old age is my divine inheritance."

Ouch! Makes you wince, doesn't it? Who would say such things, especially in light of what we now know about the power of our words?

Yet it's shocking to learn that many of us broadcast the equivalent of such dreadful statements every day. How? By following the powerful words *I am* with something less than God's will for us:

"I am *so afraid* of failing."

"I am *sick and tired* of your behavior."

"I am *too poor* to afford it."

"I am *too old* to travel anymore."

These are the kinds of pronouncements we hear all around us, maybe even say ourselves. But such statements are dangerous, even lethal. This is because they all contain those two little words *I am*.

The words *I am* are so powerful that they must be used with extreme care. Why? Because the words *I am* are your actual identity. They are your spiritual name, the identity of your spiritual self. Your I AM is the name of the God nature in you and of all the divine potential in you. It is who you are at your Christ essence. I AM is your true identity.

FEEL THE POWER

If you want to feel the power of the words *I am*, substitute the words *It is my essence to be ...*, or *It is my nature to be ...*, or *... is God's will for me.* Thus a seemingly innocuous comment, "I am so worried," translates into "It is my very nature to be worried." A comment said in frustration, "I am absolutely devastated," becomes "It is my essence to be devastated." The statement "I am a diabetic" is really the assertion "Diabetes is God's will for me."

Restated that way, those statements feel so uncomfortable to you because they more clearly point out that you are claiming something you don't really want. You are identifying yourself with something far, far removed from your essence.

Yet that's exactly what happens when you use the words *I am*. You put a claim into the great Creative Intelligence of the universe to transform yourself into whatever it is with which you are identifying.

When negative feelings are put into "I am" statements, these seemingly harmless statements take on a life-altering seriousness. Can you really believe that it is your *nature* to be worried? Of course, you feel concerned and anxious at times; we all allow circumstances to bully us, but worry as part of your true nature? Never.

There are times when events can make us feel devastated—the death of a loved one, a serious financial setback, a relationship gone sour. But saying "I *feel* devastated" is significantly different than claiming "I *am* devastated." What you *feel* is transitory, what you *are* is forever.

What about identifying yourself with a sickness (for instance, "I am a diabetic")? If God's desire for us is absolute good, then how can God inflict diabetes on anyone? But if you insist on claiming it, making it part of your identity, then it's yours because you are holding on to it.

CHOOSE YOUR IDENTITY

At many conventions, name tags are put on a table in front of the main hall. You are expected to find the tag with your own name on it and pin it on your lapel. Of course, you choose your tag carefully because you don't want to be identified as someone else.

It's much the same with your use of your I AM. You are naming yourself. You are calling on the universe to identify you with what you are claiming and then to help you to produce that claim in your life.

Your I AM is your true identity. In fact, it is your *only* identity. Only you can say the words *I am*. Only you can direct the energy of these words to a universe waiting to do your bidding.

How successfully Jesus used the words *I am*! The Scriptures are scattered with His statements of identity, from "I am the bread of life" (John 6:35), "I am the light of the world" (John 8:12), "I am the resurrection and the life" (John 11:25), to "I am the Alpha and the Omega" (Rev. 22:13).

Years ago a television commercial for a stock brokerage company featured a crowded room filled with noisy people. The camera focused on two of the people who were speaking privately. One said to the other, "My broker is so-and-so, and they say ..." Suddenly the room became quiet as everyone turned to listen intently to what so-and-so thought about the stock market.

In a similar way, all of the creative energies of the universe stop and listen when we say "I am ..." since it is their function to bring us whatever it is that we're claiming for ourselves. They are always ready to spring into action whenever a claim is entered.

TAKING GOD'S NAME IN VAIN

As a child, you probably learned the Ten Commandments. Remember the third? "You shall not take the name of the Lord your God in vain; for the Lord will not hold him guiltless who takes his name in vain" (Ex. 20:7). Personally, we used to think that meant don't curse using the name of God. But the ramifications of this commandment are so much deeper than that.

When Moses confronted the burning bush and was told to return to Egypt, he asked God's name. He was told, "Say this to the people of Israel, 'I AM has sent me to you'.... This is my name for ever" (Ex. 3:14-15).

Thus we came to learn that God's name is I AM.

Now, could it be only coincidence that God's name is the very same name we use when referring to ourselves? Not a chance, when we remember that Jesus very clearly described God and the kingdom of God as being within us. He insisted that the Father and we are one. To Jesus, the focal point of God and that oneness is indeed within us. In fact, it is the I AM of us, the Christ of us.

FROM PRISTINE TO PERSONAL

In its most pristine expression, the I AM of us is Godlike—eternal, pure, and unchanging. If we attach a human limitation to our I AM, we limit its expression through us. It is no longer eternal, pure, and unchanging. It is ... well, whatever we say it is.

The I AM is impersonal and universal, but you personalize it when you say, "I am ..." I am angry. I am afraid. I am sick. However, phrases like these merely reflect the human you expressing your personal universe. Your real I AM cannot be angry. Your true I AM cannot be afraid. Your authentic I AM cannot be sick because I AM is the name of the God nature in you. I AM is the essence of the God potential which expresses as you. Therefore, I AM is all-peace, all-power, all-wholeness.

THE NAME THAT IS A KEY

Let's go back to the third commandment. We see that the name of the Lord in this commandment is really I AM. It is the presence of God, not just in a burning bush, but in you. In fact, it is the presence of God *being* you. So whenever you attach a negative or untruth to your I AM, it is then that you are taking God's name in vain.

Jesus used the words, "I am" when He referred to Himself as "the way, and the truth, and the life." He was saying His I AM—the Christ identity within Him—is the way and the truth and the life. He taught that the same I AM presence in each of us is the seed of our own salvation, our own way and truth and life. It is the key which unlocks the door to what is to become of us. The more we get into the habit of using the I AM in the right way, the more effective it becomes in creating high-quality life for us. As with any exercise, the more we practice, the better we get.

STAKING YOUR CLAIM

Think about it. When you say "I am," just what are you really saying? It is, first of all, your identity. It is what you are claiming for yourself. It is how you are identifying who and what you are. What you voice after the words *I am* reflects your state of consciousness. It reflects your own idea of yourself and what you think will eventually be projected into the visible world.

What you say after "I am" is what you are linking to God's name, and God's name, I AM, is not a static concept because God is always creating. It is God's nature to create. And since we are cocreators of our world with God, our use of our I AM is the dynamic shaper of our world. Our I AM is an ongoing creative energy, always bringing into our world exactly what we ourselves identify with. It is by the use of our I AM that we form and shape the circumstances and events of life.

PICK UP THE RIGHT TAG

The great thing about all of this is that the I AM of you, your God self, is always seeking to project itself into visibility *as* you. It is the fountainhead of your desires at their most spiritual level. What you want to be at your highest level, you *can* be because this desire is the intuitive awareness and expression of your I AM.

The power of prayer is elevated to an ever higher plateau when you join this I AM energy with your most fervent desire:

"I am healthy and well."

"I am at peace."

"I am prosperous and successful."

"I am an ageless expression of Spirit."

All of a sudden the importance of speaking only words that we want to see become manifest in our lives becomes very obvious. What we attach to our I AM is directing the creative power of infinite Mind. Whether that direction is into a negative channel or a positive channel is up to us. There are all kinds of name tags on the table for us to pick up and pin on: fear or peace, sickness or wholeness, poverty or abundance, despair or inspiration. The more intimate we become with our I AM as we practice using it correctly, the more deeply we will come to appreciate this power of God in action in our lives.

YOUR DIVINE ORIGIN

In the consciousness of your indwelling Christ essence, you can rest assured that God is your source and you are an heir to all of God's good. If you remember your divine origin and, more importantly, that your I AM is rooted in that origin, you will automatically employ this powerful asset to change your life for the better.

Your I AM is what you are. It is the wagon to which you hitch whatever you choose to carry you through life. You can hitch up to mediocrity or you can hitch up to greatness.

Hitch your wagon to a star.

Mile markers

- The words *I am* are your spiritual self, your true identity.
- I AM is the name of the divine potential in you.
- Whatever you attach to the words *I am* is what you are claiming for yourself.
- The creative energies of the universe are always ready to spring into action whenever you enter a claim.

I am grateful, God, for all of Your blessings. I am wholeness ... I am peace ... I am prosperity ... I am joy ... I am all that a child of Yours should be.

Please proceed to Adventure 21 in the Activity Book.

*R*ELEASE AND AFFIRMATION | *22*

*Sometimes you need
"spiritual training
wheels" to start you on
the path.*

Pulling weeds, planting flowers

"Let what you say be simply 'Yes' or 'No.' "
—Matthew 5:37

"Let's clear away the whole mess!" The city council
had had enough of the crime and the filth. So, in an
attempt to reclaim the downtown area, a large north-
eastern city decided to tear down their ugly, dangerous slums and demolish all the abandoned buildings,
burned-out homes, and tenements. Several city
blocks were cleared and, after years of looking like a
war zone, it was an amazing improvement. But something very unexpected happened. The shacks and
trash started slowly creeping back, and the cleared
areas were on their way to becoming as seedy and
undesirable as before.

What on earth had gone wrong? The bewildered
city council couldn't figure it out. Finally it dawned

on them. It's not enough to *remove* offensive structures. You have to *replace* them with something better. This time they would get it right.

So, after clearing away the resprouting slums, they leased out the land for the construction of theater complexes, shopping malls, and upscale apartment houses. After that, the slums did not return.

BORN AGAIN CITY

This "born again" city is a great lesson. If we expect to reclaim our consciousness, we have to get rid of our old "ugly and dangerous" beliefs. But once we clear them from our minds, we have to quickly follow up by building a God-consciousness or else the old thinking will creep back and we'll have to rout it out again. And again and again.

Releasing is the tearing-down process. Affirmation is the building-up process. We need them both. When you pull a weed, you have to plant a flower to take its place, or you'll just get more weeds. Releasing and affirming will help you keep your garden beautiful.

Release

Isn't it marvelous that we, along with all other forms of life on this planet, have been given the power of elimination! Without elimination, we would have no way to rid our bodies of toxic wastes, those life-denying poisons which accumulate daily as a result of normal living. But through our intestines, kidneys, skin, and lungs, we are able to release these metabolic wastes. By denying these life-*depleting* poisons a place in our bodies, we strengthen those life-*sustaining* forces which keep us whole and healthy.

The faculty of elimination applies not only to our physical bodies. Our free will allows us the luxury of eliminating or releasing *anything* in our lives which is not sustaining and nurturing us.

You can release any belief not consistent with what you are. If a thought or a feeling or an action—yours or someone else's—does not validate the divinity in you and all which that implies, get right to work denying it space in your life. Refuse to accept it. It's important to note, however, that when you use a statement of release, you are not denying the appearance of a situation. *You are merely denying its ultimate power over you.*

DENYING THE APPEARANCE

This can use some explaining. Let's say there's a man who chain-smokes cigarettes, and he wants to quit. He would not attempt to release the habit by saying "I don't smoke," because he cannot deny his excessive use of tobacco: it's an obvious fact. He probably can't even deny his craving for cigarettes. He couldn't honestly say "I don't crave tobacco," because that would not be true. He *does* crave it, many times a day. That's why he's still smoking! What he can deny is the thought that he is a slave to tobacco. He can deny his being completely controlled by it. A good statement of release for him might be, "I don't *need* cigarettes." By doing that much, he has taken a big step toward releasing the addiction.

Notice, he hasn't denied the fact that he smokes or that he often craves it, but he has denied the *necessity* of smoking. He has opened his mind to accepting the fact that smoking is not an inevitable part of his life unless *he* allows it to be. As this awareness expands, he soon sees that he's been given power over *all* things, not only cigarettes, and that nothing can control him unless he lets it. Tobacco then starts losing its importance in his life. He finds he doesn't need it, and so eventually he won't use it.

Let's look at another example. An X ray may clearly show a medical problem. You can't deny that there is a shadow on the X ray. What you can do is release it by denying that it belongs in your body. You can deny that it has power to affect the wholeness that God wants for you. See the difference?

Although it is always the thoughts and feelings behind the release statement which change your consciousness, the actual words themselves can be a great motivator. For instance, a woman who constantly overeats may try to convince her intellect, "I don't like chocolate," but that's ridiculous! Of course she likes chocolate and she knows that. She would have a difficult time convincing herself otherwise. It would be more effective for her to say, "I don't have to have chocolate," or "Chocolate is *not* in charge." Her intellect can agree with those words, and so she will more easily accept them into her consciousness.

How about a man with a poor self-image? When thoughts of unworthiness gang up on him he can say, "I am *not* like that," or "I refuse to think of myself that way," or "Not true!"

THE HIGHEST FORM OF JUDGMENT

Releasing is the highest form of judgment. It is a declaration that something is keeping you from expressing your best self, and so it has to go!

Remember, you don't deny something out of existence. You deny your inaccurate beliefs about it, since it is your *belief* which sets the cause into motion to bring you the result. (The law of cause and effect again!) That's why no true release is ever concerned with things or conditions. It works on your incorrect thoughts and feelings which cause all of those unwanted conditions.

OF DIAPERS AND RELEASING

Some people don't like to use statements of release. They think of them as "too negative" and will use only statements of affirmation. Yet affirming without releasing is like changing a baby's diaper by putting a clean one over the dirty one!

Before any rebuilding can take place in your life, first get rid of whatever is causing trouble. If your house were on fire, wouldn't you call a fireman *before* calling a building contractor to rebuild it? It's the same with statements of release. They allow you to first let go of what's wrong in your life—your wrong beliefs—*before* you begin rebuilding your consciousness with new thought patterns.

As you change your beliefs, you change your life. Release is an important step in this change. Just as a body can't be whole with a disease organism in it, you can't be whole until you first eliminate "diseased" thoughts like unforgiveness, sickness, and poverty.

Is there space in your life for love if you are cluttered with unforgiveness? Is there room for health if you haven't first gotten rid of the thought of sickness? Can prosperity flow into your life if you haven't first released the notion of poverty? Can you plant a flower on top of a weed and expect it to grow?

OLD RUTS, NEW GROOVES

In Alaska during the rainy season, dirt roads become thick mud. Deep ruts are gouged into them as vehicles travel back and forth. Soon after the rainy season, winter arrives and the deep grooves in the road freeze solid. At the beginning of one of these roads (a particularly long one), there is a sign which reads: "Choose your rut carefully. You'll be in it for the next 50 miles."

Each thought of sickness or health, hatred or love, poverty or prosperity cuts a very subtle neural pathway or "groove" in the brain. The most dominant thoughts cut the deepest "grooves." Once a groove is cut, thoughts just automatically keep traveling in it. Some of these grooves have turned into deep ruts. Releasing can get you out of a rut. Affirmations can help you cut some new grooves.

Repeat your statements of release often—aloud whenever possible—but whether to yourself or out loud, say them with *conviction*. A thought without conviction is like dynamite without a match! When your words are saturated with faith and sincerity and conviction, they are like powerful explosives which will blast the old rocks of negative beliefs, clearing the rubble from your path so that a new consciousness can step forth.

In the Activity Book you will find suggestions for writing your own statements of release. Often, however, if a strong negative feeling is coming at you with both barrels, nothing beats a plain, old-fashioned, down-home, rootin'-tootin', very loud *"No!"*

Affirmations

It is not enough just to pull the weeds in your garden. You have to plant flowers so weeds will have nowhere to grow. Releasing removes negative states of mind, but any release has to be followed by an affirmation.

Affirmations build into that cleared area of your mind only those ideas which tell the truth about you. And what's the truth? That you are a child of the Creator of this universe, and therefore have access to (and deserve) *total* good. Affirmations can take an idea about you from Divine Mind (God) and root it deeply into *your* mind.

CONVINCING YOURSELF

An affirmation is a tool which states the truth about a situation based on the omnipresence of God. Its primary purpose is to build a consciousness of the presence of God (and therefore your good) into every situation. An affirmation is spoken to convince the intellect and the emotions that God is the only presence and power in the universe and in your life and, yes, in any present difficulty.

As with statements of release, affirmations should be repeated, either silently or audibly, as often as possible. *"Yes!"* is a wonderful affirmation. It is simple, direct, focused, and powerful. Say it immediately to yourself whenever you catch sight of a positive outcome to a problem. In fact, reinforce any positive thoughts with a hearty "Yes!"

Also, remind yourself that these affirmations are not "making something happen." When you affirm, you are accepting the good that is waiting for you because it is yours by divine inheritance. Affirmations take the expectation of that good and lock it firmly in your mind. They help you develop a taste for what you are capable of becoming, and that's exciting.

The constant repetition of your affirmation is important because this embeds its idea deeply in your subconscious mind, into your feeling nature. And speaking it with faith, joy, and enthusiasm speeds up your good.

MIND SHAPES BODY

Affirmations work not only in the realm of invisible spiritual and mental laws. Your body is extremely receptive to the bidding of your mind. Any message that you repeat goes through your brain cortex—your frontal lobes and your limbic system, which have to do with your emotions. Hidden deep within this area is the hypothalamus, the master regulator of the autonomic nervous system and supervisor of many body functions such as pulse rate, blood pressure, hormone production, and body temperature.

When you repeat affirmations, you are actually programming your body to do those things which you are affirming. Psychologists refer to this as "cognitive restructuring," actually redesigning the thinking circuits.

Isn't the need for positive affirming clear? Imagine what happens when you are constantly telling yourself "The best is yet to be," or "I eat only healthful foods," or "God brings my good," or "I am prosperous," or "I am loved," or "God is healing me now."

LOOK FOR THE SILVER LINING

There will be times when you will be hard-pressed to find something to affirm in a situation. At times like these, you have to intellectually design a statement which reflects the real truth of the situation as your spirit knows it. Thus the chain-smoker may affirm: *I am in charge*, or *I decide when and if I smoke*, or *I have control over cigarettes*.

Sometimes you will affirm things intellectually but not emotionally. At other times the opposite will be true. The part of you which doubts must be convinced by the part of you which believes. If you can neither intellectually nor emotionally accept a truth, then it could be that you are not ready to change.

If you do really want to change, you'll be able to dig out the truth underlying a situation and come up with appropriate statements of release and affirmation. Say them often enough, and you will experience a healing—the healing of your unbelief!

TUCK THIS IN YOUR TRAVEL PACK

Now here's something worth knowing for the journey ahead: It's not important that you completely believe an affirmation before you begin using it. The very repetition of it, *if it is true*, will soon have you believing it. People who don't understand the principles of releasing and affirming may think these are examples of lying to one's self. But it's not lying at all, because the statement is based on the *real* truth of a situation, not on its appearance only. The real truth is that because God is present, there is the potential for good in even the most dreadful-looking situation.

The muscles of a leg that's been in a cast for a long

time may be so weakened from lack of use that, to all appearances, they're unable to move. But as a therapist moves the leg and coaxes the muscles to work, the muscles soon "remember" their job, slowly gain strength, and before long are able to move on their own. The more they are used, the stronger they become.

It's the same with affirmations. You may be just "saying words" with no conviction or emotion behind them when you start, but *if the affirmation is based on truth*, it will create a momentum of its own and you will finally accept that truth on a deep level.

IMPORTANT TOOLS

RELEASE and AFFIRMATION are tools you can and should use to convince yourself of God's good when things look quite the contrary.

However, *both releasing and affirming have to be rooted in truth.* If a boy jumped off a roof denying the existence of gravity, he would suddenly be shown how wrong he is. His denial of the law of gravity would not have changed his downward momentum nor the pain he felt when he landed. In the earlier example of the X ray showing a medical problem, the person cannot deny that the condition exists. There it is, showing clearly on the X ray. Can that person really say and believe the statement of release, "This problem does not exist"? Of course not. It does exist. Yet he or she can say and believe, "This is *not* part of God's plan for me," or "This has *no* power over me," or "This is *not* my inheritance from God." These statements of release can be said and *believed* because they are the truth.

The same holds true for affirmations. If ten

million people affirm that an apple seed will become an orange tree, they will still get an apple tree. All the affirming in the world would not prevent that seed from following its genetic blueprint. How about a woman with ten dollars in her bank account? Can she really say and believe an affirmation which states: *I have thousands of dollars?* She might say it, but she certainly can't believe it. The bank statement very clearly shows only ten dollars. But she can say and believe: *I inherit God's abundance.* She can say and believe: *I claim my rich inheritance from God.* She can say and believe: *My Source is unlimited*, or *God is my Source.*

These examples demonstrate a crucial principle about release and affirmation: Something is not false because you deny it. You deny and release it because it is false. Conversely, something is not true because you affirm it. You affirm and accept it because it is true. It's an important distinction.

You can release your inaccurate thoughts and feelings about something and affirm thoughts and feelings based on the fact that God's desire for you is absolute good and the fact that God is in the midst of every situation. When you do this, you change your consciousness and your changed consciousness starts setting up good things for you.

Sometimes statements of release and affirmation can do their transformational work without our repeating them over and over. Sometimes it is enough to realize them with great conviction and then merely allow them to reveal to us the truth of a situation.

Jesus was simplifying things for us when He advised, *"Let what you say be simply 'Yes' or 'No.'"* If something is true, affirm it, accept it. If it's not true, out it goes with a strong and well-placed "No!"

Releasing and affirming. Like spiritual training wheels, they steady you until you find your divine equilibrium.

$\mathcal{M}$ile markers

- Release is a tearing-down process.
- Affirmation is a building-up process.
- You do not deny the existence of something. You deny its ultimate power over you.
- True release works on your thoughts, feelings, and beliefs.
- An affirmation states the truth about a situation based on the omnipresence of God.
- Statements of release and affirmation should be repeated often, aloud if possible, and with great passion.

I freely release all that is not part of my divine pattern. I freely affirm and accept all that is part of my divine pattern. Thank You, God, for the wisdom to know the difference.

Please proceed to Adventure 22 in the Activity Book.

$\mathcal{M}$OVING INTO ACTION | 23

*A desire without a deed
is a dead end.*

$\mathcal{P}$ut feet on your prayers

"Stretch out your hand."—Matthew 12:13

It is said that when Paganini performed, there would be *two* stars upon the concert stage: the great virtuoso himself, and his violin, a wonderful Stradivarius. With this remarkable instrument, Paganini could move his audiences to smiles as well as to tears.

The violin was his most treasured possession, and so it is not surprising that Paganini made special provisions for it in his will. He bequeathed his Stradivarius to a city in Italy, with the explicit order that it never be played.

Niccolò Paganini died in 1840. As he had desired, the violin was placed on public display in its exquisite diamond-studded case. True to his wishes, it remained silent through the years.

Today all that remains of the sublime instrument, so lovingly crafted by Antonio Stradivarius in the seventeenth century, is its case. While other Strads are still superb after being played for centuries, Paganini's violin is now nothing more than a small pile of dust! You see wood, if used even the slightest bit, will remain strong, but if neglected, it disintegrates. A violin must be played if it is to stay a violin.

SIGNS OF CHANGE

How much more sublime, more remarkable, are we than a Stradivarius, but if we don't use our gifts, if we don't "play our music," we "crumble" and our existence becomes meaningless, like Paganini's violin.

You are aware that any changes in your life (your relationships, your finances, your health, and so forth) will be a result of any changes you have made on the inside, in your soul. Inner change is the only way to improve your life. *The Quest* is really a process of your own inner change. The work is done on yourself only.

You have been involved in self-transformation since you began your journey on *The Quest* and maybe even before that. By now you are able to perceive signs of inner change. New reactions to things, a different way of looking at a relationship, good feelings which were not there previously about a certain situation, these are all examples of a shift in your consciousness toward the high road. Make a mental note of things like this and rejoice in the change.

FROGS AND BUTTERFLIES

Once the inner changes start happening, however, they have to be reflected in your outer world. It becomes time to move into action. A frog in a well, no matter how wonderful a frog he is, can never talk about the ocean. A summer butterfly, no matter how beautiful, can never talk about the winter ice. The frog and the butterfly, even if perfect, have never moved beyond their limited worlds. Their experiences remain the same. Probably frogs are not meant to know the ocean, nor butterflies designed to live in ice. They have reached the boundaries of their potential. They can proceed no further.

But we have not yet reached ours. We humans were designed for greater things than we have yet attained. Our potential is beyond anyone's speculation. It is, in fact, unlimited. Our souls are on a continuous journey upward toward perfection, and as we evolve on the inner levels of our lives, we must let these changes be translated into our outer world as well. Humankind is meant to know the "ocean" and the "ice." We are meant to stretch ourselves continually to new and more meaningful experiences.

Moving into action denotes applying the teachings to every situation in your everyday life, right where you are. It doesn't imply running off in all directions in search of new and exotic experiences. The broadened experience takes place wherever you find yourself. Every incident, no matter how trivial, is an opportunity for a greater experience and can be brought to whatever height you want to take it.

FROM DESIRE TO DEED

"Stretch out your hand." Jesus directed the man who wanted to be healed. The man knew that Jesus could help him discover his wholeness. Although the desire for healing was there, Jesus instructed the man to do something about it, to move into action, to extend his desire into a deed. "Stretch out your hand."

A desire without a deed is a dead end. It is like a high-powered sports car waiting patiently for a driver to start the engine. We can plan, dream, wish, hope, and inwardly change all we want. This is not only beneficial but necessary, but if we don't bring these forth into our practical lives, they eventually lead nowhere. We have to *do* something with what we know! Our lives have to reflect the inner change. We have to, as the expression goes, "put feet on our prayers." Even the greatest teachings lose their power if they are not put into practice.

Do our actions always mirror what we know in our hearts to be true? Are we really *doing* something about getting onto the highroad, whatever that means for each of us?

DOING OUR SHARE

Certainly we want God's will for us at all times. "Thy will" rather than "my will" is the goal we all should be desiring to express. We have to be open to our inner guidance, most assuredly, for here is where we obtain our true answers, the way which is for our highest good. It is by listening to our inner guidance that we actually discover just what God's will for us really is.

Having received the guidance we were seeking, we then "speak the word." We begin verbally declaring the truth about a situation. Then what do we do next? We *act* upon it. This is the way we cooperate with the universe, with God. In other words, we do *our* share.

Spirit can (and will) reveal to us the way if we sincerely ask, seek, and knock. Spirit can show us the path, but having been shown the path, it is *we* who must take the steps and walk that path.

Sometimes the best decision is no decision, merely to live in the now and do our very best to let Spirit express Itself through us, to be loving in every situation. It isn't necessary to constantly search and strain for guidance, watching for "signs" and trying to interpret insignificant things as monumental fiats of the Almighty! This often results in confusion, instability, a scattering of mental powers, and a drain on the energy level.

So, what do we do? We live each moment, as best we can, aware of the presence of God which is always with us. We also take at least one regular period each day to become still and listen to our inner guidance. But—and here's the secret—once we feel nudged by that Spirit within to go in a certain direction, it is time to move into action, to set our hearts *and feet* in that direction and follow through!

"WALK THE TALK"

It's time, at this point in your journey, to be on the lookout for these things. Now that you are making good inner progress, are you starting to move into action with it? There are inviting resting places along our trail which may beckon to you to stop and dally. It is necessary to move forward, however, without delay. Keep checking to see that you are applying Truth teachings to the way you deal with everything in your life. As some people would say, you have to "walk the talk."

But serendipity is at work here. It just so happens

that when we make inner changes—true changes—
they cannot help but spill over into our outer experiences. It becomes almost automatic. Little by little
you find your life guided by your own inner Power.
You will keep turning up at the right place at the
right time, saying the right things and doing the right
things. It is almost as if you were on automatic pilot
and your course were laid out straight before you. As
you continue your journey on *The Quest*, the foliage
will part and your path will be clear.

God can work best when we show our willingness
by moving into action. God supplies the breeze but
we must hoist the sail.

Stretch out your hand ... now.

$\mathcal{M}$ile markers

- You must use your gifts.
- The Teachings must be applied to every situation in your everyday life.
- A desire without a deed is a dead end.
- Once you receive your guidance, it is time to move into action. Spirit will show you the path, but you must walk that path.

Thank You, God, for showing me the path. I know that Your desire for me is absolute good. As I move into action to do the things that are mine to do, I feel You guiding me every step of the way.

Please proceed to Adventure 23 in the Activity Book.

Faith is tricky.
You have to be
very sure it is
pointed in the
right direction.

What do you expect?

"According to your faith be it done to you."
—Matthew 9:29

"Oh, if only I had more faith. If I just had a little more faith!"

Ever said that? If you have, you might be surprised to learn you already have all the faith you will ever need. It's true. You don't *gain* faith, you discover it and you direct it. The issue is not how much faith you have, but where your faith is invested. You have faith on many different levels and in many different ways, but its most perfect expression is in your spiritual nature. True faith is that deep inner knowing that the good you desire is already yours. True spiritual faith is complete trust in God's will.

The following two stories took place many years ago, but they are such dramatic yet very different examples of faith that we decided to use them here.

Although there have been thousands of good examples of faith before and since these two, these continue to remain our favorites.

A CASE OF INTELLECTUAL FAITH

There is a very famous, well-documented case[1] of a man who had an advanced form of cancer, a lymphosarcoma. Gravely ill, he was completely bedridden, on oxygen, and needed fluid removed from his chest regularly. Huge tumor masses covered his body.

The man heard about a new "miracle drug" and asked to be included in the clinical trials. Within ten days of receiving the drug, he made a spectacular recovery and was released from the hospital. He remained *symptom-free* for two months.

Then he read some negative publicity about the drug, and a few days later he was back in the hospital again with the massive tumors, the fluid-filled chest, and the need for extra oxygen.

His physician, desperate at this point, told the man that he wanted to try an improved batch of the drug which was far superior to the last batch. The man enthusiastically agreed. But the physician had no new drug. He injected his patient with *sterile water!*

Yet again the man made "remarkable" improvement. The tumor masses melted, the fluid drained from his chest, and his need for oxygen diminished. He again returned to work completely symptom-free with no trace of cancer in his body.

1. Richard Jafolla, *Soul Surgery—The Ultimate Self-Healing*, DeVorss & Co., Marina Del Rey, Calif., 1987, p. 66.

233

Sometime later the man read a newspaper story reporting that the drug was judged "worthless in treatment of cancer."

Two days later the man was dead.

A CASE OF SPIRITUAL FAITH

Contrast that story with the great Nobel prize-winning surgeon Alexis Carrel's story of an incident which he personally observed and later wrote about in his book *The Voyage to Lourdes*.[2] The story deals with Dr. Carrel's journey, as a young physician, with a trainload of sick to the shrine at Lourdes, France. His intention was to debunk the reports of healing from the pilgrimage site.

During the train ride, Dr. Carrel was kept especially busy with a girl named Marie, a young girl with what Carrel described as "a classic case of tubercular peritonitis."[3] She was so ill that her personal physician considered her case "hopeless."

On the train to Lourdes, she lapsed into a coma several times, saved only by Dr. Carrel's medical intervention. After arriving at Lourdes, Carrel was called again to minister to the girl. This time he brought another physician with him to examine her. They both agreed, "She may last a few more days, but she is doomed. Death is very near."[4] Carrel felt, "If she gets home again alive, that in itself will be a miracle."[5]

Yet Marie was determined to be bathed in the

2. Harper & Row, New York, 1950.
3. Ibid., p. 9.
4. Ibid., p. 24.
5. Ibid., p. 23.

water at Lourdes. Dr. Carrel describes the girl: "She lay on her back, all shrunken beneath the dark brown blanket which made a mound over her distended abdomen. Her breath came quick and short... The sick girl was apparently unconscious... Her pulse was more rapid than ever. Her face was ashen... It was obvious that this young girl was about to die."[6]

But Marie did not die. Two hours after having the water poured over her, all symptoms of her illness had vanished! Dr. Carrel reported: "She was cured. In the span of a few hours, a girl with a face already turning blue, a distended abdomen, and a fatally racing heart had been restored...to health."[7]

BEWARE THE SHIFTING SANDS

Jesus said, "Thy faith hath made thee whole" (Mt. 9:22 KJV). It was Marie's faith which made her whole. Hers was a spiritual faith anchored in the spirit of God within her. When faith is so unshakably anchored, it brings forth a demonstration which many would call miraculous.

Marie had faith that when she was bathed with the "holy water" she would get well, but her faith went much deeper than that. She was aware that no one else from her group was healed. Imagine the deeply rooted faith this girl must have had, seeing such failures all around her and yet never wavering in her expectation of her own healing.

If Maria had had faith only in the water, that faith would have crumbled in the face of such overwhelming evidence of failure. That would have been an

6. Ibid., pp. 26-27.
7. Ibid., p. 36.

intellectual faith. But "miracles" are never possible with intellectual faith alone because intellectual faith is built on the shifting sands of circumstances and appearances. When the circumstances change, the faith shifts and all that was built on such faith falls apart. Intellectual faith by very definition is restricted to what the intellect says is true, and the intellect is based on limited information.

Marie's faith did not fall apart because the water was merely a catalyst which fanned the flame of her deep, spiritual faith. Marie had complete trust that God's desire for her was absolute good. This is true spiritual faith.

ACCORDING TO THY FAITH

The cancer patient, on the other hand, had a faith which was purely intellectual. It was based *totally* on an outer appearance, which convinced him that it was strictly the miracle drug that had made him well. Even the powerful evidence of his healed body could not overcome the negative news reports.

Yet once again the life-force within him made him healthy, this time with only sterile water! Yet the man's faith was so firmly rooted in the drug that he disregarded his own wellness and let the news of the drug's failure kill him.

Aren't these two stories remarkable? Can you see that you *have* the faith, it is merely a matter of where you place it? The man doomed himself because he couldn't even accept the evidence of the life-force in his own body as proof of his health, so fixed was his faith on something in the outer.

To all outer appearances, Marie was fatally ill and *her faith made her well.* To all outer appearances, the man was well *and his faith made him fatally ill!* We all have the same amount of faith, but each of us invests that faith differently.

Since "like attracts like" (the law of mind action), whatever we have faith in, we eventually attract. Faith can be invested in sickness or invested in health. It can be invested in hatred or invested in love. It can be invested in poverty or invested in prosperity. You get what you expect.

WHAT DO YOU KNOW?

True faith, the kind you can always rely on, is a spiritual process based on eternal Truth. Faith is "knowing."

The question is, what are you "knowing"? Are you knowing that God is in charge of your life and therefore you will be led to the perfect means of healing? Are you knowing that the right job is waiting for you? Are you knowing that wonderful blessings will come out of the heartache you're feeling over a loved one? Or are you knowing your life will be ruined because your spouse is an alcoholic? Or that you will become diabetic because your father was? Or that you will never have enough money because your family has always been poor?

Plainly stated, faith is expectation. Whatever you strongly and consistently expect to come into your life is invariably what you will experience.

Here is something especially important: Faith, whether in the positive or negative, is always attached to a strong emotion. In fact, faith is not faith unless it has a strong emotion attached. You feel it so strongly that it is almost a reality already.

IS FAITH ENOUGH?

Jesus taught that "if you have faith as a grain of mustard seed, you will say to this mountain, 'Move from here to there,' and it will move; and nothing will be impossible to you" (Mt. 17:20).

If this is the case, why should you make any physical effort on your own behalf? Wouldn't it be easier to bring forth something into your life by merely directing your faith toward it? The answer to this, of course, is a resounding "Yes!" Your faith *can* make you whole. In fact, complete faith in God is the best route to instantaneous healing.

But hold on, we have to note two important things. First of all, it takes work to move your faith in the right direction. Secondly (and most importantly), although your faith is limitless, *faith can only extend to the self-imposed boundaries of your present consciousness.* It can go no further. Your present consciousness creates an "artificial boundary" which limits your faith, and limited faith can only express in limited ways.

How can your faith in abundant prosperity not be limited if your consciousness has faith that, "I'll *never* be able to afford that"?

How can you direct much faith in your innate wholeness if your consciousness has faith that, "I'll get heart disease because it runs in my family"?

This idea is so important that it bears repeating: *Faith can only reach to the self-imposed boundaries of your present consciousness! It can go no further.* Jesus had a consciousness which expanded to the limitless reaches of His spirit. Because of that, His faith was limitless and the acts He performed seemed miraculous. But Jesus was able to perform them because He let Spirit flow freely through His soul, expanding His consciousness without limit.

While your present consciousness may not be that of Jesus, the law still holds true that "substance responds to your faith in it." Faith can be invested as strongly in sickness as in health, as strongly in poverty as in prosperity, as strongly in hatred as in love. Which will it be? It's your call.

INVESTING YOUR FAITH

As you travel deeper into *The Quest*, you are beginning to contact your eternal, unchanging essence. As you tap this constant source of inspiration, your consciousness will steadily expand and change. As it does, your faith will shift in the direction of good, always nudging at the boundaries you have imposed on it, always anxious to spread into every corner of your soul and bring forth your most fervent desires.

We have been given clear instructions for obtaining the good that we desire, and these instructions are actually quite simple: "Whatever you ask in prayer, believe that you have received it, and it will be yours" (Mk. 11:24). Expect it. Expect it so much that you can almost taste it, almost see it already accomplished. That's where your heart is, that's where your faith is, and that's what you'll get.

Your faith is unlimited. Invest it wisely.

$\mathcal{M}$ile markers

- True faith is that deep inner knowing that the good you desire is already yours.
- True spiritual faith is complete trust in God's will.
- You have unlimited faith. The question is, where are you investing it?
- You get what you expect. Plainly stated, faith is expectation.
- Faith is always accompanied by strong emotion.
- Faith can only extend to the self-imposed boundaries of your present consciousness.

God, help me to keep my faith directed to You. I thirst for the comfort of complete trust in Your will. I accept the truth—right now—that everything is all right. Thank You, God.

Please proceed to Adventure 24 in the Activity Book.

$\mathcal{A}$ RANDOM WALK

"You Are What You Eat!" shouted the poster in the health food store window. It seemed to make sense.

After all, the raw materials which our cells use to repair and replace their tissues are obtained from foods. Our bodies are really the vitamins, minerals, proteins, carbohydrates, and fats in food, reorganized and reconstructed! Common sense dictates that the healthier the food, the more wholesome the food, the better the raw material and the healthier the body.

Yet the poster wasn't entirely correct. Not quite as catchy but far more accurate would be, *"You Are What You* Digest!"

Simply *eating* healthful food is not enough to change anyone's body. Swallowing even the most nutritious product is no guarantee that the nutrients will go where they are needed. For example, ingesting a vitamin pill rich in nutrients will do no good at all if it has a hard, indigestible coating.

TAKE TIME TO DIGEST

It is one thing to "ingest" *The Quest*, to study its teachings. It is quite another to "digest" it, to live it. Unless you are able to make the teachings a part of your life, it will forever remain an intellectual exercise and, like the hard vitamin pill, unable to be incorporated into your life and help you to become spiritually healthier. That's why it is important to take time every so often to rest from the teachings you have been working on and to digest them.

Now is such a time of digestion. It's time for another break, another Random Walk, so that you can have an opportunity to consolidate the teachings of this second quarter of *The Quest*.

The trail has been steep. You have been faithful and unflagging in your journey. You deserve a rest. Make this next week a seven-day period of relaxation and quiet introspection. Relax and enjoy life. Don't actively think about *The Quest* anymore than you would think about food after you've eaten it.

We'll be here when you come back. In the meantime, just relax and release, let go and let God.

*W*ELCOME BACK!

Hello, friend. It's good to be together with you again. We hope your vacation was beneficial and that you were able to digest lots of good spiritual "nutrients."

Are you faring well on *The Quest*? Do you have a sense of how far you have come? You should have a good feeling of accomplishment by now, since you are at the halfway mark.

This next leg of our journey will take us into more mystical and personal territory than before, so be sure you bring a good supply of patience, openness, and quiet time for prayer.

Now, if you're ready, let's gear up and move on out. This way ... turn the page.

If your life is not all that you want it to be, it may be that you have some forgiving to do.

How can I forgive?

> *"But I say to you, Love your enemies and pray for those who persecute you."* —Matthew 5:44

The walls of Santa Maria delle Grazie, the old church in Milan, are in a ruinous state. It is difficult to discern the fabled painting which the master Leonardo da Vinci brushed into the plaster in 1495, and observers often come away disappointed.

Still, in spite of its pathetic condition, *The Last Supper* remains one of the great art treasures of the world. Linger for a while in the dim room and the emotional power of the faces and the gestures of the thirteen figures begin to emerge, drawing you into the mystical moment captured so ingeniously by Leonardo.

One cannot help but be especially captivated by the face of Jesus, the focal point of the fresco.

Through the peeling paint and faded pigments come feelings which touch the heart of anyone who takes the time to discover them there, feelings brushed onto a plaster wall, standing throughout the centuries like silent witnesses to all of the pains as well as the joys that humankind can experience. What exquisite sensitivities the artist must have had to express such a panoply of emotions with his paints and brushes.

A significant event occurred while Leonardo was working on the face of Jesus. He had become very angry at someone. While the details have long been lost, we do know that a violent argument took place, during which the artist threatened the man with bodily harm.

When Leonardo resumed his work on the fresco, he did so with a heart full of hatred and resentment. Try as he might, he could not paint the face of Jesus. Over and over, he attempted to apply subtle touches to the wet plaster, only to be frustrated and upset. Something was terribly wrong inside his heart.

Finally realizing that his anger was depriving him of the peace necessary for him to create, the great artist laid aside his brushes and sought out the man to apologize to him and ask his forgiveness. Only after doing that was the master able to return to his work with a loving, peace-filled heart, a heart capable of creating the face of Jesus Christ.

AT THE GATE

We have now passed the halfway mark of our journey together on *The Quest*. You have discovered and have put into use many spiritual teachings, teachings presented by Jesus Christ. By now you have first-hand knowledge of how these teachings function to create more harmony and happiness in your life.

In this second half of *The Quest*, we will be traveling at higher altitudes. We will be making our way among the peaks which heretofore may have seemed too misty to traverse. Yet easier will be our way because by now our footing is surer and our desire for transformation even stronger than when we began.

You have come to a turning point in your journey. A gate now stands before you. Beyond the gate lies a special trail which, while carrying you sharply upward, is incredibly easy to climb. Major overcomings and great spiritual progress bringing much joy and peace are to be found on this trail. So much of what your soul longs for can be experienced as a result of journeying there.

Yet there is only one access to the trail, and that is through this special gate. If you cannot go through the gate, you will find yourself at an impasse and your travels will come to a standstill. You are at the point where you can make no further progress without going through the gate. You will discover that other paths lead backwards or sideways, not forward, and will eventually bring you back to where you are right now. The only way to avoid this, of course, is to open the gate. It is the gate of forgiveness.

WE ONLY HURT OURSELVES

Harboring unforgiveness and resentment in our hearts does not hurt others. It hurts us. It eats away at the soul, filling it with bitterness and blocking the free flow of God's love, which is the essence of our true nature.

Holding grudges and hanging onto anger and hatred are *self*-destructive. Of that, there is no doubt.

No matter how educated we are in spiritual principles, unless there is complete forgiveness in our
lives, we wither and die spiritually, emotionally, and
sometimes even physically because we are working in
such opposition to our basic nature, which is to love.
Without complete forgiveness, we ultimately deny
ourselves access to total healing (emotionally and
physically), abundant prosperity, permanent peace,
and all of the other good which God wants us to experience. Our way is blocked. It's as if we have come
up against a stone wall which says: "God's gifts not
available here. Please use gate."

ASK TO BE SHOWN

What's going on in your heart these days? Is there
any trace of anger or hatred? Sometimes we know
only too well whom it is that we are having trouble
forgiving. On the other hand, sometimes we're not
even aware of a long-past disagreement which we've
been hiding in a dark corner of the soul.

Sitting quietly and asking God to reveal to you
whatever needs revealing will usually quite quickly
uncover where your work must be done. If your life is
not exactly what you know it can be, chances are
there is some forgiving work for you to do. If you
don't believe that, take it on faith and ask to be
shown.

TRUE FORGIVENESS

Let's talk about forgiveness, what it is and how to
do it. There are several levels of letting go of hurts
and grievances, but most are not true forgiveness.

A woman told her husband she would forgive his
philanderings, but she vowed she would not be

subjected to anything like that again. "I'll forgive but I won't forget." This is not true forgiveness.

A young man insisted that he had forgiven his brother for his heavy drinking and irresponsible behavior. He claimed he now understood why some people act as they do, and so he no longer required them to live up to high standards. This is not true forgiveness.

A mother's aching heart professed forgiveness after she discovered her husband was molesting their little daughter. She said she wanted to know the kind of forgiveness which Jesus taught and was able to recognize the deep soul needs in her husband and eventually have great pity and compassion for him. While her intentions and efforts were commendable, she was still not able to take that final subtle step into the forgiveness which Jesus taught.

Then there were the parents whose young son was brutally murdered. We had the beautiful experience of observing these people move almost unbelievably from horror and shock, to hatred, to bitterness, to acceptance, to forgiveness, and finally toward total release of the tragedy. They even visited the murderer in prison, expressed their love for the Christ within him and know that although he stumbled and grossly misused the power given to him by the Creator, he is still a child of God. He is *part* of God, which means he is part of them and part of their son and, therefore, there is nothing to forgive. Their forgiveness had a profound impact on the man responsible for the tragedy.

It may sound impossible to believe, yet the only forgiveness this remarkable couple sought was their own! They asked the man who took the life of their son to forgive *them* for having initially judged him as less than a child of God. This was not a matter of "I forgive *you*" but of "Forgive *me*. Forgive *me* for judging you wrong in the first place." And *that* is the Jesus Christ kind of forgiveness. *With true forgiveness there is nothing to forgive!*

People often say "God forgives," or they might pray to God for forgiveness, but God *cannot* forgive because God has not judged. God cannot see anything which needs forgiving. God simply cannot help loving us unconditionally, and we must view all others in the same way, just as that couple did. Obviously, not everyone would do what they did, but everyone *can* do what they did. And if we want to attain the spiritual heights, *we must do what they did!*

"YES, BUT THIS IS DIFFERENT ..."

Ah, yes, there are some things which have been done to all of us which seem unforgivable. Aren't there some hurts that are just *too* big to release? Sometimes it seems as if we even love to cradle these hurts in our arms and nurse them along through the years.

But every hurt, every resentment—no matter what the cause—wreaks a corresponding amount of destruction in our bodies and/or souls. We really cannot afford the harm it does to us, the toll it takes. You are welcome to stand outside the gate of forgiveness and feel justified in passionately nurturing your hatred, but then you must also be willing to pay the price.

Ideally, we have to reach the point where we refuse

to let anyone or anything come between us and our awareness of the presence of God, either in ourselves or in anyone else. We have to be able to say and mean, "There is nothing you can ever say or do which will stop me from loving you. Nothing!"

The teaching on judgment showed us that we can refuse to stay around dangerous or negative behavior, but this doesn't mean we refuse to recognize the presence of the Christ within that person whom we are avoiding.

TIME TO OPEN THE GATE

How are you doing on your quest? Are things going well for you? Do you thirst for more?

Your faithfulness has led you to the gate of forgiveness. Whatever old baggage of resentment and unforgiveness you have been dragging around must be left outside. Put it down, now. Ask the Holy Spirit within you to reveal what and who needs releasing. If you are unable to do this unconditionally, at least let God know that you *want* to do it. That sincere desire to forgive, in itself, will open the gate.

Apologize in your heart to anyone, past or present, here or on another plane of existence, whom you have judged as less than a child of God. You will soon feel the enormous rush of freedom which comes from realizing that there was never anything to forgive in the first place.

Open the gate wide, friend, and go through to meet your good.

$\mathcal{M}$ile markers

- Your spiritual progress is at a standstill until you practice true forgiveness.
- Harboring resentment and anger hurts you spiritually, emotionally, and even physically.
- True forgiveness is part of your basic nature.
- Without a consciousness of forgiveness, you deny yourself permanent access to God's good.
- Ask God to reveal to you the areas which need forgiveness work.
- With true forgiveness, there is nothing to forgive because it means seeing everyone as a child of God.

Holy Presence within me, I am willing to release all feelings of hurt and anger and resentment. Help me to know true forgiveness and to see each person as a part of me and a child of Yours. Thank You, God.

Please proceed to Adventure 25 in the Activity Book.

Jesus based His whole life on love. You can do what He did with phenomenal results.

Your built-in God gauge

"This is my commandment, that you love one another as I have loved you." —John 15:12

It's a familiar story by now, well documented in research journals: infants in orphanages or similar institutions tend to be lethargic, smaller in stature than normal, and have weaker vital signs than other babies. They are given the physical necessities—food and drink, and medication if needed—but these are not enough to keep them well. However, if someone holds and caresses the children, rocks them in their arms as often as possible, gently talks to them, and loves them, suddenly the children begin gaining weight at a normal rate and their health and mortality rate is dramatically improved.

Conventional wisdom would say that the children improve simply because they are given massive amounts of love, and that love was the medicine which released the natural hormones and enzymes needed for normal growth and health. Scientific evidence seems to confirm this conventional wisdom.

Yet in an earlier teaching, we learned that God has created all of us as complete, that like the egg developing in its shell, there is nothing that can be added to give us more potential. On the surface, it would seem that the children were suffering because they needed love to develop normally, and that having been deprived of love, they developed abnormally.

But we are spiritual beings. As creations of God, we are whole and complete and, therefore, nothing has to be added *to* us, only released *from* us. *Love must be released.*

If we reflect on this story spiritually, we come to a different conclusion: the children became healthier not because they were loved, but *because they were given the opportunity to love!* That's a crucial difference. Love was not given *to* them; it was released *from* them. We cannot be fully alive until we express the love we have. We don't have to receive it from others. In fact, we can't receive love from others! We have no room for it. All that we can do is to allow others' love for us to be a catalyst for the release of our own love.

We receive true love only from God. Only when we allow love to pour from the God of love *through our hearts* to the hearts of others are we expressing love the way Jesus told us we should.

EVEN SCROOGE LEARNED TO LOVE

Scrooge, the protagonist of Dickens' classic tale *A Christmas Carol*, was an unloving, mean-spirited, unfeeling, cruel, utterly distasteful man who was completely unloved and, ostensibly, unlovable. He lived a miser's life. He hoarded everything, not giving of himself, his feelings, or his possessions.

However, when he finally was forced to recognize his greater self, he made a complete turnaround. He began loving everyone and found such joy in giving to and helping others that his life took on new significance. Although his love was not immediately reciprocated, he was so caught up in releasing the love that he had, that it didn't matter if anyone loved him in return. It didn't stop him nor did it discourage him from loving.

Scrooge felt good, not because he felt loved, people were too suspicious of his motives to love him. He felt good simply because he loved. Suddenly, Scrooge loved loving! The very act of loving others was satisfaction enough for him.

In this wonderful novel and through this extraordinary character, Dickens has communicated the great lesson of love: Love is not a commodity that we can acquire and hoard. Love can only be released.

"HOW CAN I GET MORE?"

The real question is not, How can I get more love? It is, How can I express more of the love that I already have?

We may resist this idea because we have always given love so that we could receive love. This is conditional love. Implicit in this love is, "I'll give you love as long as you give me love." Yet love doesn't work that way—not *true* love, not *Christ* love. True love is expressed not to be reciprocated but to make us completely alive.

Children instinctively do this. When unhappy, when feeling unloved, a child hugs a favorite stuffed animal. In the hugging, in the loving, the child feels better. Why? Was it the teddy bear that loved the child? Hardly. The teddy bear is just a heap of wool and cotton and thread and button eyes. Stuffed animals contain no love, *but the child does!* As the child hugs and cuddles the animal, *love*, the essential truth of that child's being, is expressed and the child feels the warmth of love.

As adults, we can hug stuffed animals and feel the warmth of love ourselves, but there is a more preferable method that works faster and infinitely better. It is to express love as Jesus directed: "Love one another."

JESUS' ONLY COMMANDMENT

Imagine the power of Jesus, a man who was able to command the forces of the universe. He could have made many pronouncements on how to take charge of this power, yet He chose only one commandment to pass on to us: "This is my commandment, that you love one another as I have loved you." Unconditionally was how Jesus loved.

We can love unconditionally. In fact, at some point we must. Yet it's not as hard as it may seem, because unconditional love, Christ love, is the most natural of all love. To love another is the most instinctive of all reflexes. The fact that we may have trouble doing it is not that it is an unnatural trait so much as it is a forgotten trait. We are and always have been capable of unconditional love—true love. It is the most natural part of us because it is the substance of God.

LOVE IS WHAT GOD IS

One would think that of all the places to find a definition of God, the Bible would be the first place to look. Yet John was the only writer in the Bible to define God, and he used only three words to define the Undefinable: *"God is love"* (1 Jn. 4:8). How simple. How succinct. How complete. How utterly perfect! *God is love.*

Love, then, is not a toy of human caprice—something we can trot out and use and then take back and put away when we are finished with someone. Love is a divine activity. It is a cosmic force, a spiritual gift. It is a part of our life just as the ocean is part of the fish. As long as the fish swims in the ocean, the ocean sustains it and nurtures it and renews it because the fish is taking in ocean for life and renewal. The fish is part of the ocean, and the ocean is part of the fish.

Love is God's ocean, and we live and move and have our being in that ocean. Love is God's energy, and when we let love direct us, we let God direct us and we become part of the divine energy of God.

WITHOUT LOVE, WE'RE NOTHING

Paul spoke eloquently about love. He said: "If I speak in the tongues of men and of angels, but have not love, I am a noisy gong or a clanging cymbal" (1 Cor. 13:1). In other words, no matter what I say, unless it resonates through the channel of love, it's only noise! It is meaningless.

Paul went on to say, "And if I have prophetic powers, and understand all mysteries and all knowledge, and if I have all faith, so as to remove mountains, but have not love, I am nothing" (1 Cor. 13:2).

How powerful those words are. They state that love is the single most important faculty we have. It is the hub of all good that is in us. *Nothing* else matters in our lives if we are loving.

LOVE DOESN'T NEED A FOCUS

Love can be felt for another, but love is not *primarily* a relationship to a specific person. In other words, it does not need an object on which to focus. It's like a powerful floodlight which brightens an entire room, rather than a flashlight which illuminates only where it is pointed.

Love is an attitude which determines how we relate to the world. If we love one person and are indifferent to the rest, we are like the flashlight. This is not love, but a dependent attachment to something that makes us temporarily feel good.

Yet most of us have believed that love begins with an object to love, rather than its being an indwelling faculty to be lived. If we don't see love as an activity of our spirit, then we can easily believe that all that is necessary to express love is to find the right object. This attitude is like the person who wants to learn to paint but won't take art lessons, claiming that when the right scene is found, he or she will paint it perfectly.

The fact is that we don't need "the right person" in order to express love. When you *truly* love one person, any person, you are able to love all people. You love the world and, most importantly, you know that you love yourself. If you say to somebody, "I love you," then you are saying, "I love God, I love myself, I love everyone."

SELF-LOVE

The power that is love begins with God, to be sure, but we need to accept that love as our own before it can be sent to someone else. This is true self-love, and this type of self-love is not ego-centered. It is, in fact, anchored in the greatest of humility because only in loving self can we act as clear conduits for God's love. The more we accept God's love, the more we allow it to pass on to others.

Loving others is impossible until we love ourselves.

Also, without a love of ourselves, there is no "baseline" to measure other love. Without a love of ourselves, we feel unworthy of any other love. "After all," we reason, "if I can't love myself, how can I expect anyone else to love me?" Only when you can love yourself can you remove the obstacles to the expansion of yourself.

Too often, however, we consider ourselves unworthy of love and therefore are not able to express love. The danger is that when we believe ourselves to be empty of love, we look for someone to love us to "fill the void." When we look to someone for love, we fail to experience true love. It is only when we *release* the love we have accepted for ourselves that we experience love.

OUR *NEED* TO LOVE

There is an innate need in each of us to express love. The inability to express love is a common cause of our problems. We see this in children and teens who have been deprived of love. We see it in adults who spend their lives looking for approval and acceptance. Neither the children nor the adults know how to accept love, and so neither can adequately express love. They stop growing because of the fact that as human beings our soul's growth depends on how much of God's love we can accept. When we stop accepting love, we stop growing.

ALL YOU NEED IS LOVE

"This is my commandment, that you love one another as I have loved you." It is probably the only commandment we have to know.

If you feel you are out of practice, that you have trouble expressing love, know that love is not something you have to master, but only allow. There is something you can practice over and over again, however, and that is the *decision* to love. Make up your mind to love, and then let love do what love will.

The mind is extremely powerful. It can take you to the very gates of heaven, but only your heart can utter the password to let you enter.

$\mathcal{M}$ile markers

- Love cannot be added *to* you. It can only be released *from* you.
- When you allow God's love to come through you and then out to others, you are loving in the Jesus Christ manner.
- You express *true* love not in hopes of having it reciprocated, but simply to make you completely alive.
- Love is the most natural part of you, because it is the substance of God.
- Love is a divine activity, a cosmic force, a spiritual gift.
- True love for God and others is not possible until you love yourself.

I open my heart to Your love, God, letting the warm radiance shine out to all the world. I make the decision, right now, to bless everyone and every situation with true love, for when I love, I am most like You. Thank You, God, for Your gift of unending love.

Please proceed to Adventure 26 in the Activity Book.

How many times have you longed for an unmistakable sign, showing you how to proceed?

Show me a sign, God

"Watch therefore, for you do not know on what day your Lord is coming."
— Matthew 24:42

High on a hill in a midwestern town stands an old post office. The building just happens to be situated so that rain falling on one side of the roof flows down the hill into a stream which joins a river that empties into the Great Lakes and on into the Atlantic Ocean. Rain falling on the opposite side of the roof travels by way of a small brook into the Ohio and Mississippi rivers and into the Gulf of Mexico. So tenuous is the position of a raindrop over this post office that the slightest breath of wind will determine the direction of its fate!

Do you ever have the feeling that your own fate is waiting to be determined? Have you felt suspended tenuously between two choices and wished some gentle breeze would come along to direct you one way or the other?

Often, our options seem equal. The Gulf of Mexico or the Atlantic Ocean—either choice would seem favorable to a raindrop. Our choices, too, can offer equal advantages—or disadvantages! In such a case, we usually pray for guidance as to what choice to make. "What should I do, God? Give me a sign."

IT JUST "FEELS RIGHT"

In Teaching 13, "God's Will," you saw the importance of living your life according to God's plan. You were given guidelines for discovering what the will of God is, and you have been aware, ever since, of allowing this will to be expressed in your life.

In this Teaching, we want to move another step inward. You will draw closer to your inner sense of guidance, which will never fail to direct you in ways that will protect you, prosper you, heal you, and lift you. The reason you can follow this guidance with positive assurance is that it comes from your own Christ essence, and this is *always* working on your behalf.

Although inner guidance may announce itself through the intellect, it operates through the "heart"—through your feelings. It comes to you not as a logical, calculated decision, but more as an insight or a feeling, and it *always* has with it a sense of rightness and joy.

FEELINGS, NOT LISTS

Perhaps you haven't been in the habit of listening for (or to) this kind of inner guidance. Ironically, it takes practice and patience to regain a process which should come very naturally to us but which we probably somehow lost as children. It is time now, if you are not already doing so, to redevelop an ear for your unfailing inner direction. Maybe an experience of ours will be of help to you.

A while back we suddenly found ourselves face-to-face with the largest decision of our lives. If we chose one road, it would bring a major upheaval in our contented way of living. It would involve leaving most of our very dear friends, moving to an area of the country which had no strong appeal for us, and making a drastic change in our very comfortable life-style. If we stayed on our present road, we would be giving up a once-in-a-lifetime opportunity. What did we do? We pondered our dilemma and talked for days about our choices. Like two raindrops heading for the post office roof, we were looking for a gust of wind to make the decision for us.

We also made lists, lo-o-o-o-ong lists, of the pros and cons of the two choices. Each time we made a list we would review it, shrug our shoulders and toss it away, only to eventually make another. We soon discovered that list-making was a fine intellectual exercise and was valuable in helping us to define the two choices, but it wasn't getting us any closer to our decision.

Meanwhile, we prayed for guidance, that we would be shown in unmistakable ways what to do. We knew that if we trusted the inner Christ guidance, our answer would come in a way that would be clear. In fact, we both ended each prayer session with the words, "God, speak to me in a way that I cannot possibly ignore." Finally, we felt a sense of peace about the whole matter and were able to release the outcome as we waited to receive our sign.

We will never forget the exact instant the sign appeared to us. We wanted to get a feel for what it would be like if we followed the new road, and so we visited the new location and physically experienced the overall scene and situation which would cause such drastic changes in our lives. One moment, we were emotionally neutral and still open to weighing both sides. The next moment, we were overcome with a feeling of joy and enormous peace. There was not a shadow of a doubt that this was the right choice. Our inner Christ spoke to us in a way we could not possibly ignore. In our complete nonresistance, the wind had blown us to the side of the roof which was best for us.

"WATCH THEREFORE ..."

That's how it will be for you, too, when you rely on your inner guidance. It can come suddenly, without warning. As Jesus cautioned, "Watch therefore, for you do not know on what day your Lord [your inner Christ guidance] is coming." You just have to remain open to it, whenever it arrives. In the meantime, release your concern for any decision with which you might be wrestling. In fact, we can say that the prerequisites for receiving inner guidance are release, peace, openness, and trust.

Sometimes we can go overboard in trying to interpret *everything* as a sign. We become hypervigilant, analyzing and projecting the smallest incident into a sign to be heeded. However, if we are asking God to speak to us in a way "we cannot possibly ignore," our inner guidance, when it addresses us, will be clear.

The more aware you become of the divine potential

within you, the more in tune you will be to your inner guidance. You will rely on it more and more, because you will know that it is your God-nature. It won't take long for you to discover that it will always put you on the side of the roof that will lead to your greatest good. It will speak to you in a way that you cannot possibly ignore.

Mile markers

- Your inner guidance will never fail to steer you right.
- Inner guidance comes from your own Christ essence, which is always working on your behalf.
- Inner guidance comes through the feelings, rather than the intellect.
- Prerequisites for receiving inner guidance are release, peace, openness, and trust.
- As Jesus cautioned, your inner guidance can come at any time, often when you least expect it.

Christ spirit within me, speak to me in ways I cannot possibly ignore, so that I may follow Your will and Your way. Help me to recognize the unmistakable signs, as I release all concern and trust Your unfailing desire for my good.

Please proceed to Adventure 27 in the Activity Book.

Everyone is afraid at some time or other. But you do not have to live with fear. It is unnecessary and interferes with your good.

Why am I afraid?

"Why are you afraid, O men of little faith?"
—Matthew 8:26

There was once a mouse who was afraid of the cat. His fear grew and grew until at last he wished with all his might to become a cat. His wish was granted, and the mouse did indeed become a cat. But the cat was afraid of the dog, and so he wished and wished to become a dog. Once again his wish was granted, and the cat became a dog. But the dog was afraid of the lion, and so this time he wished and he wished to become a lion. Eventually the dog did become a lion, but now he was afraid of the hunter. The lion wished and wished with all his might to become a hunter and, surely enough, his wish was granted. But the hunter, poor man, was afraid of his wife. So he wished and he wished to become a wife. His wish was granted, and the hunter was now a wife. But, alas, this was not the end of the chain of fear, for the wife, too, was afraid. She was afraid of the mouse!

FEAR BREEDS FEAR

And so it goes. One fear leads to other fears, which can only lead to other fears. If we live in a fearful state, there will always be something of which to be afraid. We can even be afraid without being able to identify the cause of our fears! We're just plain afraid, and we go from day to day, carefully picking our way through a fear-filled existence.

Our lives can take on the aspect of a war, as we spend our energy trying to avoid the land mines which lie hidden all around us, land mines of fear which can explode into bouts of worry and anxiety, or even panic attacks. We can begin to fear the feeling of fear. The reaction, the experience, of fear is often worse than the actual object of our fear.

As long as we stay in the fear mode, it's like being on a battlefield and there will always be something to fear, another land mine to avoid, another decision based not on what is best for us but simply on how to avoid whatever we fear. Then it's so easy for the fears to multiply. They have an insidious way of reproducing, spawning countless arrays of new fears without our being aware. They rob us of a great deal of our freedom—especially the freedom to grow.

SOME FEAR IS NORMAL

We have all experienced fear, and there are certainly times in our lives when fear is a perfectly normal reaction. We recall the fear we felt when we found ourselves in the middle of a Texas shoot-out!

Turning onto an interstate highway, we were suddenly surrounded by state troopers shooting at some fugitive who was careening at full speed in his bullet-riddled car. It was quite a while before our own emotions could calm down. That was certainly a time when we were afraid—no, *terrified* would be a better description. No doubt you have instances of your own which were frightening to you, leaving you with a racing heart and weak knees. These immediate reactions are natural instinctive reactions to survive.

Spontaneous fear, the kind which is difficult to control and which passes when the danger is over, is not the fear we're addressing. That kind of fear is perfectly normal. We're talking more about being afraid of things over which we have been given dominion and over which we should have complete control. Fears which we have fabricated in our own minds: fear of not being quite good enough, fear of expressing our opinions, fear of being alone, fear of becoming sick, fear of not getting well, fear of being ourselves—these are only a few of the countless fears which can plague us.

They are very real to us, and there are understandable explanations for why these fears take hold. Yet in spite of the terror they strike in our hearts, a simple change in our perspective can change them from an object of fear into just another fact of life. When we can accept the fact that God's will for us is only good, then what we have feared will be seen as a stepping-stone to our good.

ONE ANSWER TO FEAR

Virtually all fears are educated into us and can be educated out. How is this done? How do we rid ourselves of fear? There are excellent books available which address various phobias and offer solid help in overcoming them. The final hurdle of fear, however, can only be overcome with the realization that there is always a great "safety net" under you. This safety net is the knowledge that God will never let you fall. You are a child of God, precious and indispensable to God's plan. As your unity with God grows, your immunity to fear grows as well.

Imagine for a moment that you are a trapeze artist. Without a safety net, there are few tricks you will try. In fact, you may just swing back and forth all day and who would blame you? Put a safety net under you, however, and you'd know that you could attempt all of your tricks and even experiment with new ones. If you fall, so what! You would be safe and can climb up the ladder and try again.

Such is the courage we acquire to live a full and rich life when we know that God is the safety net under us. Like King Arthur's courageous knights of the Round Table, we are able to leave the familiar and venture into the mysterious unknown.

FEAR HAS ONLY ONE FACE

Fear seems to wear many faces: shyness, anxiety, insecurity, worry, panic, terror, dread. In whatever way it expresses itself, fear is basically a lack of the awareness of the presence of God as a real force in our lives. With the realization of God's active presence in our lives, the specter of fear disappears into the mists of the unreal. Like a snowball dropped into a pail of hot water, fear dissolves and its energy is transmuted into positive faith. Fear itself no longer exists.

When we surrender ourselves to God and allow God to take over our lives, fear cannot coexist with this great Power that runs the universe. How could it? It has no choice other than to disappear, just as the snowball could not coexist with the hot water. It had no choice other than to melt and become one with the water. When we surrender our fears to God, when we take even a small step toward God, our human "weaknesses" become absorbed into our divinity, and all is well in our lives.

No matter what in your life you are now afraid of, it does not change the fact that there still exists a Power supporting you which knows no fear. Know at the very depths of your being, the level where you know your oneness with God, that there is really nothing to fear.

$\mathcal{M}$ile markers

- If you live in a fearful state, there will always be something of which to be afraid.
- With fear in your heart, you can never fully accept God's good.
- You are meant to have dominion over all things.
- The final overcoming of fear is in the realization that the presence of God is a great safety net under you at all times.
- There is a part of you which can never be afraid.

Sweet Christ spirit within me, I feel the strength of Your supportive arms, holding me safe and secure. There is nothing to fear. I am free—alive—joy-filled. Thank You, God.

Please proceed to Adventure 28 in the Activity Book.

LIVING IN THE NOW | *29*

*Your present circumstances
are loaded with potential
for good. Right where you
are is the best place to
start.*

When will things get better?

*"Do you not say, 'There are yet four months, then
comes the harvest'? I tell you, lift up your eyes,
and see how the fields are already white for
harvest."*   —John 4:35

Hot and tired from an all-day drive across the
desert, we quickly checked into our motel and began
searching for a restaurant where we could relax in
comfort and eat a simple meal. That's all we wanted,
but this proved to be the start of a two-hour adventure of many miles and much frustration.

The first restaurant we entered was so dark that
only after we were seated and our eyes adjusted from
the desert sun did we discover how dirty it was. We
politely returned our menus and groped our way out.

Next was a large restaurant where we were confronted by a grumpy host puffing on a cigar and

coughing uncontrollably. He grunted for us to follow him and headed for a table. We headed for the door!

Our next try was a place where the music was so loud that the hostess had to ask us three times how many were in our party. To have eaten there would have been like eating in the middle of a rock concert, so out we went.

The next restaurants were as bad.

How did it all end? Two hours and many miles later we ate at the restaurant adjacent to our motel. How was it? Excellent. It was clean, simple, and the food was served with a smile. The lesson? The grass is *not* always greener (and neither are the salads) somewhere else.

AS GREEN AS IT GETS

Right where you are is as green as the grass will ever get. Within you is a potential for happiness that does not diminish nor ripen over time. Happiness doesn't need time to ripen, it only has to be called forth. It is ever available, ever waiting. Your present circumstances may look discouraging and may lead you to play the "if onlys" that we spoke of in an earlier Teaching: "*If only* I were richer," "*If only* I weren't sick," "*If only* someone loved me," "*If only* I were happier."

Actually, you will never have more potential for prosperity and wholeness than you have now. There will never be more of an opportunity for peace and love than exists for you right now. You will never be closer to complete happiness than you are right now. When you were conceived in the mind of God, you were given all that you needed. God holds back nothing, but it is your life choices which decide if and how you use those gifts.

THERE IS ONLY NOW

"Now" is rather an enigmatic concept when you ponder it for a while. No time exists other than *now*. Think of it—the past is over and gone. It will never be in your life again. Whatever happiness or grief it deposited in your life has already been delivered. The future? It's not here yet and when it does arrive, it will no longer be the future. It will be now. So now is really all you have and all you ever will have. The past is compost, the future is a seed not yet planted, the present is the only soil in which you can grow. So lamenting a missed chance for love in the past or nervously anticipating a need for prosperity in the future is wasting precious opportunities for all of your good in the present.

Why not begin doing the best you can *right where you are*? You can't get on an airplane that left yesterday, and you can't board one today that will leave tomorrow. You can't grow from where you were yesterday, and it's impossible to grow from where you will be tomorrow. The only growing has to take place exactly where you are planted.

You are planted where you are because that soil is best for you at this time in your unfoldment. The soil, the circumstances, in which you now find yourself contains all the elements that will make you grow best. Trust the process of growth. Trust God. Pay attention to the details in your life, doing your very best with each challenge that presents itself.

Of course, growing where you are planted does not mean that you should accept the limitations of your present circumstances. No indeed. The flower planted in the shade still seeks the sun. Any problem that you are now facing does not have to be accepted at face value. It can become a chance to grow, a chance to claim more of the good that God has for you. God's desire for you is absolute good, so do not be satisfied with less.

THE GOOD OLD DAYS

Sometimes we have a tendency to walk backwards through life. Like travelers facing backwards in the observation car of a cross-country train, we don't quite know where we are or exactly where we are going. We only know where we have been, and too often we find ourselves longing for those "good old days." Through the mist of the past, things often seem to take on an attractive patina. We have trouble seeing the blessings in the now because we view things only through the filter of the past.

Yet the past can include problems like growing up in a dysfunctional family or the early death of parents or a very sad love affair. These often have a devastating effect on us, and we allow them to affect us throughout our entire lives. Anchored in these past events, we cannot stretch into the newness that each day presents to us. Entrenched in the past, we frustrate our present potential.

KINGDOM OF GOD

Paul said "forgetting what lies behind and straining forward to what lies ahead, I press on toward ... the upward call of God" (Phil. 3:13-14). In other words, seek *first* the kingdom of God. The kingdom of God is not in the past. Staying in the past is meandering in the dark caverns of the mind. The past is illusion, mere memory. It is only what our mind is able to selectively recall. The longer something stays in the mind, the more it changes and the less it resembles what really happened. The past, like the future, is only our perception.

THE PAST IS IMPORTANT ... BUT!

The past is the raw material of the present, *but the past is not a blueprint for the present*! Give thanks for the lessons of the past. No matter how painful they were, they have given you an awareness of who and what you are. Many people recovering from an alcohol addiction state, "Thank God for my alcoholism" and mean it! What they are grateful for is the fact that the disease utterly forced them to connect with their own spirituality.

Instead of fearing the past or resisting and resenting it, use all of the raw material of the past, the good as well as the "bad," to design a new blueprint for the present. Looking back with fear or resentment is dragging the limitations of the past into the now, and that's like a boat dragging an anchor. Life is progress, and each now moment is a stepping-stone that leads to the next now moment.

You can't change the past. In fact, there is no need to because the real you doesn't dwell there anymore.

THE FUTURE IS IMPORTANT ... BUT!

What about the future? Can you believe that if you keep on thinking the same thoughts, saying the same words, doing the same things, going in the same direction, the future will be any different than now? To look to the future as a savior without changing the present is to think an orange tree can grow from an acorn.

Yes, you can change the direction of your life, but changes can't happen in the past or the future; they can only happen in the now. At each now moment there exists an unlimited amount of possibilities, which makes anytime a good time for a new beginning. In fact, every moment *is* a new beginning.

You don't have to wait for a new year to resolve to make a new life. You are, right now, at the junction of what you were and what you can be. This junction of your life, this now moment, is ripe with possibilities. This is the Possibility Junction mentioned in the first Adventure. Possibility Junction, this "now" moment, contains all of the good that you can ever hope to have. At each of these junctions, *you decide* what road you will take.

When you think of how you want your life to unfold, it may seem awesome, but when you are at Possibility Junction, everything is possible. All you really have to remember is that God is with you, because God lives at Possibility Junction. The God which dwells within you and has given you a new vision of yourself will keep you on course. The God which has allowed the vision will, with your cooperation, fulfill that vision.

BEGIN WHERE YOU ARE

Look for the seed of good in every situation, and you will see that the fields are already ripe for harvesting. All you will ever need is yours—*Now*.

Begin where you are. Do what you can. Even a small effort to change, to grow, to improve, will bring astonishing results. When you desire to change and you make an effort to change, God rushes forth to meet you. As in the story of the Prodigal Son, God waits for us to return "home." When we do, God immediately responds to us with an outpouring of everything we need—*Now*.

So walk forward and don't turn back. (You can't drive a car by looking in the rearview mirror.) If you want to discover the genuine you—the person that you really are—release the person that you were. When you *yearn* for the past, you make yourself a slave to the past. When you *learn* from the past, you become a master of the present.

You can choose to build on what you were, but you are *not* what you were. You can focus on what you will be, but you are *not* what you will be. What you are is what you are right *now*—the inheritor of all of God's gifts.

Now, this moment, is the first moment in the rest of your eternity. You can start it fresh with God.

*M*ile markers

- You will never have more potential for good than you have right now.
- God withholds nothing from you.
- There is no time but now.
- You are planted where you can grow best at this time.
- Use the raw materials of the past to design a new blueprint for the future.

I thank You, God, for my past, that I can learn from it. I thank You for my future, and I know there is good in it. But most of all, I thank You for the newness that I am today. I savor each moment.

Please proceed to Adventure 29 in the Activity Book.

*When the full impact of
your relationship to God
really hits you, you will
move up to a new level of
self-worth.*

Step up to the banquet table

*"Fear not, little flock, for it is your Father's good
pleasure to give you the kingdom."* —Luke 12:32

The shrill whistle of the *River Queen* pierced the
stillness as the majestic paddleboat rounded a bend
in the Mississippi. A handful of fishermen along with
a small boy waved from the levee in excitement and
awe.

"Let me ride! Let me ride!" yelled the boy, waving
wildly and jumping up and down as the boat was
about to slip by. One of the fishermen tried to calm
the child, explaining that the *River Queen* was a large
and important boat and could not stop to give rides to
little boys. Yet the boy persisted, and all the more
animatedly waved and shouted, "Let me ride!"

Imagine the stares of disbelief when the great boat
edged its way to the levee and a gangplank was

lowered so that one small boy could scamper onto the large deck.

Then all at once the captain appeared, arms outstretched toward the child. "Daddy, Daddy!" called the boy, as he jumped into his father's loving arms.

YOUR REAL PARENT

Jesus explained that earthly fathers want to give their children everything they can, and yet so much greater is God's desire to give us everything. "Fear not, little flock, for it is your Father's good pleasure to give you the kingdom." God denies you nothing.

It's true that not every earthly father is a paragon of loving kindness who gives the very best he can give. (Who of us is always operating from that divinity within?) While in general it is natural for fathers to want to protect and nurture their young, even the most perfect of earthly fathers, no matter how loving and well intentioned, is unable to know exactly what is best for his child or is capable of endlessly giving unlimited good to that child. Yet God is.

In a very real sense, God is the true parent of us all. We were created to be the vehicles through which God can best express. Surely this gives us some hint of the absolute love and care which are invested in each of us.

OUR FATHER

It is easy to say, "I am a child of God." Many of us learned to say it in Sunday school when we were small: "I am a child of God. I am a child of God." It trips off the tongue so glibly, yet how many of us know what we are saying? How many of us understand what those words imply? How many of us, when we say it, internalize it and feel the far-reaching impact of those words?

Jesus often referred to God as "Father." The prayer which He taught us began with "Our Father," and those two words alone contain just about everything we have to know about ourselves and our relationship to God and to each other. This one small phrase tells us we are all created by and loved by the Creator, which makes the entire human race brothers and sisters in the truest sense of the words. Each of us has an equal claim to all that the Father has.

ACCESS TO ALL THAT GOD IS

To be a child of God is the ultimate gift the universe can bestow. We are told, we are made in the image and likeness of God. Just as humanly we carry the genes of our parents, so we also bear the characteristics of our cosmic parent. The difference is that we may not carry all of the characteristics of our human parents. One parent's eyes may be brown and the other's blue. They may be short and we may be tall. Hair color may vary and personalities too. But in the case of our divine inheritance, we inherit everything. God is love, and so we, too, are love. God is wholeness, so also are we. God is absolute abundance, and that is our nature as well. Whatever God is we are part of, because we are part of God. Any attribute of God must automatically reflect itself in each of us. How could it be otherwise?

Regrettably, we don't always realize who and what we are, and that leads to all kinds of unnecessary detours in the journey. In our frenzy to find what we already have, we search for something that was never lost.

Why is it that we often refuse to claim what is ours by divine inheritance? Seldom taking advantage of all that is ours, we too often settle for so much less.

Being a child of God means we have complete access to all that God is. That's stupendous! It means we lack nothing, that each of us is special and crucially important to the Creator. All that "the Father" has is ours. What an incredible endowment! It's as if we have a bank account that can never be depleted, no matter what.

WE BECOME WHAT WE THINK WE ARE

The ugly duckling could never be more than a duck until it realized that it was a graceful swan. A duck is all that it thought it was. What we believe about ourselves determines our lives.

When we know, *really* know, that we are children of God, we will begin acting as if that were true. Children of God! Offspring of the Creator of the universe! Inheritors of all that God has!

It is God's good pleasure to *give* us the riches of the kingdom. A feast has been prepared for us. If we haven't begun to claim this absolute good, it is not too late. It is never too late. No matter how far we might have drifted, that unlimited good is always waiting quietly in the wings for us to accept it. Everything is there for us: peace, joy, health, prosperity, love. Whatever the Father has is ours.

It is yours, today, because you are a child of God. Take your place at the banquet table.

$\mathcal{M}$ile markers

- More than any earthly father, God wants to give you everything ... absolute good.
- God is your true parent.
- We are all brothers and sisters, and we each have equal access to all that "the Father" has.
- You bear the characteristics of your cosmic parent.
- What you believe about yourself determines your life.

God, I am Your child. Thank You for the safety of Your loving arms as I go about the work which is mine to do. I know that nothing can harm or overwhelm me, for I am Yours. I acknowledge that You are my Source, my Creator, my Sustainer, and that all which You have is mine. I also acknowledge my kinship with all humanity and give thanks that I and You and they are one.

Please proceed to Adventure 30 in the Activity Book.

*Things are not always
what they seem. Judging
them correctly can turn
your life around.*

It ain't necessarily so

*"Do not judge by appearances, but judge with right
judgment."*   —John 7:24

• "Ouch! Watch out for that prickly cactus. Can't
you see how dangerous it is? Just look at those
stilettolike spines." The large saguaro cactus practi-
cally screamed out to us, "Don't touch me. Hands
off!" What a worthless plant! It looked to us as if
nature goofed on this creation.

• "Oh, please, not *this* dog," was the one thought
racing through our minds as the veterinarian placed
the leash in our unwilling hands. At the other end of
the lead was Stormy April, a bedraggled and confused
greyhound whom he had recently operated on and

whom we had agreed to adopt, sight unseen, after she got injured racing. "This isn't going to work out at all," we whispered to each other as we reluctantly lifted the sorry beast into our car.

• Well, it certainly was obvious that those people who had just moved into the house across the street were going to spoil our friendly neighborhood. When they first arrived, we smiled and waved a warm hello, but they put their heads down and looked the other way. "Maybe they didn't see us, or maybe they're just very shy," we conjectured. "We'll try again."

This time we knocked on their door with the idea of introducing ourselves and offering the use of our phone or anything else they might need before getting settled. But we never got the chance, because they never came to the door. "Oh, oh," we muttered as we walked away. "This looks like trouble."

SECOND LOOKS

Take a guess. What do you suspect gets us humans into more misery than anything else? Could it be our tendency to be judgmental?

The hostile-looking cactus, which we so judgmentally dismissed as one of nature's mistakes, contains life-saving water which has rescued many a desert traveler from death by dehydration. The seemingly undesirable greyhound which we strongly suspected would be an unwelcomed addition to our family, soon became the most elegant, endearing, intelligent pet we have ever owned. And that unfriendly, rude couple across the street? They are now two of our best friends! It turned out that one of their children had been killed by a hit-and-run driver only a few weeks earlier, and they were understandably overcome with grief.

Judging people and situations and things only by their outer appearances is always a mistake. How would you like people to totally judge you only by the way you look right now? Things are *rarely* what they seem. Yet we can waste so much energy in dealing with what we *think* they are rather than staying centered in our Christ essence and allowing people and situations and things to present us with the good they always contain for us.

A RIDICULOUS HABIT

Often we are quick to condemn or judge but when we do that, what we are doing, of course, is forgetting that God is present in *every* situation, no matter how bleak it looks. Or we are overlooking the Christ presence within a person or group of people.

When we practice the ridiculous habit of judging by appearances, we cut ourselves off from the good which the situation or person holds for us. It is such a destructive, unproductive habit that it's hard to believe anyone would want to engage in it, and yet how many of us still persist?

Jesus was absolutely on target when He taught that we must not judge others. We have no right. After all, each human being, regardless of appearances, is a child of God and has the Spirit of God within. Disapproval or condemnation of someone is, when you distill it to its essence, disapproval or condemnation of God!

Every person on earth is divine on a deep level. Someone may be skillfully concealing this divinity, not fully realizing it exists, but that doesn't alter the fact that the Christ is within and must be recognized and honored by us.

As you allow yourself to do this, you will find that the people turning up along your trail seem to be more wonderful, more friendly, more appealing than ever before. That is because *you* are more wonderful, friendly, and appealing as you acknowledge the Christ first in yourself and then in each person you meet.

EVEN WHEN IT SEEMS IMPOSSIBLE

When you consider some of the strange, hideous, and inhumane acts some individuals commit, it sounds ludicrous to suggest that such people are divine at their essence. Yet they are.

You see, whatever a person does or does not do can in no way negate the fact that he or she is a divine creation. How can they be otherwise? They, too, were created by God and are, as much as you, children of God. Realizing this fact, it then becomes incumbent upon us to see the light of the Christ within that person, even when it seems to glow so dimly that they don't even see it themselves.

Within each of us is the same essence which Jesus recognized in Himself and in all humanity. True, it is expressed in varying degrees, to be sure, but be assured that It is there. The man who commits heinous atrocities is still a child of God. To judge him as anything less is to put yourself in a position of judging God; it is to say that God made a terrible mistake.

BUT ...

But there is a great difference between being *judgmental* and using your good *judgment*. To acknowledge that the Christ dwells in every individual is using your judgment. However, it does not mean that you have to hang around with a misguided soul who is dangerous to you, either physically or emotionally. Just as your judgment would direct you to get out of the path of a runaway truck, you would also get out of the path of a person who, not recognizing or expressing the Christ within, is destructive. The divine potential is there, to be sure, but until it is recognized by the person and called forth, it is often a good idea to steer clear of such an individual as much as possible.

Angry, mean-spirited people who bask in negativity are as much children of God and have the Christ within fully as much as happy, positive, spiritually centered people. It's not our job to change them but merely to see the Christ in them, do our very best to see them as children of God. Yet at the same time we must also use our judgment, which may lead us to choose not to spend time with them.

Operating from this perspective, you are not denying the presence of the Christ in someone. You are not being judgmental by seeing him or her as less than a child of God. You are simply using good judgment to avoid something which is not contributing to your good.

LIKE VERSUS LOVE

Jesus encouraged us to love one another, to see and love that Christ essence of every person, but He never required us to *like* the inappropriate behavior of someone. This is where our wise judgment enters into it. There is no one in all of history who is not lovable at the divine core, because God is at the center of that core. However, there have been many whose *actions* are unlikable and unacceptable and downright repugnant. Jesus was constantly castigating the scribes and Pharisees about their pompous and rigid behavior. He was not being judgmental of them as being less than children of God. Rather He was using His judgment and acknowledging their actions as inappropriate and harmful and a bad example for others to follow.

There is nothing wrong with choosing not to associate with or accept unlikable behavior, as long as we remember that somewhere within that person there is still the Christ.

HURTING OURSELVES

If we ignore this obligation and proceed to condemn and judge by outer appearances, we are really hurting ourselves. Our harsh judgment returns to haunt us because it keeps *us* out of "the kingdom." It bars *us* from operating in the Christ mode, and that restricts our spiritual growth. When we are judgmental, we are not being authentic or true to our divine nature, and we on *The Quest* cannot afford such wasted energy and setbacks.

Pick your way carefully among the sharp boulders of condemnation and false judgment. Get past them once and for all, because they are "trail-blockers," holding you back on your quest. They don't belong in your life.

*M*ile mark*e*rs

- Judging only by outer appearances is a mistake, because things are rarely what they seem.
- When you harshly judge or condemn, you are overlooking the Christ presence in that person.
- Disapproval of a person is disapproval of God.
- There is a great difference between being judgmental and using good judgment.
- You have to *love* each person's divine essence, but you do not have to *like* someone's inappropriate behavior.
- Wrong judgment impedes your spiritual growth.

Thank You, God, for the Christ presence within me. I now look for the same presence in everyone else. Help me to use my judgment rightly, to see as You see. If I am faced with actions which I do not like, help me to understand that this is done by a child of Yours, so that I may turn away with a loving heart. Thank You, God, for my good judgment.

Please proceed to Adventure 31 in the Activity Book.

*Spirit speaks in quiet
ways within your heart.
There are some things
too deep for words—
beyond human language.*

Spirit has its own language

*"God is spirit, and those who worship him must
worship in spirit and truth."* —John 4:24

In medieval times, people hung wind harps in the open windows of their huts. The wind, moving through these wind harps, would be transformed into music.

The little instruments would never know, or even care, from what direction the wind blew or how gentle or gusty it might be. They were simply open to the flow of the currents of air, allowing the currents to play whatever music they desired at the moment. It was as if the wind harps sensed that their purpose was to serve as instruments for the wind, for without the wind there could be no music.

Neither would there be music if the instruments

resisted the wind. By their complete cooperation, the wind harps were capable of an infinite variety of music as the wind was free to be the wind through them.

INSTRUMENTS OURSELVES

There is a marvelous and mystical passage in The Gospel According to John, in which Jesus compares Spirit, the Spirit of God, to the wind. "The wind blows where it wills, and you hear the sound of it, but you do not know whence it comes or whither it goes; so it is with every one who is born of the Spirit" (Jn. 3:8).

Like those medieval wind harps open to the moving currents of air, we must be open to the movement of the Spirit of God as It comes to us in unexpected moments and in unexpected ways. We must be willing to serve as instruments for Spirit to play through us in whatever manner It desires, because we sense in our hearts that this is the only way for us to make music and that without the music we are hollow and dull.

THE ELUSIVE MYSTERY

The Spirit of God, like the wind, moves where it wills, not seen by the human eye or heard by the human ear but only sensed by the human heart. The actual experiencing of the Spirit of God, what some call the baptism of the Holy Spirit, is an uttterly private, personal, and individual experience which no one can know for you or explain to you. God is Spirit, and the only way to know this Spirit is not through the intellect but through our own inner spirit.

To *try* to experience the presence of Spirit is to move yourself farther from It. You cannot capture

Spirit by trying, anymore than you can capture the wind by pursuing it with grabbing hands. There is only one way to know Spirit, and that begins with a desire in your heart and then a willingness to allow Spirit to reveal Itself to you.

IN THE MISTS

This is the stage of your quest where you will temporarily have to lay aside your maps and your walking stick and step out in absolute trust. When it comes to the personal experience of Spirit in your life, there are no directions or landmarks to guide you. It is too deep, too involved with levels beyond your human modes of communication. Yet it's there all the same.

Spirit is longing to make that contact with you. To allow yourself to be willing to receive the experience, to be touched however briefly or lightly, is never to be the same again.

THE DAY WILL COME

There are people who have not yet experienced the presence of the Holy Spirit in their lives. This does not mean that they cannot be God-guided, able to transform their lives and continue on *The Quest*.

If you feel you are one of these people, that you have not had the experience of Spirit, you are in no way a failure. Do remember, however, that if you maintain a simple willingness, the experience one day will come.

At the right hour and in the right way, probably when you least expect it, the Spirit of God will make Itself known to you. Having had the experience, you will then understand why things of the Spirit can only be known spiritually.

Meanwhile, keep in your mind the image of the little wind harps. Beautifully nonresistant to the ways of the wind, they are ever ready to be played through, to serve as instruments of music for the wind.

You, dear one, are an instrument for Spirit to play through as It wishes. Be willing ... for the music will come.

Mile markers

- The Spirit of God will come to you in unexpected moments and unexpected ways.

- You must be willing to serve as an instrument for Spirit to play through in whatever manner It desires.

- The harder you try to capture the experience of Spirit, the more elusive Spirit becomes.

- A desire and a willingness is the only way to open yourself to receiving the Holy Spirit.

- The "baptism of the Holy Spirit" is something so personal and so mystical that it cannot be described in words.

- You are not a failure if you have not yet experienced the presence of the Spirit of God in your life. It will come.

Sweet and holy Spirit of God, I invite You into my life. Play through me as Your instrument for peace and healing and joy and love in this world. Create the music in me that I was born to sing. Touch me with Your grace and goodness that I may serve and glorify You more.

Please proceed to Adventure 32 in the Activity Book.

‎THE JESUS CHRIST PRESENCE | 33

*You can establish a deep
and lasting personal
relationship with Jesus
Christ.*

The prevailing presence

*"Behold, I stand at the door and knock; if any one
hears my voice and opens the door, I will come in."*
—Revelation 3:20

How comforting, how reassuring, to realize that no
matter what road you take on your quest, there will
be markers to let you know you are not lost. Someone has gone before you to lead the way.

Jesus Christ, the Way-Shower, has clearly blazed a
trail for you. His teachings serve as guideposts as
you encounter what you feel may be bewildering obstacles (such as relationship problems, loss of a job,
addictions, ill health) along the path. His teachings
will not only keep you heading in the right directions,
they will arm you with powerful weapons with which
to make your overcomings.

Moving onward in your quest for transformation,
you will discover Jesus' teachings ever waiting for

you, like familiar ribbons tied to trees, letting you know you are on the right trail and leading you higher and higher in your awareness of God.

The teachings of your Master Trailblazer about the nature of God and the kingdom of heaven as well as His principles of healing and love have been thoughtfully and lovingly placed before you, so that you will always know you are not alone.

LIFESAVING REVELATIONS

The teachings of Jesus Christ stand on their own. Without any involvement with Him personally, they are entirely sufficient to help you be the person you were created to be. In fact, His teachings can (and were meant to) transform the entire world. That was, and is, their purpose: to bring to all humanity the news that we are part of God and that God's desire for each of us is absolute good.

In your personal quest you yourself are making the same discoveries that Jesus made, and you are, no doubt, having the exhilarating experience of realizing your life is getting better and better all the time. More than ever before, you are able to handle whatever is yours to handle as you increasingly understand that you have a power within you which makes all things possible. To be sure, the teachings of Jesus Christ are, in a very real sense, lifesaving, "miracle-working" revelations. We join with you in sincere gratitude for them and for Him for sharing His quest with us.

WHEN DID HE PASS THIS WAY?

Yet have you wondered, as you journeyed on *The Quest*, how long ago these teachings—these trail markings—were left there for you? How far ahead of you is the Master? Did He pass this way two thousand years ago to be gone forever and never to be seen or heard or felt again? If you were to stand completely still and barely breathe, might you hear His footsteps somewhere up ahead? Could He be waiting for you in a nearby glen, or will you come upon Him resting for a moment beside that stream beyond the trees? Or is He just around the next bend?

Not everyone who follows these universal teachings is interested in knowing the Teacher, but maybe you, like us, desire to know Jesus Christ. Knowing His beautiful teachings, perhaps you now crave a personal relationship with Him who revealed them.

It's very likely that the more you travel on your quest, the more this craving will grow, until one day you will see fresh footprints on the forest floor. Your heart will quicken as you pick up your pace. Is that the wind in the trees, or was it His voice whispering, "Come, follow me"?

HE MAKES HIS PRESENCE KNOWN

Just as you can have a personal experience of the Spirit of God, you can also have a personal experience of Jesus the Christ. Once again, this will not be an intellectual knowing. Rather it will be a mystical, indescribable perceiving. If you are sincere in your hunger to know the Master, call upon His name and ask Him to make His presence known to you.

The consciousness of Jesus Christ has never left our world. It is available to all who truly seek it, and by calling it forth, we gain access to all that Jesus Christ was and still is. We can establish a deep personal relationship with Him, a relationship which lifts us and imbues us with His own consciousness. The consciousness of Jesus Christ is the consciousness which never doubts God as the source of good, or humankind as heirs to that good.

Others have made an intimate connection with Jesus Christ. They have "felt His hand" upon their shoulders or spoken quietly with Him or seen His radiant visage in their times of meditation.

OPEN THE DOOR

How will the Master come to you? We cannot say. We can only tell you that if your heart is open to Him, if you are one of those who wish to make Jesus Christ your friend, or personal Lord, He will not disappoint.

Behold, He stands at the door. If you hear His voice and open the door, He will come in.

Mile markers

- Jesus' teachings serve as guideposts in *The Quest.*
- The teachings of Jesus are sufficient to transform the entire world.
- Some of us desire a personal relationship with the Master, Jesus Christ.
- A personal experience of Jesus Christ, while beyond the realm of intellectual comprehension, is attainable to those who call upon His name.

Jesus Christ, I call upon Your name. I open the door that You will come into my life. Reveal Yourself to me that I may know You more. I desire to follow You and to consecrate my life to Your will and Your way. In Your name I pray.
Amen.

Please proceed to Adventure 33 in the Activity Book.

*Learn the secret of get-
ting along harmoniously
with all the people in
your life.*

Understanding ... and being understood

*"Do not be anxious how or what you are to answer
or what you are to say; for the Holy Spirit will
teach you in that very hour what you ought to
say."* —Luke 12:11-12

We can react hostilely to each other as individuals,
feud with each other as families, and battle each
other as nations. At one time or another virtually all
of us have had episodes of just not seeming to get it
right with our fellow humans. Yet, our connection
with others is basic to our existence.

Why do we so often fill ourselves with anger and
bitterness toward people, building walls around ourselves, when touching someone soul to soul can be
one of the most beautiful and satisfying experiences
available to us?

Personal relationships are a major cause of

unhappiness in people everywhere, and an avalanche of books, tapes, workshops, and television shows has been directed toward improving them. We are told that for every personality type there is a particular strategy which must be employed if we would have harmony. However, the harmony which these ideas would have us establish is not really harmony at all, not genuine harmony, that is. It is often more like one-upmanship, self-assertion, and saving face.

Trying to find successful ways of dealing with people according to their personality traits is futile and time-consuming, and it puts the emphasis on outer characteristics rather than where it belongs, which is on the inner. Imagine all of the time and mental effort we save when we don't have to figure out what words to say to appease someone or quench a fiery outburst or soften a hateful attitude. If we wanted to, we could let our entire lives be preoccupied with figuring out which words work best for which people. This works well for some people sometimes, but there is a much easier way to handle relationships and that is not to "handle" them at all.

LOOK FOR THE GOLDEN THREAD

Since each of us is part of the One, there is an underlying sameness to us all. Although present situations, yours and others, may be filled with conflict, it is nevertheless natural to long for close contact with other humans. Parts of the One seek to connect with other parts of the One. Relationship problems can be merely a thin veneer which we use to cover a doubt or fear we have about ourselves.

There is a level in every human soul which knows no conflict, competition, or contempt, a level which knows only peace, harmony, and love. In fact, it *is* peace and harmony and love, because it is the Christ essence of us. It is our innate divinity, and on that level, there is no distinction between you and every other individual. It is one unbroken and unbreakable golden thread stitching all of us together. If we will allow ourselves to search for it, every one of us can find that golden link to all humanity. We can find it in ourselves, and we can find it in others.

GETTING IT RIGHT

Is there a relationship which has you upset or frustrated or depressed? It doesn't matter if it's with a spouse, a child, an acquaintance, a relative, or a friend. If you want it to improve, the method is the same: lift yourself up in consciousness. Lift yourself out of any negative emotions and reactions and become aware of the presence of God within you. It is as simple as that! The reason it *always* works is because when you feel this Presence, it will automatically be communicated from that level in you to the same Presence in the other person.

Your awareness of the Christ presence in you will cut through all of the hurts and angers and fears which have built up in this relationship, and you will focus directly on the divine Presence in that person. In other words, you will be dealing directly from Christ to Christ.

Relating to others this way has an amazing and often immediate effect. Years and years of unforgiveness and hardened attitudes can break up and dissolve in a matter of minutes!

Dropping all the superficial adornments and focusing directly on the Christ is a wonder-worker for any relationship. It has to be. Why? Because the Christ operates only with love—knows only love and therefore sees only love.

Every human heart yearns for love and responds to love. That's the way we are made. Some people do a good job of hiding that craving from others and even from themselves, but the Christ love, sincerely radiated, eventually proves irresistible. Barriers come down, fences fall, and walls crumble in the face of the Christ. No one is exempt because the Christ is all-inclusive.

Our human relationships are meant to be light and joy-filled, for it is in the connecting with others that we most easily discern the Christ. It is in the looking deeply into the eyes of a fellow being that we see the Christ. That precious moment brings a sweet exhilaration to which few things can compare.

WE ARE EACH OTHER

In the space-time continuum, the normal "worldly" dimension, society teaches us to differentiate ourselves from others, to look for and to accentuate the differences between us. The news media make a living by doing so. However, in the spiritual dimension, we realize our oneness with others. Operating from the space-time continuum, it is too easy to see others as different from us, to see boundaries, to be *ex*clusive. Operating from our spiritual center, however, is to see others as part of ourselves, to see no boundaries, to be *in*clusive.

Scientifically, we know that the molecules of our bodies are in a continual process of exchanging themselves with molecules of other bodies. Each time we inhale, we are breathing in new molecules which were once part of countless other people. Each time we exhale, we are releasing molecules which had taken up temporary residence in us, sending them forth to be part of others' bodies. It is a constant exchange, and it shows how, on a physical level, we are part of all creation. (Although not a provable fact, according to many reputable scientists, it is highly likely that because of the incredible number of molecules in one human breath, there are molecules in each living person that were once a part of Shakespeare, Julius Caesar, Alexander the Great, and, yes, Jesus Christ!)

On the spiritual level as well, we are linked to one another. In light of this, the answer to Cain's "Am I my brother's keeper?" (Gen. 4:9) becomes not "I am my brother's keeper" but "I *am* my brother," for we are all one.

GO DIRECT

Do you want a better relationship with your mate? Are you hoping for more harmony between you and your child? Do you wish there were better understanding between you and your parents? Do you long for a new, more intimate relationship with a friend?

Put the relationship on a Christ-to-Christ basis. Cut right through the outer facade. Put aside your old hurts and attitudes, never mind your feelings of embarrassment or fear or timidness. Don't let these kinds of emotions dictate what your relationships will be. There is too much at stake to allow yourself to be a victim of old ways of thinking, of old habits.

Make contact Christ to Christ. Pray to God for understanding, so that you can put yourself "in the other person's shoes" and have a realization of why he or she is *really* acting in this manner.

But most importantly, nothing can match your being centered in the Christ light and looking lovingly into a person's eyes, speaking lovingly and warmly, validating his or her hurt or anger or fear. By allowing yourself to show your Christ identity, you will plainly see the Christ in the other person who will then be able to see it much more clearly in himself or herself.

What words should you use? There is no need to be concerned with that, because the Christ within you knows exactly what to say—always. That is why things become so infinitely easier when we deal on the Christ level.

Trust the Spirit within, within you and within other people. When you do, relationship "problems" will be a thing of the past. Like smoldering campfires no longer capable of casting light, you can unburden yourself of them and leave them below in the valley.

$\mathcal{M}$ile markers

- Trying to deal with people on the personality level is futile and time-consuming.
- It is natural to long for close contact with other humans.
- There is a level in every human soul which knows no conflict, competition, or contempt; it is the level of the Christ.
- To heal any relationship, cut through all of the hurts and angers and fears and go directly to the Christ level of that person.
- When we are in contact with our spiritual dimension, we realize our oneness with others. There is no need to be concerned with choosing words, because the Christ always knows exactly what to say.

Christ of my being, I acknowledge Your presence within me, and I allow You to harmonize all of my relationships. Help me to see the Christ in all others and to know that I am truly one with them and they are one with me.

Please proceed to Adventure 34 in the Activity Book.

$\mathcal{H}$ELPING OTHERS | *35*

$\mathcal{H}$ow to be a light in a dark world

"Unbind him, and let him go."—John 11:44

Once upon a time a young soldier was sentenced to death by a king. The king decreed, "He will be hanged at the ringing of the curfew bell tonight." The soldier's betrothed, desperate to help him but finding no other way, climbed up in the bell tower a few hours before curfew and tied herself tightly to the bell's gigantic clapper. When the curfew hour arrived, only muffled tones were heard from the tower, and the king demanded to know why the bell was not ringing. His investigators discovered the young woman, terribly battered and bleeding from being knocked back and forth against the huge bell. The king was so struck by the woman's willingness to suffer such pain in order to save her loved one that he released the soldier with the decree, "Curfew shall not ring tonight."

THERE IS SOMEONE

This very moment there is someone in your life whom you want, perhaps desperately want, to help. You know who it is. It's the person with that great challenge: a life-threatening illness or a grieving heart or a consuming addiction or a crippling financial lack. You, like everyone else, will always have someone in your life whom you feel needs some kind of help. What can we do about it? Is there really a way to help another person?

Yes, there is, but help does not begin with any of our human resources. Certainly a helping hand can be useful. There can be tangible, practical things we can do to assist others. Jesus felt the need to take action on many occasions. He placed mud on a blind man's eyes (Jn. 9:6), He ordered jugs to be filled with water so that it could be changed into wine (Jn. 2:7), He had the burial linens removed from Lazarus (Jn. 11:44). We, too, can take practical action to help others. But trying to help someone by using *only* our human resources is a great waste of energy.

EYES DON'T ALWAYS SEE

Looking at someone's situation with our human eyes often gives the impression that this person is less than complete, that he or she is lacking in some area, and therefore needs "fixing." We think we know what is best for the person, offer a little (or a lot) of our well-intentioned "wisdom," and then get upset when it's not gratefully received or satisfactorily acted upon.

By then we have begun to alienate and discourage the person, who now knows we view him or her as inadequate in some way. You yourself know that you don't like to be with people who think of you as less than whole. It's too easy to believe them and to begin to see yourself that way!

If we try to help someone out of a challenge by working only from a human level, we are acting out of desperation. Our actions are motivated by fear or worry. The implication is that we can't wait for God to act, it's too serious for that. Something must be done now!

What the person is really looking for is not help but direction. What is really needed is someone who sees him or her as complete and whole, someone who looks beyond the appearances to the truth. The truth, of course, is that God wants absolute good for your friend, for you, and for all of us.

Seeing through the problem to the truth is seeing with the eyes of Spirit, and it is the *only* way we can ever truly help someone else. (It's the only way we can ever truly help ourselves too.) A situation can only change when the change comes from within the person involved. A change in a person's consciousness is what changes his or her life. There is nothing we can do, no matter how brave or dramatic or drastic, no matter how much we love the person, no matter how much we want our friend to experience happiness. There is nothing we can do that can ever provide the help we desire for that soul.

It's a sure thing that the soldier who was saved by his fiancée was destined to end up in trouble again if he did not go through some kind of inner change.

Unless he did, her desperate act was all in vain, a great and painful waste of energy. Ultimately, it was the soldier's consciousness which had to be lifted.

GIVE YOURSELF A LIFT

How can you lift another? You can't, but you can lift yourself. You can believe in yourself by believing in the Christ power within you. That Christ power can help, guide, heal, prosper, comfort, or do anything else necessary for your well-being. Then, believing in the Christ power in you, it is only one small step to believe in that same power in everyone else. The view from this level shows there is nothing which must be "fixed" in that person for whom you were so concerned. The view from the Christ level shows that everything is fine and whole and good in every way.

This method of helping another person by centering yourself will seem ridiculous to anyone who looks at it only from the human vantage point. Most people will think it can't possibly work, because no effort is being directed to helping anyone, but as a traveler on *The Quest*, you do not think and act like most people. You see the greater perspective because you spend the majority of your time these days close to the mountaintop. Your trips down into the valleys grow less and less frequent as you find yourself more often listening at the feet of the Master Teacher, Jesus.

JESUS SAW THINGS RIGHT

Jesus' own method of helping others is very clear. He did not put things right, He merely *saw* them right.

You will recall the incident when He was on His way to restore a girl back to life (Lk. 8:42-55). The crowds were pushing at Him as He trod the road when suddenly He stopped. "Who was it that touched me?" was the question which rang out to the puzzled masses. His disciples were incredulous. How could Jesus ask such a question when there had been so many people pressing against Him?

Yet Jesus was not speaking of someone's touching His clothing or His body. He was referring to His consciousness when He asked, "Who was it that touched me?" He had felt a connection on a spiritual level to someone in the crowd, and He was right. There was a woman who had been hemorrhaging for twelve years who, lying ill in her bed when she heard that Jesus was approaching, ran out to meet Him, saying that if she could just touch His garment, she would be healed. She knew it!

She managed to get close enough to touch the hem of His garment, but it was really symbolic of touching Jesus' consciousness, touching His awareness of the Christ within Him and within all people, including her. Jesus automatically viewed her with the eyes of wholeness and perfection with which God views us. The woman followed Jesus' view: she looked at herself through His eyes, saw her innate perfection, and was healed.

"If I only touch his garment, I shall be made well." The woman knew—absolutely knew—that by touching the consciousness of Jesus she would be healed. He did nothing. He simply *was*. It's a thrilling and faith-lifting story, and it shows us that Jesus did not try to change the woman or "fix" her. He simply *was*. Centered in the firm awareness of God, Jesus constantly drew people to Him who were healed and restored by spiritually connecting with His beingness.

He was able to see only the wholeness of a situation, and that was enough to help the person, no matter what the particular need. That is how He helped others, and that is how you can help them too.

Right now you can probably think of at least one person who needs your help. The fact is that there are many, and you will never know when a receptive soul runs out to "touch the hem of your garment," that is, touch your consciousness. If your consciousness is high and you are aware of the presence of God in your life, you will be an instrument of healing or help for that person, although you may not ever know you were. There will be no need to do anything other than just *be.*

YOU ARE A BEACON

All of this is a radical departure from the old way of looking for solutions: advising, counseling, manipulating, worrying, and often just plain meddling. We cannot presume to know what's best for another soul. We have no way of knowing where that soul has been, what road it has traveled, what its secrets are, and what lessons it needs in order to attain spiritual awareness. What we *can* know is that the Christ mind, which *does* have all the answers, is present in that person and will respond to our own Christ mind when we allow it to radiate from us.

By allowing your own light to shine, you serve as a beacon to draw others to their own light. Then each person who needs help will be free to find his or her own way. It may not be *your* way but rather the way which is right for that individual. Your strong faith in the Christ within yourself and in all people becomes a mighty magnet, attracting others to touch the "hem of your garment," your consciousness which sees them as whole.

No matter how dire their need or how desperately you want to help them, your new role is simply to *be*. That is the best way to help people. It is the method Jesus used. It is the *highest* way.

$\mathcal{M}$ile markers

- Seeing someone through the eyes of Spirit is the *only* way you can ever truly help that person.
- By believing in the Christ power in you, you lift your own consciousness, which then perceives nothing to "fix" in other people.
- From a higher level of awareness, you see only the wholeness and good in someone.
- If your consciousness is high, your very *beingness* is enough to help those who need it. They "touch the hem of your garment," they touch your consciousness.
- You serve as a beacon which draws others into their own light.
- Your most effective role as helper of others is simply to *be*.

God, my only prayer is to know You. I allow You to lift my soul higher today than ever before. Aware of Your abiding presence within me, I am a blessing to all who cross my path.

Please proceed to Adventure 35 in the Activity Book.

*T*HANKSGIVING | *36*

An attitude of gratitude will smooth the way before you. There are so many things for which to be thankful, once you begin to look.

A grateful heart opens many doors

"Father, I thank thee that thou hast heard me. I knew that thou hearest me always."
—John 11:41-42

Picture the scene. It's a hot, dry day in Bethany. The air is heavy with dust and almost chokes the mournful group of people clinging to each other before the cave which serves as a tomb.

Lazarus, brother of Martha and Mary, has been dead for four days. Jesus stands there with the small band of mourners and weeps for his friend. "If only Jesus had arrived earlier, He could have saved Lazarus," is the word circulating among the group. "But now, now, it is too late."

How it must have dumbfounded Martha and Mary and the others, in the midst of this grieving moment, to hear Jesus suddenly giving thanks to God! What could their reactions have been? What would yours have been? "Father, I thank thee that thou has heard me. I knew that thou hearest me always." What kind of words were these? A man has been lying dead in his tomb for four days and now his friend is giving thanks!

But any surprise or bewilderment no doubt quickly turned to awe as Jesus, with His next breath, cried out for Lazarus to come forth out of the tomb. The atmosphere must have been electric as the mourners watched in utter astonishment as the dead man, still wrapped in his burial cloth, came out to them.

The power of the moment, the extreme emotional mixture of joy, shock, and disbelief, must have been beyond our imagination. Lazarus was alive! And the catalyst which had made it all happen, the key which had opened the passageway from death to life, was Jesus' prayer of thanksgiving.

FAN THE FLAME

It's interesting to muse about that incident and imagine how it all came about and what eventually happened to the people involved. Surely their lives were changed forever by the experience. How could they not have been? Yet in their quiet reflections of reliving the scene and thinking about it in the years which followed, every one of those who had been present must have realized that it was the simple prayer, the giving of thanks, which set the "miracle" into motion. "Father, I thank thee that thou hast heard me."

Thanksgiving isn't just words, however. Jesus' words represented the feelings in His heart. His thanksgiving was a verbal description of feelings He had for God. In thanking God, He was acknowledging that God's desire for Him and for Lazarus was only good. The feeling of thanksgiving is an emotion, a visceral reaction, and not an idea.

We can intellectualize about all of the things we have in our lives for which to be grateful. We can make lists, long lists, of the innumerable reasons we should give thanks. This is good, because it helps us realize just how extremely blessed we are. We all have something, *many* things, for which to give thanks.

Still the lists, the realizations, the words, are not enough. They are only helpful if they lead us into that *feeling* of thanksgiving. We need the feeling, the inner fullness of a grateful heart in order to tap that power within us.

We learned a long time ago in our journey together on *The Quest* that strong emotions will overpower an intellectual idea virtually every time. *Feelings* activate the powers which make the changes and do the work. Feelings are the catalyst and the sustaining fuel of our actions. When feelings cease, action ceases. In fact, you would not even continue walking across a room if you didn't *feel* like doing it.

It is your responsibility, then, to ignite the feeling of thanksgiving in yourself. It is nothing anyone can give you, or anything you can take in from outside of yourself. While you may be feeling ungrateful because of a present challenge, deep within you are the embers of thanksgiving, waiting to be fanned into full blaze. With enough fanning, an attitude of gratitude will easily become a habit.

PEOPLE, PLANTS, AND ANIMALS RESPOND
We have seen how sincerely expressing

thanksgiving, as Jesus did at the tomb of Lazarus, unlocks the door to seemingly impossible over-comings. Whether dealing with people, animals, or plants, when someone or something is appreciated and praised, the best is brought forth.

Words and feelings of thankfulness and praise cause people, adults and children alike, to reach higher and to express more of their true Christ natures. Praising animals and showing thanks by rewarding them with treats and loving pats reinforce their good behavior and encourage them to do even more. Plants, too, respond to loving words of praise and thanksgiving by growing stronger and more rapidly.

All forms of life really love to hear the truth about themselves, which is that they are radiant expressions of the eternal God. Even the cells of our bodies respond and regenerate when they are told that they are appreciated and loved. "Thank you for bringing me health and strength. Thank you for your intelligence which knows what to do and how to do it. I love you and I bless you as you radiate new life throughout my body."

Myrtle Fillmore, co-founder of Unity, regained her health through this method. Told that she had a terminal condition, she began blessing and thanking each organ of her body, praising the intelligence within it, and encouraging it to come forth into new life. Try thanking your cells regularly and see how eagerly they respond with increased health.

You know from your own experience how well you respond to appreciative words and feelings from anyone. We all want to be appreciated. What's more, we all deserve it because we all are special creations of God, all part of the Divinity. It comes back to the idea of seeing the Christ within ourselves and others and being grateful for that Presence.

THANKFULNESS MULTIPLIES YOUR GOOD

Most of all, we should express our thankfulness to God, because it helps us to recognize and accept more of the God activity in our lives.

Do you want to know God more and to allow the perfect plan for your life to present itself to you? Then praise and thank God now. Do you want more wholeness in your physical body? Then praise the evidence of life and health which you already have, for the divine intelligence within your cells will be encouraged to create even greater wholeness and well-being. Do you want more prosperity? Bless and give thanks for whatever resources you do have, and they will multiply in new and creative ways.

GIVING THANKS ON THE HIGH ROAD

You are traveling higher and higher in your journey now, lightening your load of old, stale, and outdated attitudes and behavior. The demons and dragons which inhabited the forests at the beginning of the trail are not real threats to you anymore. While now and then the dim echo of a fearsome cry may ring out across the valley of your soul some starless night, it is only an echo after all and you rise up with an overwhelming sense of joy and thanksgiving. Life is good. God is good. Give thanks that the best is yet to be.

*M*ile markers

- It is your responsibility to ignite the feeling of thanksgiving in yourself.

- People, animals, plants, and even the cells of our bodies respond in a positive manner to sincere words and feelings of appreciation and praise.

- All forms of life love to hear the truth about themselves: that they are radiant expressions of the eternal God.

- Thankfulness multiplies the good you already have.

Thank You, God, for hearing me. I know You always hear me, and that You meet my every need. I give thanks for all of my blessings, and my only prayer is to know You more.

Please proceed to Adventure 36 in the Activity Book.

$\mathcal{A}$ RANDOM WALK

We have arrived at a place of peace and gentle beauty. It has no geographical location other than within our minds. It is a state of consciousness. Although our trail has been leading us higher and higher, we stand now on a level ground which seems to invite us to rest and relax for a time.

The air is clean and sweet with clover here. The sun shines every day, and the only sounds are the cheerful songs of birds and the occasional hum of a honeybee as it busily goes about its work among the flowers.

Flowers are everywhere in this high mountain meadow. Wildflowers, they are, children of the wind which had dropped them there as seeds.

The past twelve weeks have taken us into the elusive land of forgiveness and love and divine guidance. We moved among the teachings of how to overcome fear, how to live in the now, what it really means to be a child of God and how to judge rightly. From there, the trail turned sharply upward as we entered into the areas of Spirit, the Jesus Christ presence, good relationships, and help for others. Just before coming upon this mountain meadow miles above our base camp, we filled our hearts with such thanksgiving that our feet barely touched the forest floor beneath them. Such lightness do we feel, such buoyancy, that we can skip across this grassy lea as if we were weightless spiritual beings, which, of course, is exactly what we are.

So we leave you here for one week's time. This is your week to rest and do whatever pleases your soul. The Spirit of God within you does Its work regardless, and the rich teachings will be absorbed into your very tissues even as you play.

Rest well. Leave your Guide Book and your Activity Book in your travel pack for the next seven days and just enjoy the beauty and serenity of this high mountain meadow. After the week is over, we will rejoin you for the final leg of our journey together.

*W*ELCOME BACK!

Hello once again, friend.

Are you as eager as we are to get started on these final twelve weeks of our journey on *The Quest*?

Some of the mountain flowers haven't yet opened their faces to the new day, and the dew still coats each blade of grass with tiny silver beads. Yet the birds' songs echo their morning music all around us, and it is not too early for us to start out.

Let's hold each other's hand as we step up onto the high trail just ahead and continue on our journey of spiritual rediscovery.

*Prosperity could very
well be the easiest of
God's laws to prove.
You can test it for
yourself.*

Your streets are paved with gold

*"Give, and it will be given to you; good measure,
pressed down, shaken together, running over,
will be put into your lap. For the measure you
give will be the measure you get back."*
—Luke 6:38

It often happened that an old-time sailing ship,
exploring and trading in new lands, would find itself
becalmed in the doldrums just east of South America.
A Spanish galleon could sit for days or even weeks,
baking in the torrid tropic sun off the coast of what is
now Brazil. With their ship unable to move in the
windless sea, unable to reach land and a supply of
fresh water, the men were doomed to dehydration.

Sometimes a local vessel would drift near one of
these pitiful ships. The appeal from the dying sailors
was always the same: "Please, give us some of your
water!"

At this, the local seamen would deliver an amazing piece of information: they were sitting in the mouth of the mighty Amazon where it empties into the sea. This river is so vast that its water extends two-hundred miles out into the Atlantic. Although they couldn't see land, the ship with its crew dying of thirst was adrift in *fresh* water! All they had to do was lower their buckets over the side. They believed themselves to be helplessly in need, but they were literally surrounded by exactly what it was that they needed.

ADRIFT AND HELPLESS

We don't have to be at sea to feel adrift and help-less. There are times when we think there is no way out of the lack into which we've gotten ourselves. Those are the exact times when we have to stop and re-examine the situation and adjust our thinking to the truth: if God's will for us is absolute good, then prosperity (having our needs met) is everyone's right by divine inheritance.

As children of God, we are created to have an abundance of all things, whatever we feel we need in order to be comfortable so that we can proceed with our spiritual development. This abundance includes plentiful opportunities for creative expression so that we live fulfilling and satisfying lives.

We do not prosper because God throws money at us or leaves it under our pillows while we sleep. Prosperity comes through God's creative ideas when we are awake or even in our dreams when we are sleeping. It is those *ideas* which we can then trans-late into the actions which will bring us prosperity. The more in tune we are with God the more opportunities for prosperity come to us, whether it's an exciting idea, being at the right place at the right time, or meeting the people who can help us. When we are continually aware of the presence of God within us, good things happen!

OLD BELIEFS

The old belief was that there is not enough abundance to go around, and so we thought if you get yours, I lose mine. If I get some abundance, I have to deprive you of yours. We have believed that people are constantly waiting out there to take our good from us. We thought that there is only so much substance in this world, and therefore it can be used up.

The human race has had it all wrong. We have to re-educate ourselves so that we firmly realize that God's source of good is unlimited. God, by nature, is a creative process, always capable of (and desirous of) bringing new and more into our lives.

The key to prosperity is the realization that prosperity doesn't come by getting more. It comes by giving more. The law of prosperity is actually 180 degrees from what most of us have been taught. We prosper not by concentrating on what we are getting but by emphasizing what we are giving. There is simply no way to circumvent this law, and it may take a quantum shift in your thinking to bring yourself around to the truth.

But once you do this and you grasp the exciting concept that you can only truly prosper when you give, the law of prosperity will be very easy for you to prove. In fact, it works so quickly that at first you may be tempted to dismiss your results as merely coincidence.

PROSPERITY IS GOOD

A second old belief which has to be changed is the idea that it is wrong to be prosperous. Have you ever felt guilty and apologetic for enjoying God's abundance? Have you ever felt apologetic about buying a new car or a bigger house in a nicer neighborhood? Perhaps you have believed that it is pious to be poor and a sin to be rich.

The truth, in fact, is quite the opposite. Remember, God's will for us is absolute good and that means God *wants* us to prosper. Jesus never preached poverty, although He certainly taught that we should put the proper perspective on money and possessions. You will not find any suggestion of possessions being a bad thing anywhere in the Scriptures. On the contrary, Jesus preached that all of our needs must be met. It is the "Father's good pleasure to give you the kingdom" (Lk. 12:32). (What a beautiful legacy!) Jesus Himself lived a life-style which required few possessions, but there's no indication that He was ever in need. In fact, you will recall that He wore a seamless robe. This was a specially made and very expensive garment, so valuable that lots were cast for it when He died.

So, it's important that we get rid of those old, erroneous beliefs about the evil of prosperity. They have no foundation in truth and will, if embraced, keep our good from us, and that good, that abundance, is our right. It is part of our birthright as children of God to have our needs met.

DIFFERENT NEEDS

This is not to say that all of our needs are the same. What one person needs in order to be

comfortable in his or her present state of consciousness can be vastly different from that of another person. Each of us has a unique abundance quota. A
monk in a priory has very simple material needs, for
instance. He might be quite satisfied with some books,
his daily food, and a Spartan room in which to sleep.
The great composer Richard Wagner, on the other
hand, insisted he could not create music (let alone
survive!) without velvet clothes, lavish furnishings,
sumptuous meals, and a palatial dwelling in which to
house it all.

With his simple needs met, the monk is able to
devote himself to a fulfilling life of prayer and service
to God and others. With his extravagant needs met,
Wagner was able to devote himself to the creation of
some of the most soul-satisfying music the world has
known. Our own needs, no doubt, fall somewhere in-
between those two extremes.

The point is that we each define prosperity for ourselves as that amount which allows us to be free to pursue our spiritual imperatives, free to develop our souls
without fear of not having our most basic needs met.

There is a craving deep within all of us to attain a
greater spiritual awareness. Often we cannot identify
this craving, this void we feel, and so we try to fill the
emptiness with "things." If you've tried that, you know
it doesn't work. No matter how many material possessions we own, they, in themselves, do not satisfy.
They can never satisfy and so the sense of emptiness
grows larger and more pressing as we get caught up in
a frenzy of buying and accumulating in order to satisfy
an ache that grows even larger with each purchase and
each disappointment. We try to quell the sense of lack
by acquiring even more, but it is never the answer.

The void is a spiritual yearning that only Spirit can fill.

WHERE TO START

Prosperity is not something you sit around and wait for. Like the fresh water of the Amazon, it already exists. In order to "make it happen" in your world, you must first of all be aware of it. Then ask for it by presenting a consciousness of prosperity to the universe.

What is a good way to start? Thank God *beforehand* for what you want. Everything you need is already part of your divine inheritance, but you just haven't accepted all of it yet.

Jesus thanked God in advance on numerous occasions. Jesus was also a great practitioner of starting with what you have. When He fed the five thousand, He started with only a few fish and a few loaves of bread, hardly enough to feed a crowd of thousands. He began with what He had, gave thanks for it, and used it wisely. Perfect advice for us today if we want to demonstrate prosperity in our lives: begin with what you have, give thanks for it, and use it wisely. More will be given to you when you need it.

GIVING IS MORE THAN TITHING

Whenever the subject of prosperity comes up, the subject of tithing is sure to follow. The Old Testament teaches the principle of giving back to God ten percent of your assets. Many people are faithful ten percent tithers and know that it is a vital part of their abundance.

With the appearance of Jesus, however, the emphasis on the *letter* of the law has been replaced with an emphasis on the *spirit* of the law. Love and kindness replace obligation and fear. Turning the other cheek replaces an eye for an eye. Rather than give ten percent because it is an obligation, how much better and more meaningful to give from the heart just because it feels good to give, whether it's ten or five or twenty percent! Once you get into the habit of lovingly and unconditionally giving to support the source of your spiritual nourishment, and you see the phenomenal flow of abundance which continually comes to you, you will automatically desire to give.

It seems to be a law of creation that we are meant to return a portion to the universe. We are dealing here with principles that work. It is like the law of gravity. Step off the top of a building and you always get the same result. Plant one seed and it will yield many fruits. Lovingly and unconditionally give of your assets, financially as well as time and assistance wherever you can, and the results again will always be the same: more abundance. All of nature operates this way, and we are meant to operate this way too.

If you are living with the laws and working with them, you can trust them completely, because they are infallible. Yet how can you expect to prosper if you are not practicing prosperity laws?

Support the source of your spiritual nourishment, where you are being spiritually fed. It could be a place of worship, an uplifting author or publication, a television ministry, or an inspirational group. These are some examples of where you might be finding your spiritual food. Wherever you are fed is where you should give your support.

FURTHER CONSIDERATIONS

Forgiveness, too, is essential to permanent

abundance.   By self-forgiveness, we get rid of our guilt, and by forgiving others (actually recognizing that there is nothing to forgive in the first place), we get rid of anger and resentment.   A mind cleansed of such emotions opens us to receive our good.

The principle of cleansing states that we must get rid of what we don't want so that we have room for what we need.   We get rid of the lesser to make room for the greater.   There must always be a continual intake as well as outlet in life.   Imagine not being able to breathe out after we inhaled?   The Dead Sea in Galilee is a wonderful example of what happens if there is not a giving out.   It takes in fresh water but it has no outlet, and so it is briny and will not support life.   It is dead.   We, too, become "dead" if we do not continually give.

We live in an opulent universe, friend.   God's nature is to forever create newness and abundance for us, so that all our needs are met.   We can never run out of supply when we look to the true source of our abundance.   The source of our prosperity is not a certain job or a certain person.   They are only *channels* through which prosperity can come.   There are unlimited channels through which God works, and we must never restrict ourselves to thinking we can only survive and prosper if our good comes through one particular channel, be it a job, or a payment due you, or a rich uncle.

We are ever in the richness of universal Source. Like the becalmed mariners, all we have to do is become aware that we are in the midst of our supply right where we are.   Recognize God as your unlimited Source, bless what you have, and lovingly give.   You are the rich child who inherits the kingdom.

$\mathcal{M}$ ile markers

- Prosperity is your right by divine inheritance.
- True prosperity comes not through getting but through giving.
- You do not deprive someone else when you prosper, as the Source is unlimited.
- It is not sinful or impious to have your needs abundantly met.
- Material possessions can never satisfy your soul's yearning to be filled.
- Giving thanks in advance helps to multiply the good you already have.
- It is necessary to lovingly and unconditionally share your good with the source of your spiritual nourishment.
- Forgiveness is necessary for prosperity.
- You live in an opulent universe, a sea of prosperity. Use what you have, share what you have, and give thanks.

*I see abundance everywhere I look.
Opportunities for new good flow toward
me daily, and I acknowledge You, God,
as my true Source of good. Thank You,
God, for the blessings in my life and
for the security of knowing that all my
needs are met.*

Please proceed to Adventure 37 in the Activity Book.

You are a spiritual being, but you are living in a physical world. That means there are certain rules you have to observe.

Render unto Caesar

"Render therefore to Caesar the things that are Caesar's, and to God the things that are God's."
—Matthew 22:21

"Ouch!" Stub your toe, and you'll cry out in pain. Lose a dear friend, and there will be a great emotional hurt. Be in great need of something, and you feel a visceral yearning. But wait just a second, that doesn't sound very "spiritual," does it?

We have been saying that we are so much more than the flesh and blood and bone and sinew that make us up. We are infinitely more. In fact, the real of us transcends our physicality and roots itself deeply in our divinity. Yet if the real of us transcends our physical self, why the pain and the hurt and the yearnings?

The answer is that we are spiritual beings living in a physical body, inhabiting a physical world. Since we live in a physical world, we must obey the laws of that physical world.

There is a great order in the universe. We live in a cosmos—orderly, harmonious, and whole. It follows specific laws. The same physical laws that apply to the orbits of the stars in the farthest reaches of space apply just as compellingly to the orbits of the electrons in the atoms of our cells. The universe needs laws to survive, and it is incumbent on us to learn and to obey these laws if we are to survive.

These laws are universal. The elemental hydrogen burning in the farthest sun is the same as the hydrogen in every water molecule in your body. The iron in the bowels of the earth is the same as the iron in your hemoglobin molecules, assisting in the delivery of oxygen to your waiting cells. The iodine in the depths of the ocean is the same as the iodine in your thyroid gland, helping to beat out the tempo of metabolism.

So the question becomes, how can I—a spiritual being—be under the influence of physical laws? Aren't physical laws lower laws than spiritual laws?

ONLY GOD'S LAWS

In fact, they are not! There is no hierarchy of laws. We may tend to think that there is a realm called "physical laws," and that these laws are subservient to "mental laws," and that these mental laws are subordinate to "spiritual laws," but this is not the case. The "physical" laws of physics and chemistry and biology and nutrition and medicine are as much a part of God's laws as is the most sublime theological insight. There are no "physical," "mental," and "spiritual" laws. There are only God's laws. Nature—God—is not in conflict with Itself.

Those laws which we have identified, we call "physical laws," and we accept them as normal. Thus seeing a comet or an eclipse of the sun is easily explainable and fun to watch. Hearing a human voice from around the world over a telephone is the most normal of occurrences. Seeing a figure on a small TV screen is certainly not a spectacular feat. The physical laws involved in getting a helicopter off the ground may not be understood by many but seeing one flying overhead is certainly taken for granted.

What if we could expose those who lived three thousand years ago to these modern marvels? Would they think these were outworkings of "physical laws"? Comets and eclipses that occurred even hundreds of years ago caused great consternation. Most likely if people living three thousand years ago saw a helicopter flying overhead, they would think that they had offended the gods and would prepare to sacrifice someone in order to appease the gods. To them, hearing someone's voice over a thin wire, seeing a tiny figure in a box, seeing and hearing a "metal bird" in the sky would have been examples of laws higher than physical laws.

In the same sense, mental and spiritual laws are not abrogations of natural laws. They are simply examples of things we cannot yet explain.

For example, if a block of iron were to be placed in the middle of a lake, it would sink. It would be obeying many laws, one of which was the law of gravity. Yet shape that same block of iron into a bowl and now it floats. Does that mean that the laws of equilibrium are higher than the law of gravity? No, not higher, just different.

What about an airplane? An airplane is essentially twenty tons of metal which seems to be defying the law of gravity. But there are other laws it is following when it flies, and they are the laws of aerodynamics. If a plane is in the air, does that mean that the laws of aerodynamics are "higher" than the law of gravity? Certainly not, they are just different. If the laws of aerodynamics were higher than the law of gravity, the airplane would never come down! A good pilot is aware of all of the laws governing flight. He has studied them and is able to manipulate the airplane, not by breaking one law and obeying another, but by cooperating with all of the laws.

DID JESUS USE HIGHER LAWS?

What about Jesus' healings? Weren't they examples of using higher laws? After all, He healed the sick, brought sight to the blind, raised the dead. He must have been utilizing laws higher than those on the physical plane.

Jesus did not use "higher" laws. He used "other" laws. Because He was at one with God and with the universe, He was able to tap into *all* of the laws of the universe. Just because we don't understand exactly how He did His work, let's not be tempted to think that He tapped into an energy that is not available to everyone. Remember His promise: "He who believes in me will also do the works that I do; and greater works than these will he do" (Jn. 14:12).

We can do all the works that Jesus did, that's true, *but we cannot do them unless and until we assume the same consciousness that He had when He did them.* That's an absolutely crucial qualifier.

BOUNDED BY OUR CONSCIOUSNESS

We said in an earlier teaching that *we can only act within the self-imposed boundaries of our present consciousness.* Jesus' consciousness did not have boundaries. His was not limited by what He saw or heard. He saw people who were blind from birth, yet His consciousness was not limited by this physical fact. He saw past the blindness into the perfection. Utilizing laws other than those physical laws which we know, He was able to go beyond what His senses told Him was true to the real essence of what had to be done, and He did it.

OBEYING PHYSICAL LAWS

There are laws of nutrition and exercise and right thinking that affect our body temples. We may think we are above obeying these laws, that we can eat whatever we want and not exercise and engage in stressful thinking and destructive habits and then pray our way to health.

But isn't this putting God to a foolish test? Remember the allegory of the devil's taking Jesus up to the pinnacle of the temple and saying, "If you are the Son of God, throw yourself down" (Mt. 4:6), claiming that if He were really the Son of God that the angels would save Him. Jesus refused, saying that this was a foolish test of God (and probably of the law of gravity too!).

It's so tempting for us after we've had a spiritual insight to feel that we are somehow exempt from the natural laws of the physical world. Yet until our consciousness expands beyond a reliance on only those laws, we will have to pay attention to them.

Praying for the healing of a faulty heart while

continuing to smoke cigarettes is putting God to a foolish test. Praying for weight loss while continuing to eat two desserts at each meal is putting God to a foolish test. Praying for love in your life while continuing to hold hatred or unforgiveness toward another is putting God to a foolish test.

PUSHING AT YOUR BOUNDARIES

Becoming more spiritually aware does not exempt you from physical laws. It puts you in touch with more of God's laws. In learning and utilizing those laws, you are then able to accept more of God's good.

Rather than trying to outmaneuver God's laws, doesn't it make better sense to gently push at the boundaries of your present consciousness, to expand it so that you can incorporate all of the laws of God's universe into your life?

Rather than accepting a minimum wage and minimum health and minimum love, doesn't it make better sense to expand your consciousness so that you can open yourself to accept more of these gifts from God?

The spiritual journey is done through the course of daily living. You can't achieve a higher destiny except by working in your life with the events and circumstances that present themselves. Your life is a perfect laboratory for your unfoldment. Don't resist—rejoice. In you is the power to change yourself—surrender to it.

There are laws governing the universe. In that understanding is your freedom.

$\mathcal{M}$ile markers

- You are more than your physical body.
- The laws of the universe apply to the atoms of your body.
- There is no hierarchy of laws. There are only God's laws.
- Jesus did not use "higher" laws; He used "other" laws.
- You can only act within the self-imposed boundaries of your present consciousness.
- In learning and utilizing God's laws, you are able to accept more of God's good.

Thank You, God, for the gift of physical life. Reveal to me ways in which I can learn and obey Your laws which will nurture and sustain me in this physical world. I know You have given me a body for a reason, and I make the commitment to honor and protect it. Thank You, God, for physical life.

Please proceed to Adventure 38 in the Activity Book.

*Every time you
seek to get well,
you are doing the
will of God.*

You can be healed

"Do you want to be healed?" —John 5:6

In the past few weeks you have taken into your body over a quadrillion atoms. That's how incredibly changing and new your physical body is.

Every part of you is continually being replaced, some parts completely new every few days. The lining of your intestines, for instance, is virtually new every three days. Each atom of the entire body is replaced over and over and over in a perpetual dance of resurrected life.

With all of these replacement atoms and given the fact that we're so continually new, the obvious question is, Why do the old symptoms of illness remain? It's a logical question, the answer to which is the key to all healing.

NEW IDEAS BRING NEW RESULTS

Each day thousands upon thousands of thoughts issue forth from our minds. How remarkable are these minds of ours. Perhaps even more remarkable is that about 99 percent of today's thoughts are exactly the same as yesterday's. (This is something we learned in an earlier chapter.) So here we are with the ability to step into something new, with a field chock-full of possibilities, and we usually choose to stay rooted in the old belief patterns which no longer serve us well. (If we analyze them, perhaps they never did!)

Rather than fearing the unknown and its marvelous frontier of new and transforming thought patterns, we may be better off fearing the *known*, with its rigid ideas and outdated thought patterns, for they are what may have gotten us into trouble.

Why do the old physical patterns remain? Because the old mental and emotional patterns are unchanged. All of that fresh, new influx of atoms teeming with every possibility, and we end up pouring it into the same old molds—new wine in old wineskins. The body has no choice but to conform to the patterns provided and we, sons and daughters of the living God, are the providers of those patterns. Our bodies are fields of ever-changing patterns which *we* control with our thoughts and feelings and willingness to open ourselves to Spirit.

WHAT DO YOU WANT?

When someone came to Jesus for healing, Jesus often asked, "Do you want to be healed?" It seems like a foolish question. After all, the person had approached Jesus with healing in mind. But the question is not as foolish as it might seem, because there are many of us who think we want to be well yet do not believe in and expect wholeness at the deepest level of our beings.

"Do you want to be healed?" translates into "Do you want to exorcise your belief in and expectation of illness? Do you want to banish the ghosts of disease patterns at the quantum level—a level beyond the tissues, the cells, and even the atoms—a level touched and known only in the silent empty spaces beyond all physical matter?" The new awareness of wholeness is what changes one's beliefs and, subsequently, the patterns we provide for the new cells which continually are born in us.

CANCEL THE SUBSCRIPTION

There are scores of techniques for healing—some new, some old. There is probably some validity to all of them, and each has its roster of people who have been healed by following it. It used to puzzle us, the authors, how so many very diverse methods could each bring about a cure for the same malady. Upon deeper investigation, we realized that all techniques have one thing in common: they bring about a shift in awareness in the person. A change in belief patterns takes place on the most basic level of existence. The very core of that person is outfitted with a new pattern, a new mold, into which new life is poured. The old, outworn pattern is simply not reused. Its subscription, so to speak, has run out and it will not be renewed. It is replaced with something else.

What is that "something else"? It is an awareness that the life-force, the Spirit of God within us, provides us with exactly what we ardently expect at the deepest level. Unless that basic awareness is changed, modern medicine and scientific techniques as well as any alternatives will merely be stopgap measures because the old patterns are still there expecting to be filled. No matter how many different ingredients we put into our waffle batter, if we pour it into the same waffle iron it will always look the same.

A new awareness that we have the power to change the pattern—just that awareness alone—will bring about new faith, a new mold, and the physical body has no other option than to follow it into wholeness.

ALL IS RIGHT

Are you in need of physical healing, friend? Speak to the organs, tissues, and cells of your body, praising and encouraging them with words and feelings and thoughts of radiant life. See them shouting for joy, eager to do your bidding of health and wholeness. Your body loves to hear the truth about itself, which is that it has power to resurrect and become filled with new life.

Secondly, work at becoming aware that you have the ability to change any pattern that is not part of God's will for you, and that this awareness in itself is enough to call forth the healing forces within each cell. This is the awareness which Jesus Christ had, and which He evoked in others. If you do not have this awareness, pray for it.

When all is said and done, the essence of healing is the simple awareness, the joyful expectation of only good, the unwavering feeling that, in spite of any apparent condition, everything—*everything*—is all right!

Mile markers

- All of the atoms of your body are continually being replaced by new ones.
- Old disease patterns keep replicating themselves when the old thought patterns stay the same.
- All healing techniques serve to bring about a change in consciousness, which means a new expectancy of wholeness.
- What you expect at the deepest level is what you get.
- Your body loves to hear the truth about itself.
- Your body cannot help but respond to an awareness of and an expectancy of wholeness.

The cells of my body shout for joy as they resurrect into new life. God's powerful healing presence touches every atom of my being, calling forth a radiant wholeness, and I am healed. Thank You, God.

Please proceed to Adventure 39 in the Activity Book.

You didn't begin when you entered this world. Your soul is on an eternal journey.

Have I lived before?

"Whoever drinks of the water that I shall give him will never thirst; the water that I shall give him will become in him a spring of water welling up to eternal life." —John 4:14

Isn't the view of life getting more and more spectacular with each day of our journey? Let's stop here for a while by that sign marked, "Scenic Overlook."

As you stand out on this belvedere of higher consciousness, you can almost see forever. To the right and to the left, in every direction, the endless panorama of life stretches into eternity. You grasp the sense that this present life is but a moment in time, part of a seamless continuum with no beginning and no end.

We speak of the ongoing of a soul after it leaves this physical plane. Something placed within the heart of humans, since humans came upon the scene, has told us that we never really die, that our true identity is immortal. Our persistent desire to live is, perhaps in itself, a proof of our individual survival.

Many of us believe in an eternal life as it applies to the future. We believe that we will continue to live after death. But not all of us see eternal life, if it is truly eternal life, as endless life—that it is eternal on both ends, past and future, before our birth and after our death.

LIFE BEFORE LIFE?

Where was the soul before it was born in a physical body? Have we been here before? Accepting the existence of the soul prior to its earthly appearance seems as logical as accepting its existence after it departs from its earthly sojourn.

Jesus referred to the pre-existence of the soul when He said, "Before Abraham was, I am" (Jn. 8:58). If we can get the picture of life as an unbroken circle, with the earthly experience as merely one segment of that circle, we can start to see the unending aspect of us all.

The question—from where do we come and where do we go?—is fascinating as well as basic to each of us, and believing in an endless soul journey, open at both ends, does seem to answer many questions.

Since we never know exactly where the soul has been or what secrets it brings with it, we cannot fully know or understand the motives of another person. We do not know what soul needs are brought into this earthly existence, needs which must eventually be met or transmuted or resolved in some way.

There are countless examples of special talents and abilities and prior knowledge which appear to have no source in the person's present existence. The idea of a prior life (or lives) seems the most satisfying explanation for many otherwise unexplainable phenomena.

It is not part of our journey together on *The Quest* to learn or speculate about past lives and pre- or postexistence, however. If such is your interest, you may explore this later on your own. *The Quest* is involved with life right here, right now. This is more than enough material with which to structure your transformation.

As a part of God, that which we are eternally had no beginning nor does it have any end. It is really enough for us to know—that life persists, that it is indeed eternal—and then to get on with the life that we are experiencing in the here and now. We are always greater than what we express, and the purpose of our life is to express more and more of what we eternally are. We do that by living each moment of life as a joyful song of exultation to God. Like the traveler, Christian, in John Bunyan's *The Pilgrim's Progress*, we view each event in our journey as stages of an unfolding spiritual process.

THE PLAN FOR PERMANENCE

Living life on the "high wire"—following that path which brings us the most bliss, being divinely guided and whole and prosperous and the best that we can be—this is a project worthy of our finest attention. This is the fulfillment of God's plan for us.

Since it is the will of God for us to be well and strong, since the creative process of the universe

(God) is always moving in the direction of newer and better, and since the life-force (God) continually is at work within us to heal and perfect us, could it be possible that we are intended to remain permanently in this physical milieu?

When you consider the journey life has taken from its earliest beginnings as single cells up to the present inscrutably complex beings called human-kind, one might quite easily conclude that since it is moving inexorably in the direction of improvement, life is meant to be lasting.

Unthinkable? Outrageous?

The idea is worth considering, if not now, then sometime in the future. When a person can link up strongly with the idea of oneness with God and the idea that what God creates, God can and does main-tain, and the idea that God actually lives through us, the life within that person is quickened and regener-ated. It then becomes a small step to the belief that since God put us into a human form and loves us so infinitely, perhaps—just perhaps—God wants us to stay around!

THE BODY RADIANT

The idea of eternal life in the physical body raises many issues, of course. It would have to be a well body, engaged in useful and soul-satisfying activities. A physical life which would last indefinitely would have to be able to sustain harmonious and loving relationships, be a radiating center of peace so that people everywhere would live without war or rivalry and be a faithful steward of our planet and even be-yond.

We have a way to go before we reach this ideal

state, but physical permanence is, possibly, the direction in which life is moving.

Yet regardless of what you think about the idea, the fact remains that here and now you have been given the gift of physical life by God. Cherish that life, because it is part of God. Perhaps it is the ultimate gift which God can give.

$\mathcal{M}$ile markers

• Accepting the existence of the soul prior to its earthly appearance seems as logical as accepting its existence after it departs from its earthly sojourn.

• Since we never know exactly where the soul has been or what secrets it brings with it, we cannot fully know or understand the motives of another person.

• The idea of a prior life (or lives) seems the most satisfying explanation for many otherwise unexplainable phenomena. Physical permanence, possibly, is the direction in which life is moving.

Dear God, I know that I am on an eternal journey. While I don't know the past or future steps of my immortal soul, I know that I am ever traveling safely within You. There is no place that I can go where You are not, and my heart sings with joy and praise that I am part of You.

Please proceed to Adventure 40 in the Activity Book.

Jesus gave this teaching as a "how-to" for those who are ready to experience transcendence.

The strangest paradox of all

"Whoever exalts himself will be humbled, and whoever humbles himself will be exalted."
—Matthew 23:12

"There is only one Presence and one Power in this universe ... *and I'm not It!*" Herein lies the secret to humility.

Whether we wield power as a parent, a boss, a judge, the President of the United States, or an absolute dictator, if we claim that power as a *personal* power, we are believing a lie.

We have no personal power. We may think we have, but there is only one Power and that is God-power. All else is evidence of this one Power.

Think of a waterwheel. It may seem to have a power of its own as it generates electrical energy, but, in reality, it is evidence of the power of the mighty river that flows through it. It humbly accepts its role of being a channel of the flow. Yet, to the degree that it were to separate itself from the river, it would lose power. Similarly, if we claim any power as our own, we become powerless to the degree that we separate ourselves from God.

HUMILITY BEGETS POWER

True humility is the absence of false pride. It is complete authenticity. Strange as it seems, the more humble you become, the more potential for power you actually have. (The more the waterwheel allows the river to flow through it, the more power it transmits.)

Humility is allowing the Christ within to express what you are to the world, rather than making that assertion yourself. While it may seem to be a power-less state, there is unlimited potential in true humil-ity—great power in genuine authenticity—because you are not limiting yourself to your worldly assets. You are, instead, tapping into the rich resources that are your gifts from God.

As an example, let's say you wanted to exalt your-self. What is the absolute highest you could hope for—Supreme Ruler of the World? Even if you were to become supreme ruler of the world, so what? You would be the unchallenged master of a trivial planet revolving around a minor star in an insignificant galaxy of trillions of stars in a universe of billions of galaxies. That would be the most exaltation you could hope for, but on the other hand, to become humble is to be exalted as part of That which *made* those billions of galaxies.

"GAINING" THE WORLD

Sound foolish? After all, it's what happens in the

world that counts, isn't it? History seems to imply that the world belongs to the strong, not the weak. It is replete with examples of powerful and aggressive leaders whose impact was worldwide: Alexander the Great, Julius Caesar, Ivan the Terrible, Napoleon, Hitler, Stalin—these men are not what one would call shrinking violets! Yet at what price were their conquests? "What shall it profit a man, if he shall gain the whole world, and lose his own soul?" (Mk. 8:36 KJV)

And, in truth, these dictators never did "gain" the world. They never even possessed their piece of conquered land. The fact is that they had to victimize people to get what they got and had to fight to keep what they temporarily possessed. If we must victimize someone to get something and fight to keep it, it's not really ours. This applies to a possession, to a job, to a relationship, to finances.

In seeking to transcend our problems, we may feel that we should be able to use God's power to overcome our circumstances. Humility, however, doesn't use anyone or anything. It allows. Humility is getting ourselves out of the way so that God can be more active in us! The more God is involved, the less problems will appear in our lives, because problems do not exist in God's world!

So rather than striving for power, isn't it better to strive for humility? Rather than striving to be *somebody*, isn't it better to strive only to be yourself? Who could be better at being you than you? If you are dissatisfied with what you are, it is not a spiritual dissatisfaction. It is really a dissatisfaction with what you have allowed yourself to become. Humility puts you back on track.

Humility is an admission to yourself that God did a better job than you did and that you want to reclaim your true identity. Humility is simply being yourself. It is the acceptance of the one Presence and one Power that is God in you and in the world.

Since humility is the key to *releasing* the one Presence and one Power that God is, humility then becomes the only road to *true* power. When you admit to yourself your true powerlessness, when you get yourself out of the way, you are automatically putting yourself in touch with the power of God in you, allowing it to move through you.

THE START OF A NEW UNIVERSE

Truly you are made in the image and in the likeness of your Creator. God created you for a specific reason, and you are important to God's plan.

If you strut upon the stage of life clanging cymbals and banging drums, flaunting diamonds and gold, flashing your social status—all this just to be noticed—what have you gained? Whom have you impressed? What does it matter in this infinitely endless universe what a group of ever-changing atoms called "you" has accomplished? Will it change the brightness of one star, the rotation of one planet, or the position of one moon? Will it even change the color of one blade of grass?

But the realization of your fundamental oneness with God is an explosive idea, the "big bang" that is the origin of your new universe of thinking and acting. It is the creation of a new world—your world. In your humble realization of the Christ within you, the entire universe rejoices.

$\mathcal{M}$ile markers

- You become powerless to the degree that you separate yourself from God.
- True humility is complete authenticity.
- The more humble you become, the more potential for power you actually have.
- If you must cheat to get something and fight to keep it, it isn't yours.
- Humility doesn't use anyone or anything. It allows.
- Humility is simply being yourself.

God, it is You who created me and sustains me, and not I, myself. It is Your power which moves through my mind and body, leading me higher along the path. It is Your presence which stirs my soul and gladdens my heart. Thank You, God, for blessing me so. Yours is the kingdom and the power and the glory forever.

Please proceed to Adventure 41 in the Activity Book.

*Knowing the truth carries
with it an extraordinary
responsibility. Meeting
that responsibility can be
your most rewarding
experience.*

$\mathcal{Y}$our part of the bargain

*"You are the light of the world.... Let your light so
shine before men, that they may see your good
works and give glory to your Father who is in
heaven."* —Matthew 5:14,16

*I stood frozen to the deck of the cruiser, not because
of the temperature—it was July, and we were in the
Mediterranean—but because of the scene before me,
stabbing its way into my soul. I felt an icy chill as the
submarine on which I'd served and which had just
dropped me off pulled away and sped menacingly
toward the horizon. It was a nuclear sub, carrying on
it enough destructive capability to blow our planet
apart. Nuclear submarines—their speed, their stealth,
the deadly potential of their nuclear warheads, had
been my life for the last two decades.*

Like an ominous angel of death, her wake trailing

for miles behind her, she made haste for her next ren-
dezvous point to watch and to wait. Now, the full im-
pact of what I had been so proudly serving cut into me
with a pain I'll carry with me always. "My God, what
have we created? What have I done?" I whispered to
myself as the last trace of her gruesome presence disap-
peared.

That was seven years ago, when I retired from active
duty, but I still feel the same icy chill whenever I recall
that final scene and its despairing message that I had
spent my adult life serving the power of destruction.

Our friend, a former chief petty officer, now devotes
his time and energies to serving the forces of goodness
and love. He movingly related to us how the vision of
that sinister submarine as it fled out of his life had
brought immediately to mind the compelling biblical
command: "Choose this day whom you will serve"
(Josh. 24:15).

WHOM WILL YOU SERVE?

To many of us, the term *serve God* has conjured up
pictures of pious people with hands clasped before
them and eyes looking upward to heaven. Serving God
was something only the "holy" did. What it really
meant was not having any joy or fun and was therefore
only for the more saintly types. But such pictures are
inaccurate. They completely misrepresent what serving God really means.

Each soul must one day come face-to-face with the
question of whom it will serve. Chances are that you
have already answered this question for yourself or are
at least trying to answer it. If you have not, it is time
now that you do.

You have studied the Teachings. You have achieved the realization that there is only God, and that the presence of God is to be found in every person and every situation, no matter what the appearance. You have discovered certain truths which are literally transforming your life and which have the ability to transform the world if put into practice.

Yet simply to know the truth is not enough, for with knowledge comes responsibility. The truth must ultimately be served. You, because you are the custodian of certain truths, have the responsibility to use these truths in your life, not only to lift yourself but to lift others. Having learned these truths, it is now your sacred obligation to serve God in this way.

There are many people who are serving causes of negativity, their own and others. Serving God means devoting our complete attention to the awareness of good. It means using the energy of our thoughts and feelings and words and actions to serve only good.

Although this may sound like a monumental undertaking, it is actually very simple because it is done through the hundreds of choices we make each day. There is not a thing which can stop us from living this way if we decide this is what we want. The only thing which ever holds us to a life of less than serving God is our old patterns of serving negativity, of thinking or acting in a way not consistent with God's will as we know it.

By choosing to serve God each day, we are serving that indwelling nature of God in us and in all people. With enough practice, it eventually becomes unthinkable to serve anything less than good, because we have the full realization that to do so would prevent us from journeying higher on our path.

WITH GAZES FIXED ON GOOD

Let's keep reminding ourselves that the potential for a fulfilling and glorious life is accessible to us this very day. Whatever path each of us took in the past has led us to where we are right now, to serving the good, the God presence of love, in our world.

There is so much evidence of goodness all around us. Let us vow to keep our eyes forever fixed upon the good and find, each day, new ways to serve it. Let us not be dissuaded by anyone or anything or any circumstance. If in the past we have served negativity, let's let it vanish from our sight as did that submarine, so that we need never look at our lives and utter with a sense of despair: "My God, what have I created? What have I done?"

$\mathcal{M}$ile markers

- If you have not yet answered the question of whom to serve, it is now time that you do.
- To *know* the truth is not enough. It must be *served.*
- You have the responsibility to put into practice the truth you know.
- Serving God simply means devoting your full attention to the awareness of good.
- The only thing which can prevent you from serving God is an old pattern of negativity.
- The potential for a glorious life is accessible to you this very day.

I now release all unwanted patterns of thought and emotion. I choose this day to see the good, to let my love radiate to all people, and to be an inspiration to help lift others. God, I choose to serve the truth and live my life to glorify You now.

Please proceed to Adventure 42 in the Activity Book.

*T*RUSTING GOD | *43*

God has a plan for your life which is far beyond anything you can possibly imagine.

God has a plan just for you

"The sheep hear his voice, and he calls his own sheep by name and leads them out." —John 10:3

Many years ago when we began studying spiritual teachings, we discovered that God always has the perfect answer for every situation and should therefore be trusted to reveal the right plan for our lives.

In light of the fact that God is the essence of good and therefore wants good for all of Its creations, it seemed very logical for us to trust that there is a divine order. When we considered that God can totally be relied upon to bring spring each year and to turn the tides each day and to hold the planets in their orbits and constellations in their patterns, it became quite obvious to us that this Creator knows what It's doing.

"Yes, clearly," we decided, "God can be trusted to

bring about the best for all creation." We were convinced. Or were we?

TRUTH WENT OUT THE WINDOW

It wasn't long before a crisis appeared in our lives. What did we do? We reacted to it the old way—with fear, worry, and a good amount of anxiety. After expending a lot of human energy on those negative emotions, which no doubt impeded the natural process of resolving the situation, everything eventually worked out extremely well. Finding our lives back on an even keel again, we resumed our truth studies and admonished ourselves that we really should have trusted God.

Not long after that incident, we found ourselves in the midst of what we thought was another "glitch" in life. What did we do? Why, just as before, we simply forgot all ideas about trusting God and lapsed into the familiar pattern of worry, anxiety, and fear. Once again the natural plan of events took hold and things worked out better than we could have imagined. When the dust settled, we picked up our teachings where we'd left off and went back to trusting God!

Over the course of several years, we again faced situations in our life which had the appearance of being "worthy" of our worry and fear. Each time one of these situations passed, we would berate ourselves for not having trusted God more and vowed that we would never again fall into the old negative reactions. "Next time, for sure, we'll trust."

Gradually, we did. Each new troublesome situation was less anxiety-provoking to us than the previous one. We were able to go for longer and longer periods of holding to our trust in God's creative process before giving way to doubt and worry about the outcome. "There! That proves it. We will never, ever doubt again," we would announce to each other after a perfectly beautiful resolution would occur.

Little by little, we are getting the message—*really* getting the message, deep in our hearts and minds—and are now much more willing to trust God completely to bring about the perfect solution for all concerned.

We can't say it came easily or that it is easy to sustain. It took years of practice, although why that had to be so is a mystery. One would think that such a basic truth would have been the easiest thing in the world to practice. It wasn't easy for us. Hopefully, for you it is or soon will be.

DIVINE ORDER

We are so often programmed with negative responses to events in our lives that it might take some practice to get to the point of completely trusting God to bring about the perfect plan. If you are not now living a life of total trust in God's plan for you, then it is time to get that trust established as soon as possible.

God, the Creator of all, does have a plan for every part of creation. We cannot know specifically what that plan might be. There is really no reason for us to know. What we can be sure of, however, is that there is a divine order to things. By not attempting to predict outcomes, by not fretting about the means of our getting there, we smooth the way for God's plan to reveal itself easily and quickly. Our part is to keep centered on God as the Source of all good, and then to trust, simply trust.

It almost sounds too easy, doesn't it? When faced with situations which seem threatening or even tragic, our human tendency is to allow the flow of appearances to get us involved in a negative way. But the solution to a problem is never to be found on the level of the problem. The only way out is up. Up ... up in consciousness, in thought and feeling, to the level where Spirit dwells, to the level of divine order. We touch that center of God in us, and having contacted it, we feel the assurance that all is well.

BETTER THAN GOOD

The outcome? It is always better (and usually different) than what we expected. If we are truly centered in Spirit, each outcome is exactly what we need at the time, for God knows us better than we know ourselves and always sees the *grande image*, the big picture.

If we view our lives from this broader perspective, we see that each episode along the way, no matter how difficult at the time, has proven to be a stepping-stone to greater good. It was part of the plan of our lives and we, in viewing the overall pattern, can recognize the hand of God present every step of the way. Out of every twist and turn, we've been divinely led further along the pathway to the awareness of God.

Trust God, friend. There is always a divinely perfect solution underlying every challenging situation. No matter how far you have strayed from your good, God knows a direct route back to where your bliss is. Centered in Spirit, you can walk with sureness of foot because the way is prepared before you, and God is making everything, *everything* right.

$\mathcal{M}$ile markers

- It requires diligence and purpose to break free of any habitual old patterns of negative responses.

- God has a perfect plan for your life, but it might take some practice to get the point of completely trusting God to bring about that plan.

- By not investing in a specific outcome, you smooth the way for God's plan to reveal itself easily and quickly.

- When you contact the center of God in you, you feel the assurance that all is well.

- To live your life to the fullest and best, it is imperative that you trust God.

I do not know the answers, God, nor do I know the steps that I should take to get me there. I only want to know You more. My only need is to savor Your sweet presence in my life. I trust, truly trust, that I am in Your care and that all is well. Thank You, God.

Please proceed to Adventure 43 in the Activity Book.

*Would you ever have
thought that you can be
joyful in the midst of any
situation? You can,
because joy is your
natural state.*

Happiness is a God-job

*"These things I have spoken to you, that my joy
may be in you, and that your joy may be full."*
—John 15:11

Stripped of their freedom, their dignity, even their
clothes, the prisoners of the Nazi concentration
camps during World War II had little reason to feel
hope or joy. Separated from their wives and husbands and children, many would never see them
again. Viktor Frankl was one to lose his wife along
with everything else. He remembered the men who
walked through the huts comforting others, giving
away their last piece of bread. He observed, "Everything can be taken from a man but one thing: to
choose one's attitude in any given set of circumstances, to choose one's own way."

In this time we have been together, we have discovered several reversals in the beliefs with which we may have been operating. The truth, we have seen, is often quite the opposite of what we had been taught and what we had been practicing.

The secret of prosperity, for instance, lies not in getting, but in giving. Love warms our hearts, not so much when we are loved as when we are loving. True forgiveness is not in forgiving someone else, but in asking forgiveness of ourselves because we judged another in the first place.

Now we come upon still another "reversal." We will see that true joy is completely independent of what happens to us from the outside. No person or event has any real power to make us happy, and that may come as a surprise to most people because they spend their lives waiting for events and people to change so that things will get better.

To many, it would seem incongruous that joy has nothing whatsoever to do with circumstances. After all, hasn't each of us been guilty at one time or another of saying things like, "If only my marriage were smoother, I would be happy," or "When I get a new job, my life will be great," or "How can you expect me to be happy when I have to take care of my invalid father?" or "Once the kids are out of college and on their own, I'll be able to enjoy my life"?

If we keep looking to the people and events of our lives to supply us with joy, life becomes like a shooting gallery at a carnival where as soon as you succeed in knocking down one target, another one pops up! We can end up trying to "shoot down" one trial after another, never getting a breather and never getting the chance to relax and enjoy life right here, right now. We spend our lives chasing what we envision as happiness only to discover that whatever we may have caught in our nets turns out to be only a temporary stimulation and never lasting joy.

WHERE THE JOY IS

If you had been looking for happiness in people and events, you discovered that it is not there. If you look to outer circumstances for your satisfaction cues, you will stay on an emotional seesaw.

There is the old story of the father who was so happy because he had a son. The son fell off his horse and broke his back, and that made the father sad. Then because of his injury, the son was not called to war, and that made the father happy. Because he didn't go to war, the son married a terrible woman, which made the father sad. Then the son had a child, which made the father happy. And so on, and so on, one event gladdening, one event saddening. This is how most people live their lives, always reacting to whatever pops up and searching for joy in all the wrong places: outer events.

True joy is actually part of your nature. It's built into your very being. Yes, even in spite of outer circumstances which may appear to range anywhere from fair to awful, the experience of joy is always present deep within you. It is not something you take in from without, but something you let out from within you. Events merely give us an excuse to feel it.

No matter what situation you find yourself in, once you make contact with the Christ center at the core of your being, you feel an immediate rush of joy, because you know that you can trust God and that everything is going to be all right. There is no true joy without trusting God, for when you trust God you are aware that, whatever the situation, you are just an observer passing through, that things will work out right for all concerned, and that everything really is okay.

JOY HEALS

When you touch the Christ of your being and can rest for a few moments in that sense of trust and peace which you find there, you automatically come away buoyed up and overflowing with joy. This feeling is totally spontaneous and, as you will discover, has nothing to do with what is happening in your life.

The feeling of true joy is a great harmonizer and healer, not only of inner emotions and human relations but of the physical body as well. In fact, it is this very feeling of inner joy which activates the healing forces by sending the message to your cells that all is well, that good is expected. When the body receives this message, it has no choice but to follow and become whole. You will recall this from *The Quest* Teaching on healing, which spoke of that deep inner knowing that everything is going to be all right. It turns out that it is joy which gives you that sense of all-rightness.

It is true joy which keeps you lifted, in spite of whatever is going on around you. True joy arises out of your contact with the spirit within you. When the contact is made, the joy breaks forth. You have already been proving this for yourself, perhaps without fully knowing what was taking place.

The lives of the great spiritual teachers throughout history have been marked by joy. If one continues to dip into that font of divinity within, the result simply has to be the sense of joy which comes from trusting God.

Joy has been implanted in you from the beginning. No one can give it to you. No one, as Viktor Frankl observed, can take it from you. It is entirely in your own hands. If you are willing to turn inward to that Power which lies at your essence, you cannot help but find joy. It bolsters the soul and strengthens the body.

It is a most precious gift, this gift of joy, to be taken lightly and used frequently. As creations of God, we were meant to live in a state of joy always. As one who is traveling on *The Quest*, you are coming more and more to bear the permanent mark of joy. Recognize it in yourself and celebrate it.

$\mathcal{M}$ile markers

- True joy is completely independent of what happens to you from the outside.
- True joy is part of your nature—built into your very being.
- No matter what situation you find yourself in, once you make contact with the Christ center at the core of your being, you feel an immediate rush of joy.
- True joy comes as a result of trusting God.
- Joy is a harmonizer and a healer.
- It is joy which gives you a sense of all-rightness about your life.

Praise God for the assurance that everything in my life is all right. I am lifted to new heights on wings of joy, and my heart sings as I radiate that joy to everyone I meet.

Please proceed to Adventure 44 in the Activity Book.

*Once you discover your
path, it takes commitment
to stay on it. It is so easy
to get sidetracked.*

Detours only slow you down

> *"Enter by the narrow gate; for the gate is wide and
> the way is easy, that leads to destruction, and
> those who enter by it are many."* —Matthew 7:13

Eyes wide, mouths open, the crowd stared up with
anxious fascination. There was hardly a sound under
the big top. High above the center ring was a high-
wire walker, slowly and carefully making his way from
one side of the arena to the other.

But his goal was not the platform at the far end of
the wire—not at that moment. In that moment and in
each succeeding moment, his goal was the precise
spot where his eyes fell, that next point a few feet
ahead of him on the wire. Pole held firmly in his
hands, he stared, not at his feet, but at the wire
stretched taut in front of him. Nothing distracted
him, nothing could deter him. For the next several

minutes, that was the path he would follow and, in this life-or-death struggle, he dared not let another thing take his attention.

LOOK WHERE YOU'RE LOOKING

What is your path? What are you staring at? Where are your feet taking you? If it is not being true to the Christ in you, be prepared for a fall.

The goal is oneness with God, nothing more, nothing less. The idea is not to aim for healing or prosperity or better relationships or any of the other "things" (noble or deserved as they may be), since their seeming absence is merely a symptom of a deeper problem: a straying from the path. Rather, the goal is the experience of the presence of God in us and in our daily lives. "Tunnel-visioned" toward God, we might say.

THINNING TRAFFIC

Staying on the path requires a strong commitment, and few are interested in making such a commitment. In fact, have you noticed how the further you journey on *The Quest*, the fewer people you encounter along the path?

Once you make the commitment to travel the path, you almost at once observe a thinning out of traveling companions. There is a direct ratio between the degree of your commitment and the number of people traveling in your direction. This is not surprising. The path you have chosen for your life is not, at this stage of collective human progress, a popular one.

At every phase of your journey, you have passed by side roads, into which many other people have turned off. Yet you, in your commitment to your quest for truth and transformation, have chosen to walk the straight path set before you, and that is what has made the difference.

There may seem to be drawbacks to your path. It can feel lonely, because few people understand your thinking and beliefs. They may even try to chide or ridicule you because you do not go along with the ways of the crowd. As Jesus said, the gate is narrow through which you must pass if you wish to enter into the kingdom of God, that kingdom of peace and love and joy which is only to be found within.

DETOURS

The path is teeming with detours, as you probably have discovered. Sometimes in their search for the presence of God, people will venture down all sorts of blind alleys, dead ends, and circuitous roads. Everyone has a hunger for the experience of God, and we will pursue all kinds of paths in order to satisfy that longing in the soul.

We can get caught up in one fruitless trail after another if we are not careful. The detours can be very enticing. Some people become spiritual dilettantes, jumping from one philosophy to another, from one seminar to another, from one fad to another. This can be intellectually stimulating, but it usually is the long way home.

There are systems based on stars or minerals or numbers or the shape of your hands. These paths may beckon you from your path. They are seductive and alluring, but no matter how fascinating or entertaining they are, to the degree that they detour you from the path, they are harmful. This is not to say that the practices themselves are harmful: that is for each of us to decide. But if we allow the position of the stars or the crystalline structure of certain minerals or the manipulation of cards or the creases on our palms to dictate our lives, we have turned from being God-centered to being star-centered or card-centered or whatever.

Astrology, channeling, tarot cards, palm reading, crystals, and other pursuits can be interesting, but if you are on a path that cannot lead *directly* to the Power within you, consider it a detour. It is true that sooner or later all paths will find their way back to God, but why waste time? If your path does not point to God within as the source of guidance and wisdom, it would be wise to consider an alternate route as soon as possible!

"DRAWBACKS" FALL AWAY

Obviously, you have remained faithful to your journey. The fact that you are reading these words right now means you have not succumbed to the lure of detours or, at least if you did, you quickly found your way back to the main trail again.

Hopefully by now you have come to realize that the path, *your* path, has been worth the seeming drawbacks. We know it is not always easy to stand firm in support of your beliefs and your way of life, especially when that stand isolates you from the masses. But eventually the drawbacks melt away, for people come to respect you for your convictions, and they begin to sit up and take notice of your loving, peace-filled manner. Eventually they start to wonder what it is you have, and how they can get some of it!

Finally, the marvelous advantages of staying on the path take precedence in your life, and each day dawns as a bright new opportunity for more joy or more peace or more of whatever aspect of God you may need.

While initially your journey may have seemed to set you apart from many of the people who had been part of your life, you now have begun to draw to you those who support your journey and who walk the same path as you. What an enriching experience this is. Now your life is blessed with people who share with you on the deepest level at which people can share: the spiritual. Life takes on more meaning and more beauty and more of everything good as you progress further and further on the path.

AN ETERNAL PATH

When you have journeyed as far as you have on the path, you develop an inner compass which keeps you on course. There is no turning back now, even if you wanted to, since the truths which you have learned are part of you forever.

For you, there is no other path than the one on which you walk. There may be times when your foot slips, and you temporarily stumble off the path, but it will not be long before you are right back on it again and moving steadily ahead. Once the journey is in your blood, it is there to stay.

Yes, our Trailblazer was right, the gate is narrow through which we enter. It requires dedication and commitment and a clear focus on what you want, which is the experience of the presence of God in your life. Yet having gone through the gate, you now know how glorious the path ahead of you is. It is the path you have chosen because you heard the summons quite some time ago.

Although the ranks thinned out quite early along the way, and it seemed a lonely place to walk, in time, great hordes of people will be venturing onto this same path, because it offers peace and love and deep contentment. Although the saying tells us "all roads lead to Rome," the truth is that, no matter what the twists and what the turns, all roads eventually lead to God.

Mile markers

- The path you have chosen is not yet a popular one.
- The path is teeming with seductive detours.
- If your spiritual path cannot take you directly to the Power within you, consider it a detour.
- You have now begun to draw to you those who walk the same path as you.
- Once the journey is in your blood, it is there to stay.
- All roads eventually lead to God.

Hand in hand I walk with You,
God. My vision is stayed on You,
and my steps are sure.

Please proceed to Adventure 45 in the Activity Book.

To really evolve as an individual, it will be necessary for you not to follow the crowd.

Getting in step with God means marching to a different drummer

"Put out into the deep and let down your nets for a catch."
                                                —Luke 5:4

The men had been fishing all night, their little boats bobbing silently on the lake of Gennesaret. Not a fish was to be caught, and at dawn they headed back to shore with empty nets.

In the morning, Jesus told Simon Peter, one of the fishermen, to put out for the deeper water and cast their nets. Peter was confused by this, questioning how there could be fish out there when there had been no catch all night. Set out they did, however, and their nets hauled up so many fish that the boats almost sank.

NO FISH IN THE SHALLOWS

It is easy to fish in shallow waters, the waters

where everyone else fishes. No one will ever question you for fishing where everyone "knows" you should fish. It's safe to stay in those waters, because that's where you are "supposed" to fish. You won't even be criticized for pulling in an empty net and catching nothing. People will understand.

Yet Jesus very clearly enjoined those men to launch out into the deep. Those deeper waters were not the accepted place to fish, as everyone knew. Why would they want to venture out into the unknown? Wouldn't they be ridiculed, misunderstood? And wouldn't it be risky to test new waters?

In a word, yes. But the lesson was given to us to show that if we are to reap the harvest, we need to launch out into untested waters, for that is where the true rewards are to be found.

You have traveled *The Quest* for almost a year now because you had felt unfulfilled in the shallows. You are making your way in the untested waters, away from the ordinary, casting the nets of your vision into unproven territories where most people are afraid to go. But that is where the treasure lies. It is your own unique way.

DISCOVER YOUR GIFT

You are not an adolescent anymore—not physically, emotionally, or spiritually. You are a person on a journey, questing for the realization of the presence of God and all which that implies.

Look at yourself in the mirror. Look into your eyes. Ask yourself, "What's it all about?" The answer will come that it's about giving of yourself, giving of your uniquely special gift which makes you *you*.

We all have a gift. Each of us is born with something unique to express, to do, to become. It is your responsibility to discover your unique gift. What is it? Do you already know?

Once having been discovered, the gift is developed and nurtured and then it is given back. Once the nets are filled in the deep waters, the fish are brought back to shore and used to feed people. Your own unique gift must also be used to help others. It is the only way you can really feel fulfilled.

Before you began to fish in the deep waters, you probably (if you are like most of us) looked to others to give to you, to fulfill you. Now you see that *real* joy comes from giving back, from being authentically you and sharing that authenticity with those around you.

THE COMMON DENOMINATOR

There are certain people whom we, personally, enjoy being with or listening to or watching on television. As we began to analyze it, we discovered that these people are about as diverse as people can get. The next and really surprising discovery we made was that these people talked about things in which we have not even the slightest interest!

We love to watch a certain chef on television, for instance. We watch with fascination as she discusses French cuisine and puts together elaborate gourmet meals. We also enjoy seeing a home carpentry show, where the host might be constructing a cedar chest or rocking chair. We especially like a television program which shows the intricacies of planting and managing a vegetable garden.

This puzzled us, since we are not intrigued by gourmet food, have not the slightest interest in doing any cabinetmaking, and don't have the time to plant a garden. Why then, we wondered, are we so captivated by these various people?

It occurred to us that the people which we enjoy so much have one thing in common: they are being true to themselves. Each one is genuine—totally absorbed in what he or she is doing and not afraid to be an authentic individual, even when it means launching out into the deep waters where others do not fish. In fact, they are unique and interesting, with so much to offer, *because* they dare to cast their nets in the deep, without concern for playing it "safe."

In her excitement, the gourmet chef often drops food on the floor, she'll wipe her counter up with a less than spanking clean towel, she'll pat the fish she's about to bake and speak lovingly to it! She is so enthusiastic about creating the meal that she doesn't even care. She is too busy enjoying being her authentic self, and so we enjoy it too.

The cabinetmaker is so skilled with his tools, so totally absorbed in creating his furniture and in being his authentic self, that we enjoy watching him work even though there are long periods of silence as he becomes totally engrossed in his woodworking.

The horticulturist is so on fire with love and excitement about his plants and seeing them grow that we enjoy watching him be his authentic self, in spite of the fact that we have little interest in his subject.

A DIFFERENT BEAT

Those who are being what they were meant to be and sharing their authenticity with others are not usually found in the shallows. They are not afraid to "march to a different drummer," as Thoreau said.

The authentic ones hear a different beat than the masses hear. They are not concerned that they might appear to be "out of step." They don't care at all if they are!

You yourself are now marching to a different drummer. You have heard the call and launched out for the deeper waters. The treasure of living a God-guided, God-centered life is yours. You are an authentic being, overflowing with the richness of your unique gift. If you have still been occasionally casting your nets into the shallow waters, now is the time to launch out fearlessly. The nets can only be filled with the treasure when they are no longer cast where the treasure is not.

Push away from the shore. Fear not, for it is the way you have chosen. It is your own unique way and belongs to you alone. Dare to be yourself.

$\mathcal{M}$ile markers

- In order to be authentically you, it is necessary to travel in untested waters, apart from the crowd.
- The treasure is to be found in the untested waters.
- You are born with a unique gift to express, which must be used to help others.
- It is now time to launch out, fearlessly, into deeper waters.

I set out for deeper waters, filling my soul with You, God. I call to You across the waters, and You answer that I am Your beloved child in whom You are well pleased. I in You and You in me— together as one, we venture forth. Thank You, God, for the safety of Your guiding presence, no matter where I go.

Please proceed to Adventure 46 in the Activity Book.

*Here is some very special
news for you: The uni-
verse is rigged in your
behalf.*

You have a safety net

*"And he arose and came to his father. But while
he was yet at a distance, his father saw him and
had compassion, and ran and embraced him and
kissed him."* —Luke 15:20

Now comes the gift. The gift is yours from God
simply because you are God's child. You didn't have
to earn it, and you don't have to prove you deserve it.
It is yours unconditionally. It comes with being part
of creation. It is the gift of grace.

Along the way, you learned many practical principles. Each has played its role in your quest for
transformation, and each one is a law on which you
can utterly rely. For a moment, think back to some
of the things we've discovered along the path together: the law of mind action, forgiveness, love, prosperity, faith, and so on. If you practice them, they

work. It's as elementary as that. Not that it doesn't take dedication and some retraining of oneself to make the necessary changes. That may not always come easy, but the principles themselves are simple to understand and simple in the way they function.

Not so with grace. There doesn't seem to be a set of rules for the concept of grace. There is no way to get more nor any way to accept less. It is the consummate by-product of God's perfect love. We deem it mysterious or elusive because we do not understand it. Yet grace is quite probably that unknown part of God's law.

THE GIFT OF GRACE

In a nutshell, grace is God's goodness given to you in *greater* proportion than you give of yourself to God.

The universe is rigged on your behalf, which means that no matter how far you reach to find God, God will reach further, no matter what you may do to connect with God, God will automatically do more. You can never outgive God.

The most beautiful example of this law of grace is Jesus' story of the prodigal son. To us, personally, it is the most powerful and poignant of all the parables.

No doubt you are familiar with the story recorded in Luke 15:16-32. A father had two sons, one of which stayed home and devoted himself to serving the father and his estate. The younger son asked his father for his inheritance, left home, and squandered the entire fortune in a far country. He ended up feeding swine and suffering great despair. He realized that even the servants in his father's house were better off than he was. Ashamed and feeling very guilty, he nevertheless turned away from the misery he had heaped upon himself and headed toward his father's home. When the remorseful son, who had wasted all of his inheritance, was still some distance from his father's house, the father saw him from afar and ran out to meet him! Ecstatic at having his son come back to him, the father threw his arms around the young man and kissed him and ordered a great feast to celebrate his return. He lavished fine gifts on the son and enfolded him at once back into the household.

There are many powerful lessons in this story, but the one which is most obvious is that the prodigal son did not have to journey the *full* way back to the father's house. He only had to be headed in that direction so that the father could see him and rush out to meet him. This is grace.

We do not have to go the full distance in order for God to rush out to meet us. We only have to be headed in the direction of that Divinity within us and be desirous of making contact with It, in order for It to find us. We do not have to earn grace. The nature of God cannot help itself from going the extra mile and lavishing upon us every wonderful gift that is God's to give.

IT'S AUTOMATIC

Grace is the most beautiful expression of our Creator's love for us. God loves us so much that everything in the kingdom is automatically ours.

By practicing the other universal laws, by sincerely seeking to know, love, and serve God, you do not have to worry about being perfect. It is enough that you are a human being, headed in the direction of the Father's house.

If there is a magical quality to grace, the magic lies in its absolute simplicity. While its workings may be enigmatic, its effects are utterly pure and basic, *so* pure and basic that we may tend to question it. We often like to make things complex, believing that they are then more important or profound. However, grace is the most simple act of the Creator. We are infinitely loved, and so we are given all.

The heartwarming story of the prodigal son is so human. It is easy and comforting to relate to God as our Father, who showers us with blessings no matter what we have done as long as we turn our eyes back in God's direction. God is always there awaiting our return, and the decision to return is enough to trigger the flow of grace.

Yet this is not entirely the whole picture, for God's grace is active even during those times when we are not heading in the direction of "the Father's house." The truth is that we are *always* given more than we give. God is *always* there, keeping us from reaping the *full* harvest of any seeds of disaster we might have sown. It only takes a brief recalling of some of the incidents of our own lives to realize that maybe things "should have been" worse than they were!

THE COSMIC VIEW

There is a more cosmic view of grace than the human story of the prodigal son. This more universal way of looking at grace is the understanding that there is a Creative Process in this universe (which we usually refer to as God), which by Its very nature has no choice other than to push toward more and better expressions of Itself. There is an eternal Principle longing to prove Itself through each one of us because we are Its major means of existence!

From this perspective then, grace is simply the natural and unavoidable drive of the Creative Process to create more of Itself and to know more of Itself. The universe is in the process of becoming. This process underlies everything, especially humankind, for it is in us that the Creator invests the most potential, the most hope.

THE PERPETUAL FLOW

It might help you to think of grace in this way. Picture yourself rowing a boat downstream, going *with* the current. The flow of the stream moves you along faster than the rate at which you are rowing. Since you are moving in the same direction as the stream, the impetus of the water carries you along faster than merely the result of your efforts.

Also, since you are rowing in the direction of the flow of the water, the extra speed and motion come as unearned "gifts." It is not simply the result of your rowing, but rather the result of your rowing in the right direction! You cannot help but be swept along by the flow. Come to think of it, even if you pulled in your oars and no longer rowed but merely kept your boat pointed in the right direction, you would still be moved along with the current.

Conversely, when you try to row *against* the flow, it is extremely difficult, requiring much effort. You won't get to your destination without the feeling that you are "rowing against the tide," which, of course, you are. You will always feel the pull of something trying to bring you back to the right direction.

The flow of the Creative Process of the universe is

always in motion. All we have to do is head ourselves in its direction—dip our oars in the water, so to speak—and we are instantly caught up in the flow of God's grace.

It's a marvelous thing, this grace. It could well be God's most unique gift to us.

$\mathcal{M}$ile markers

- Grace is God's gift to you, simply because you are part of God.
- Grace cannot be earned.
- Grace is God's goodness given to you in *greater* proportion than you give of yourself to God.
- The universe is rigged on your behalf.
- Grace is *always* active, even when you are not heading in the direction of "the Father's house."
- Grace is the natural and unavoidable drive of the Creative Force to create more of Itself and to know more of Itself.

Great Spirit of this universe, how glorious are Your ways. My human heart can't fully grasp the magnitude of all Your good, yet I know I am Yours. I know that there is nowhere I can go nor nothing I could be when I would not be in Your loving care. Thank You, God.

Please proceed to Adventure 47 in the Activity Book.

You are not just learning principles. You are practicing a new way of life. Your future is unlimited!

This is just the beginning

"I am the Alpha and the Omega, the first and the last, the beginning and the end." —Revelation 22:13

Welcome, friend, to the last stretch of our journey together. For the past fifty-one weeks we have walked the trail—almost one full year of learning, a year of changing old ways for new, old thoughts for new. With the gift of grace held in your hand like a magic, coruscating orb, you now move boldly toward these last measured meters of this particular trail.

Of course, this is not the end. It is another beginning. It is the point at which you shed the last vestiges of uncertainty about the allness of God and your intimate connection with that allness. Like the sea gulls by the water's edge who, wanting to fly, merely open their wings to the wind and are lifted above the sand, you are now experiencing the freedom of stretching forth toward the light, free to fly above the earthly scene effortlessly born aloft by zephyr currents of Spirit. Such freedom, such heights, such power, merely by surrendering to the updrafts of the ever-present Creative Force which moves through you.

By simply being available to the rising currents of love, you allow yourself to be carried to new dizzying heights of awareness. Life in the midst of every kind of human complexity becomes a simple act. All forcing, striving, manipulating, and controlling disappear as you become an observer of your life. Carried along by the gentle strength of the Spirit of God within you, your life unfolds like perfect petals of a blossoming rose.

NOTHING MORE TO GET

Trusting in the Creative Process at work in the universe, you are able to give up the struggle to re-arrange the world to suit *you*. You realize that the answers to all questions are within you as the wisdom of God-Mind. There is nothing more to get, only to be. Living each day, savoring each moment one at a time, you see that it is enough to know God, for God is all there is—the Alpha and the Omega.

Life lived from this awareness becomes so sweetly simple. The storm clouds part and great golden rays emerge. From the edge of nothingness, they stream toward you, bathing you in purest light, warming your heart, and drawing you into a vision of oneness with all life. What is this light which seeks you out, which seems to be enveloping the entire planet and dissolving all darkness? It is the light of Pure Love.

And there, in that one word, we find the universal

panacea. It is Love which emerges, after all, as the force which allows us to live the simple life. Love is the healer. Love is the harmonizer of nations, the soothing balm of relationships, the resurrector of the life-force in the physical body.

Life lived in a consciousness of love is a life without guile or struggle. Love frees us to be our true selves, expressing the divinity within us in everything we think or do. Do you realize how simple that makes things?

GOD IS ENOUGH

A simple life does not mean a life without human problems nor does it mean a life lived in barest accommodations with a minimum of comfort. No, that's not it, but in living the simple life, we become like bystanders to the human problems; we may be in them but not of them. They are merely things which are passing through our lives. We view them from a distance and are able to stay out of their webs. In living the simple life, we also may possess material comforts if we choose, but they do not possess *us*. Possessions are merely things which we can take or leave and are not relevant to our true identity, which is the divine of us.

It is an interesting paradox that the more spiritually aware we become, the more simple our lives become. Suddenly, God is enough! Love, God's healing harmonizer, is enough. The soul aware of Love, of the presence of God, is satisfied. It slakes its thirst on the living waters of Spirit and thirsts no more.

The thirst is quenched. It is done. And having been satisfied, it begins again.

$\mathcal{F}$UTURE QUEST

Well, friend, you have come a great way! You have traveled from afar, crossing wasteland, wilderness, and mountain. The frontiers of your soul have been explored: treasures unearthed of which you had not known.

You stand now on a mountaintop, prize in hand, eyes gleaming in the dawn of a new day. As you rest in the sweet exhilaration of a job well done, a gentle wave of triumph passes through you. You are at the summit. All is well.

Suddenly your eyes perceive a distant peak much higher than the one beneath your feet. How is it that you had not noticed it before, you wonder? Just when you thought you could lay down your walking stick forever, a new and greater frontier emerges out of the mists. It beckons, and something in your soul knows you must go.

NO TURNING BACK

The trail behind you is no longer recognizable. In the many months that you have been journeying, the way you came has overgrown with shrubbery and infant trees. It is no longer discernible, having yielded itself back to the wilderness from which it was carved. The only clear path is ahead. There is no turning back.

As your eyes turn from this part of your immortal journey, they focus on a new trail leading even higher. Unmarked? No. The telltale signs are clear: He's been there first.

A quiet voice calls you by name and leads you on. It seems to come from somewhere up ahead, but then again ... perhaps, it is within you that it speaks.

We leave you here, dear friend. You're in good hands. Adieu. Godspeed. Our love and blessings go with you as you set forth on new and even greater quests!

ℱURTHER READING

The teachings of Unity are founded upon the universal principles of Truth as taught and lived by Jesus Christ. This Truth is ever unfolding and revealing itself and is ultimately understood within the heart of each person.

The Quest and *Adventures on the Quest* are a present-day interpretation of the basic teachings of Unity. They do not purport to be the definitive and all-inclusive teachings, but they do provide a contemporary, relevant, and orderly exploration of many of the fundamental Unity principles.

If you would like further readings on the topics raised in *The Quest*, the following books are recommended:

Alternatives: New Approaches to Traditional Christian Beliefs by William L. Fischer

Be Ye Transformed (Interpretation of Acts through Revelation) by Elizabeth Sand Turner

The Case for Reincarnation by James Dillet Freeman

A Daily Guide to Spiritual Living by Jim Rosemergy

Discover the Power Within You by Eric Butterworth

Handbook of Positive Prayer by Hypatia Hasbrouck

Lessons in Truth by H. Emilie Cady

Let There Be Light (Old Testament interpretation) by Elizabeth Sand Turner

Metaphysical Bible Dictionary

Myrtle Fillmore's Healing Letters compiled by Frances W. Foulks

A Practical Guide to Meditation and Prayer by J. Douglas Bottorff

Prosperity by Charles Fillmore

The Revealing Word by Charles Fillmore

Spiritual Economics by Eric Butterworth

Teach Us to Pray by Charles and Cora Fillmore

Unity: A Quest for Truth by Eric Butterworth

What Are You? by Imelda Octavia Shanklin

Your Hope of Glory (Gospels interpretation) by Elizabeth Sand Turner

To purchase any of these books, call your local Unity church or center or call the Customer Service Department at Unity Village, Missouri: (816) 251-3580 or 1-800-669-0282.

Printed in the U.S.A.

148-11218-7.5C-8-05 Q